Surviving the
Nazi Onslaught

A Rifleman's Prayer

Dear God, my Father, through my son
Hear the prayer of a warrior son.

Give my eyes a vision keen
To see the thing that must be seen.

A steady hand I ask of thee
The feel of wind on land or sea.

Let me not ever careless be
Of life or limb or liberty

For Justice sake a quiet heart
And grace and strength to do my part

To God and Country, Home and Corps
Let me be faithful evermore.

I would like to thank the Royal Green Jackets (Rifles) Museum staff for all their help and support in my research when writing this book, in particular Christine Pullen and Ken Grey. http://www.rgjmuseum.co.uk/

Surviving the Nazi Onslaught

The Defence of Calais
to the Death March for Freedom

Carole McEntee-Taylor

Pen & Sword
MILITARY

First published in Great Britain by
PEN AND SWORD MILITARY
an imprint of
Pen and Sword Books Ltd
47 Church Street
Barnsley
South Yorkshire S70 2AS

ISBN 978 1 78383 106 7

A CIP record for this book is available from the British Library.

Printed and bound in England by
CPI Group (UK) Ltd, Croydon, CR0 4YY

Typeset in Times by CHIC GRAPHICS

Pen & Sword Books Ltd incorporates the imprints of
Pen & Sword Aviation, Pen & Sword Family History, Pen & Sword Maritime,
Pen & Sword Military, Pen & Sword Discovery, Wharncliffe Local History,
Wharncliffe True Crime, Wharncliffe Transport, Pen & Sword Select,
Pen & Sword Military Classics, Leo Cooper, Remember When,
The Praetorian Press, Seaforth Publishing and Frontline Publishing

For a complete list of Pen and Sword titles please contact
Pen and Sword Books Limited
47 Church Street, Barnsley, South Yorkshire, S70 2AS, England
E-mail: enquiries@pen-and-sword.co.uk
Website: www.pen-and-sword.co.uk

Contents

Foreword

by

Field Marshal Lord Bramall

KG, GCB, OBE, MC

Having joined the King's Royal Rifle Corps (60th Rifles) in 1942 and, many years later, being one of the first commanding officers of the Royal Green Jackets - into which my regiment, together with Ted Taylor's, The Rifle Brigade, had merged - it is a great pleasure to write a foreword to this account of Ted's wartime experiences, particularly the Battle of Calais in 1940. More so since Ted served with me after the war as a member of my staff when I got to know him very well and held him in the highest respect.

This is an account based on Ted's diaries and reminiscences which well captures a Rifleman's view of this hard-fought battle. The defence of Calais was a stubborn, desperate, and heroic resistance against overwhelming odds which made a great contribution to the successful evacuation of the BEF from Dunkirk, and thus to the army that, retrained and re-equipped, I was to join two years later, returning in 1944 over to the Normandy beaches to ultimate victory.

Very few survivors of that battle could be evacuated by sea, and with the weary and wounded taken prisoner, Ted was among those denied the opportunity of taking any further part in the war and who were marched off to five long years of captivity in Poland. An impressive granite memorial now stands near the harbour mouth to commemorate the 200 of Ted's comrades in the King's Royal Rifle Corps, The Rifle Brigade and the Queen Victoria Rifles who lost their lives in that battle.

In the words of the *Annals of the Kings Royal Rifle Corps*, whose Second Battalion fought alongside Ted's unit at Calais, 'To create heroic legends, successful and heroic objectives are necessary, and what better one can there be than to sacrifice oneself so that others can escape.'

In February 2007 the Royal Green Jackets found themselves once more at a point in their history where change was required - the formation of The Rifles, a reorganisation which Ted lived long enough to see. Among the rich and unique legacies that this new regiment inherits from the Royal Green Jackets are many of its battle honours, prominent among which is Calais, an inspiration, challenge, and poignant reminder to today's young Riflemen of that distant, yet still echoing battle and a central theme of this absorbing book.

Churchill's Speech to Parliament on 4 June 1940

'However, the German eruption swept like a sharp scythe around the right and rear of the armies of the north. Eight or nine armoured divisions, each of about four hundred armoured vehicles of different kinds but carefully assorted to be complementary and divisible into small self-contained units, cut off all communications between us and the main French armies.

'It severed our own communications for food and ammunition which ran first to Amiens and afterwards to Abbeville, and it shored its way up the coast to Boulogne and Calais, almost to Dunkirk.

'Behind this armoured and mechanized onslaught came a number of German divisions in lorries, and behind them again there plodded comparatively slowly the dull brute mass of the ordinary German army and German people, always so ready to be led to the trampling down in other lands of liberties and comforts which they have never known in their own.

'I have said this armoured scythe-stroke almost reached Dunkirk - almost but not quite. Boulogne and Calais were the scenes of desperate fighting. The Guards defended Boulogne for a while and were then withdrawn by orders from this country. The Rifle Brigade, the 60th Rifles, and the Queen Victoria's Rifles, with a battalion of British tanks and 1,000 Frenchmen, in all about four thousand strong, defended Calais to the last. The British Brigadier was given an hour to surrender. He spurned the offer and four days of intense street fighting passed before silence reigned over Calais, which marked the end of a memorable resistance. Only thirty unwounded survivors were taken off by the Navy, and we do not know the fate of their comrades. Their sacrifice, however, was not in vain. At least two armoured divisions, which otherwise would have been turned against the British Expeditionary Force, had to be sent to overcome them. They have added another page to the glories of the light divisions, and the time gained enabled the Gravelines water lines to be flooded and to be held by the French troops.[1]'

Extract from *The Times* quoted in *Rifle Brigade Chronicle* 1940.

'A Silence Reigned over Calais'
– Mr Churchill

'Dim was the memory of that ancient pain,
But now you have played this most heroic part,
We may tell all France with pride that once again
England has Calais graven on her heart.'
– J C Squire

Prologue
May 1945

The view from the chin gun turret of the Flying Fortress B17G^2 was impressive for those used to it. For its current passengers however, lying face down on its floor gazing at the view below, it was just something else to add to the wonder of the moment. The two .50-cal guns that normally formed part of its impressive thirteen-gun armoury had been removed to make enough room for two people to lie down in the space normally reserved for one person to sit.

However, the passengers were not interested in the capabilities of the aircraft, just in the fact that it was taking them home. It was over five years since they had left England; five long years in which they had seen things no one should ever have to see or live through. Five frightening, brutal years since they last saw those they loved and since they could relax and feel safe, but at long last the nightmare was over and life was about to begin again. There would be time to remember later. Now was for looking forward to spending time with those who had waited; those who had never given up hope.

Ted Taylor gazed out through the Perspex onto the English Channel below, unable to believe that he was at last going home. Later that day he would walk along the streets of London again and up the front path to number 62a Stondon Park, SE23. It would be as if the last few dramatic years never happened. Or would it?

The sun played off the water and created patterns on the gently rolling waves. He could even see the white-crested tips as they rolled gracefully, and the circling seagulls soaring through the air, gliding on the air currents as they hunted for fish. The scene was one of such peace and tranquillity that it had a timeless quality to it, as if it was always like that. It was so different from his memories that he could hardly believe it was the same place. The last time he had seen the English Channel his ordeal was just about to begin and it had certainly not been calm and peaceful. He fought back the memories that threatened to overtake him and forced himself to concentrate on the present. Soon he would be home, back in the arms of his Mum and his brothers, and with Brenda who had waited all this time for him.

Just thinking about them all made him smile. It was only the letters from his family and Brenda that had kept him going month after month, year after exhausting year when he was doggedly determined not to allow the camps with their ongoing brutality and sense of desolation break him.

Memorial to the Rifle Brigade in Calais.

He had also been determined to survive and eventually tell his story. The world should never be allowed to forget the madness that had engulfed it for the last six years, for by forgetting it could allow itself to slip into that same madness again. That was why his story and the stories of all those affected should be told and retold. No one should ever forget the sacrifices they made; the sacrifices of those who would never come back.

Glancing round at his companion he was suddenly shocked to see how thin and old he looked. For some reason he hadn't noticed before. Was that how he looked too? He knew his clothes were very loose but he had put that down to the fact they were borrowed. It was strange he hadn't noticed how pale the men were under their weather-beaten skin or how gaunt they looked.

Their youth had gone in the camps, lost through the enforced labour with little or no food and the continual hardships. Yet until that moment, he had not really appreciated the changes in their appearance. Although he was only twenty-five years of age, he looked much older and his eyes had the stare of someone who had seen much more than they should have. Sometimes, in his mind he only felt twenty, but at others times he could feel the full weight of those missing years. Maybe Brenda would not recognize him after all this time, maybe she wouldn't love him looking like this. He pushed the thought from his mind. He had not survived this long just to worry about things over which he had no control. He was free and nothing was going to dampen his spirits. Only a few more hours and he would be home. To his surprise and horror, he felt tears welling up in the corner of his eyes. Rapidly he blinked them away. He had not cried at the many atrocities he had witnessed in the past few years and he was not about to start now. Crying was for 'nancy-boys' not men.

'Not long now'. It was as if Harry, his companion, had picked up his thoughts.

Ted nodded, unable to trust himself to speak for a moment. Clearing his throat, he answered with a question: 'I wonder if they've changed much. Do you think we'll recognize them?'

Harry looked surprised as if the thought had never occurred to him. Looking at Ted's face, understanding slowly dawned. 'Perhaps we should worry about them recognizing us.'

He paused then added, 'Do we really look that old?'

'Of course they'll recognize you,' said an American voice breaking loud and clear into their conversation. 'They'll be so pleased to see you they won't care what you look like. Don't forget, they'll probably have changed a bit too. It's been a while after all. They're probably having exactly the same conversation right now.'

It was exactly the right thing to say and both men smiled, relief etched across their war-weary faces. Not for the first time since they had boarded his plane, the American considered what horrors and hardships his guests had endured. It just proved how indomitable the human spirit was. These guys looked like they had been to hell and back yet they had survived.

His friends had seen some of the survivors of the concentration camps and their stories made his blood run cold. He could not understand how anyone could treat another human being in that way. Even less could he understand how the victims managed to survive in such intolerable conditions. He glanced at his watch. Only another thirty minutes before they landed at Ford airfield at the foot of the Sussex Downs. Then his guests would be on their way home to their families. He wondered idly how their lives would turn out. Would they find the happiness and peace they craved? He sure hoped so. They needed a land 'fit for heroes' and he only hoped they could build it out of the ruins that were often all that was left of many of the major cities. They would find that a bit of a shock. The England they had left behind would be unrecognizable. Familiar landmarks would be gone, friends and family no more.

'Look to your right', said the American, breaking into their thoughts again. Ted and Harry looked obediently in the direction he had indicated and saw the White Cliffs of Dover rising majestically in the far distance. The iconic sight immediately rendered both men speechless. It was something they had dreamt about but had never realistically expected to see again. Ted closed his eyes, not only to hide the emotion that was threatening to overwhelm him again, but to offer up a silent prayer of thanks to whatever God had kept him alive and allowed him to experience this moment when so many of his friends couldn't.

When he opened them again the cliffs and beaches with their barbed wire and warning signs had gone and the land, like an enormous patchwork quilt, was spread out beneath them. Trees, ploughed fields with crops growing in them, villages, country lanes and people all passed beneath them while Ted watched in awe. From this height it all seemed a little unreal and dreamlike. He had to pinch himself to be sure. But that only made him painfully aware of just how thin he was.

He suddenly felt hungry. Hunger was something he had become used to over the years but this was different; it was a hunger to begin his life again, to forget everything, to relegate his experiences to the status of a bad dream. It was time to move on, to concentrate on building a future and having a family - children who knew nothing of the past and whose lives would be fresh and unsullied by the horrors he had seen.

As the aircraft circled the airfield and began its descent, Ted smiled. He turned to Harry and saw his own happiness reflected back. The two men laughed and then shook hands, still unable to believe this was really happening. For the first time in five long, terror-filled years Ted Taylor was home.

Chapter 1

The Cricket Match
Monday 21 May 1940, Suffolk

'Howzat!'

The thud of the ball colliding with the wicket was followed by the exultant cheer of the tall, lanky, young man known as Chalky. The noise resounded round the small village green in sleepy Needham Market, Suffolk.

The umpire, Major Michael Smiley, raised his hand and the batsman turned dejectedly and began the long walk back to the edge of the green where the rest of 6th Platoon were sitting. It was the afternoon of 21 May 1940 and the men of the 1st Battalion, The Rifle Brigade, were, for the most part, relaxing in the early spring sunshine and enjoying the inter-platoon cricket match. The news from the war was not any better and it seemed ages since they had been able to relax and enjoy anything. In fact the situation in Europe over the last few weeks had been even worse than the news from the sea had been over the previous months. After Poland had fallen, it had gone quiet in Europe leaving many to call it the 'bore war'. It would later be known as the 'phoney war' – an American expression - but at sea the war had been far from 'a bore'.

On the very day war was declared the *Athena*, a passenger liner sailing from Glasgow to Montreal, was torpedoed by a German U-boat with considerable loss of life. A few weeks later on 14 October, a German U-boat sunk the battleship *Royal Oak* while it lay at anchor in the naval base at Scapa Flow in the Orkneys, and in December 1939, German planes bombed and strafed fishing boats in the North Sea. On 9 April 1940 Germany invaded Norway and Denmark and the war suddenly came a step closer. This invasion was also to herald a change of leadership in Britain and on the very day Hitler's tanks invaded the Netherlands, Belgium and Luxembourg, Mr Winston Churchill became Prime Minister and Minister of Defence.

In May 1940, the 1st Battalion the Rifle Brigade was one of the most experienced regular battalions in Britain. As well as their newly trained conscripts, which included Ted and his friends, they also had within their ranks, several well-trained reservists. They were commanded by a well-respected officer, Lieutenant Colonel Chandos Hoskyns, who was appointed Commander on 27 August 1938. He had invaluable combat experience gained in the Great War, supplemented by service in India and Malta.

On 15 May in response to the continuing bad news from the continent, the 1st Battalion, a motorized battalion of about 750 men, received orders to load up their kit and equipment and move north-east to East Anglia. Here they were to continue preparing to defend the country against a possible invasion. The long journey north from Bournemouth, where they had been based, was reasonably uneventful although rumours of paratroopers in the Chelmsford area necessitated a stop en route. Enthusiastic that at last they might have a sighting of the enemy, the men made a thorough search of the surrounding area, enjoying the opportunity to put their skills to the test.

Ted before he joined up.

However, this proved fruitless and the men assumed it was just the result of another of the many unfounded rumours sweeping the country in the wake of yet more bad news from Europe. The search completed, they climbed wearily back into their trucks and continued onwards to Suffolk and the small village of Needham Market.

In the distance the church clock could be heard striking four. The gentle breeze that kept the air cool throughout the day rustled the leaves and spring blossom on the cherry trees that were set round the edge of the green. The poignancy and serenity of the scene would only become apparent to those who witnessed it at a much later date. Then it would be seen as symbolic of the calm before the storm and a memory to sustain them through the dark days that were to come.

On 21 May 1940 those present had no way of knowing how their lives were about to change. After several days of back-breaking work digging trenches in the heavy East Anglian clay soil and constructing fortified roadblocks on all the routes leading to the coast, the men of B Company were just pleased to have some time to relax. The defences they had constructed were intended to impede the progress of any enemy force that was foolhardy enough to attempt to invade the heavily fortified island. At least that was what they had been told and that's what the people of Britain hoped. Despite the continuing bad news, there was still a strong belief in the invincibility of the armed forces and a certainty that the Germans would never really get that very far.

However, despite this optimism, the continuous rumours of enemy landings, fuelled by the very real fear of invasion since the fall of Belgium and Holland, kept the soldiers busy. The surrounding countryside was now criss-crossed with defensive trenches several feet deep and the few roads were obstructed by fortified roadblocks made from 'knife racks' with barbed wire running across and ringed with defensive trenches, forming an effective deterrent to anyone trying to crash through without stopping.

Those not taking an active part in that day's inter-platoon cricket match were scattered in groups round the edge of the green, smoking, chatting, playing cards and contributing various supportive and not-so-supportive, comments. Inter-platoon cricket matches, like anything else that set one platoon against another, always generated plenty of friendly rivalry. But it also fostered the close bond between the men that an effective army relies on.

The comments and heckling of the soldiers caused much amusement to the local village children who were congregating on the edge of the field to watch the cricket. Although the soldiers had been camped there for several days now, the children were still not used to seeing so many people in this sleepy Suffolk village and made the most of this unexpected event. The arrival of the soldiers acted like a magnet to the youngsters who felt that something exciting was now happening. The so-called 'bore war' had been going since September 1939 and the absence of any real difference to their daily lives was a continual source of disappointment to many of them. The only real change was that their schoolteacher had been called up and gone to join the Navy. His replacement was an older man who had retired some years earlier. Until the arrival of the troops on 11 May, life continued pretty much in the same vein as before the war started.

Some of the older children had spent the last few spring evenings after school hanging round the edge of the hastily erected army camp on the green, chatting to the soldiers and trying to avoid the attentions of the Company Sergeant Majors and other officers. On the few occasions they were spotted, they had been shouted at to 'scarper' which made it more exciting. Rather than a deterrent, this acted as an incentive to keep coming back. Because many of the soldiers had younger brothers and sisters, they welcomed the youngsters and even let them help with some of their camp duties - although requests to help dismantle, clean and reassemble rifles were met with a resounding 'no' much to the disappointment of the older boys. Similar requests to 'have a go with your rifle mister?' also met with a curt response.

The soldiers also kept the older children busy with little 'jobs' such as taking empty beer bottles back to the shop. This was a popular task as the children were allowed to keep the 1/2d on each bottle they returned. Other soldiers gave the youngsters letters to post or sent them into the village to buy cigarettes and bottles of the local beer. The children enjoyed this too because the soldiers let them keep the change or the occasional cigarette cards they found.

Cigarette cards were now in very short supply as they were no longer included in the packets because of the need to conserve cardboard and paper for the war effort. Consequently, it was only the older pre-war packets that still had them and as it was nearly nine months since war was declared, these were virtually non-existent. Adverts on the packets had also decreased as had the posters proclaiming the virtues of one brand over another. The only posters adorning shops were either pre-war adverts or wartime information posters. These proliferated rapidly from September 1939 as the Ministry of Information sought to impart various messages to the public, most of whom were either uninterested or who complained bitterly about all the restrictions that were introduced. The posters most common at the time included those encouraging evacuees to stay in the country and warning of fifth columnists and the dangers of careless talk. Others gave information about the various penalties civilians could incur if they spent too long on the phone, used the telegraph system for anything other than an emergency or didn't save their waste paper, cardboard and other useful recyclable materials.

Despite the government's attempts to make them stay in the countryside, the majority of evacuees had returned home by this time. But for the remaining few living in the village the chance to hear London accents again was even more important. Many evacuees felt abandoned and very homesick so the chance to meet people who reminded them of home was a real tonic. There was also the added bonus that, for once, they had the advantage over the local children in that they were able to understand the soldiers' slang. This had improved the evacuees' standing among their peers and had gone some way to helping them become more accepted.

The impromptu cricket match on the green attracted most of the older village children. With them came their younger brothers and sisters, all with their gas masks slung carelessly about their persons and eager to be a part of this exciting happening in the village. Gas masks were a source of continual irritation to the children. Over thirty-eight million were distributed prior to the beginning of the war and it was now an offence not to carry one. The children hated putting them on because of the smell and the horrible uncomfortable way that wearing them made them feel. Even the novelty Mickey Mouse ones, intended to take away the fear for younger children, had not entirely overcome the reluctance to wear them. They also hated having to carry them around everywhere and resented the amount of trouble they got into if they forgot. However, inventive as always, they found they made reasonable footballs and goalposts when the adults weren't looking.

Although food rationing was introduced in January 1940, food was more plentiful in the country than in the cities and rationing had not really had time to take effect. Clothing would not be rationed for a while yet so the children were still quite brightly dressed. As the war progressed, clothing became less available and less colourful. But for now, the boys in their short trousers, shirts, braces and colourful sleeveless jumpers, and the girls in their bright tunics and cardigans with ribbons and bows in their hair, added a colourful edge to the copse of trees that bordered the green. On the whole the children looked reasonably well fed and healthy and, like all youngsters, were full of fun and mischief. Conscription meant many of the older ones were left looking after their siblings. Fathers were often away in the Forces and their mothers were busy filling the gaps that were left in the labour market. Many of the fathers who were in reserved occupations such as farming had also joined the quarter of a million men who had volunteered for the new Volunteer Defence Force (VDF) which was being formed in response to Eden's appeal on the 9 pm news on 14 May. This would later become known as the Home Guard after Churchill declared its name was unlikely to inspire anybody. Others had joined the ARP wardens. This left the children with even more time on their own which often meant finding new ways to amuse themselves. The war had given them plenty of ideas for new games and it was now easier for girls to join in because enough 'players' were needed to make up a proper fighting force. However, although rumours were already rife about paratroopers being dropped, the children's searches in the surrounding fields and woodland had, to this date, proved fruitless and there were only so many times they could play games about captured Germans without something concrete to base these on. In any case, the real soldiers were much more interesting to watch.

The bowling had now switched to the other end and it was Jones's turn. A tall well-built man with thick black hair which curled if it grew much longer than the regulation army length, Jones was an excellent all-round sportsman and was known affectionately by all as Taffy. He was a slow bowler and as the ball curved in the air, the batsman clipped it with his bat under-cutting it and sending it straight up in the air towards one of the waiting fielders. 'Yes!', shouted Jones ecstatically, but it wasn't to be as the fielder fumbled it and it fell to the ground. 'I don't believe it!'

Jones held his head in his hands groaning as the batsman took the chance to grab an extra run. But all was not yet lost as the fielder quickly recovered his wits. Throwing himself spread-eagled onto the floor and grabbing the ball, he quickly threw it towards Ted Taylor, the platoon's wicket keeper that day, who had already spotted the opportunity and had positioned himself accordingly. 'Over here, quick', he shouted from his position just to the left of the wicket. A wiry man of 5ft 7³/₄in with dark brown hair, laughing grey eyes and an engaging smile, Ted was invariably optimistic that whenever they played any team games, his team would win.

Waiting with his hands cupped he watched as the ball soared through the air towards him. As it came close, he raised his hands slightly and the ball dropped neatly into his palms. Quick as a flash his hands moved to the side and knocked off the stumps of the wicket as the batsman slid feet first towards the wicket, slightly too late.

'Got ya!' His shout of triumph was cut short as the familiar sound of a motorcycle was heard in the distance. Distracted he turned towards the sound as did everyone else.

'Aye aye – something's up'. Chalky had also lost interest in the cricket as the sound of the motorcycle broke through the silence. The heckling stopped abruptly as the gaze of the waiting soldiers followed the dispatch rider as the bike left the road and travelled the short distance across the cricket ground towards the umpire. They watched in astonishment as the rider pulled up in front of him and leapt off his bike. Without waiting to stand it up properly or even remove his goggles he spoke rapidly to the Major who then climbed on the back of the bike and went off to the Company office nearby in the village. With no one left to umpire, the game stopped abruptly and the men stood looking at each other not sure what they should be doing, but each sensing that something momentous had, or was about to, happen.

For Ted, it felt as if the world had suddenly gone into slow motion. Although he saw that the sun was still shining and the breeze was still nudging the few cotton wool clouds across the blue spring sky, it was as if a shadow had crossed the sun. He shivered as if there was a sudden chill in the air, a premonition of things to come.

In the village the Colonel summoned the 2IC2, Major Alexander Allen and the Company Sergeant Major (CSM), and after the customary salutes and a few brief words he disappeared back into his office leaving the CSM to pass on the orders. The CSM was a professional soldier with considerable experience, yet even he was taken aback by the speed of their impending departure. There were none of the usual briefings; the Battalion was to be packed up and ready to move in just four hours. There was not even time for the men to contact their families. In fact there was little time for anything other than to break camp, pack up their kit and equipment and refuel and board the trucks. The CSM shook his head, a sense of foreboding overcoming his normal calm unruffled demeanour, but the training of many years kicked in and facing the troops he barked out the orders.

'Right, everyone fall in. We're breaking camp. At the double – quick march!'

The last word was elongated and shouted and his voice echoed across the green to the watching children. 'Left, left, left, left, left'. Galvanised by the sudden change of pace, the children watched transfixed as the soldiers marched across the green at their rapid Rifle Brigade pace. Excitedly, they tried unsuccessfully to copy the frenetic marching of the soldiers as they complied with the order. These attempts at double-quick marching would normally have induced a wry smile of amusement from the CSM, but his mind was on other things. They had been ordered to break camp, pack up their kit and equipment and wait for the transport. However, other than the fact they were moving out, he had been given no further information as to where they were going or what they were expected to do once they arrived. He shook his head and tried to ignore the warning voice in his head, but try as he might it wouldn't go away. In the village the CO watched the preparations with an equally heavy heart.

What he couldn't tell them was that they were going to Southampton. They would be told that once they were on the trucks and underway. This was to ensure that there was no careless talk in the village as they broke camp. After that he had no idea where they were going. However, he could make a shrewd guess that if they were going to Southampton there was a fair chance they were going to France. But he had no idea that they would embark on the first available tide to Calais after stopping en route at Dover. He also had no idea that once in Southampton they would join up with the 2nd Battalion, the King's Royal Rifle Corps, (the 60th Rifles[4]) who were presently deployed in Bury St Edmonds and whose role, like that of The Rifle Brigade, was to stop any invasion on the east coast.

Reading between the lines, he knew that the British Expeditionary Force (BEF) was in trouble and guessed they were probably being sent to reinforce them. What he didn't know - and what was also unknown to the 60th Rifles - was that once in Calais they would join the 1st Battalion, Queen Victoria Rifles, a Territorial Army motorcycle battalion who were part of the KRRC, the 229th anti-tank battery of the Royal Artillery and the 3rd Battalion the Royal Tank Regiment (RTR) who were equipped with twenty-one light tanks and twenty-seven cruiser tanks. They had already deployed and were under fire in France. This would reunite the various elements of 30th Brigade which had originally been put together to prevent the Germans invading Norway. Unfortunately they were too late as Norway had already fallen so instead they were split up and deployed separately. Now they would be together again to do the job they had originally been intended to do, but in France instead of Norway.

Once there, they would be supported by the 1st and 2nd Searchlight Battery, the 6th Heavy Anti-Aircraft Battery (Royal Artillery), and the 172nd Light Anti-Aircraft Battery (Royal Artillery) which had been moved up from Arras and 800 French soldiers (about one-and-a-half French Infantry companies) who were based at Fort Risban in the west. There were also two field guns in the Citadel and a number of other French troops manning coastal defences. In addition, there was a platoon of Argyll and Sutherland Highlanders who were detailed to guard a Royal Air Force radar station. They would all come under the command of Brigadier Claude Nicholson.

This would leave a total of about 4,000 men facing the might of the 10th German Panzer Division, which at full strength had 15,000 men and around 150 tanks. Although about half the German tanks were out of action, the Calais Force would still be outnumbered by at least three-to-one. However, that was all in the future and to the hastily packing men their orders were no different from the orders they had received to go to Bournemouth or those directing them to Needham Market.

Chapter 2

Calais Force on the Move
21/22 May 1940

In May 1940 events in Europe were moving so rapidly that news was invariably out of date before it reached the War Office back in Britain and orders were continually changing, sometimes hourly. When the first elements of Calais Force were deployed their orders were to open up the supply lines to Gravelines and to link up with the British Forces at Dunkirk. But when they arrived in Calais the confusion was such that no one was even sure if the Channel ports were to be defended.

The first elements of Calais Force to be deployed were the 3rd Battalion Royal Tank Regiment (3 RTR) and the Queen Victoria Rifles (QVR). Lieutenant- Colonel Reginald Keller of 3rd Battalion Royal Tank Regiment, was out to dinner with his wife on the evening of 21 May when at 10 pm he received the phone call telling him to return to his unit for embarkation. Frantic calls were put out to local cinemas and pubs requesting the men return and by the time they entrained for Dover at midnight only one officer and twenty-five men were missing and they managed to catch up with the others an hour before they sailed for Calais.

Meanwhile the QVRs had also received their orders to depart. They were equipped and trained to act as divisional cavalry for the 1st London Motor Division, a home-defence formation. Their commanding officer, Lieutenant Colonel J.A.M. Ellison-Macartney, was the bursar of Queen Mary College of the University of London.

When they were ordered to deploy, many of his best men were away attending officer training courses or had returned to industry and in their place he had 200 militiamen. The unit was hopelessly ill-equipped, even to undertake its intended role. A third of the men were only armed with pistols, for which they had received no training. Having received orders to move overseas, they were then told that they could not take their transport and instead left them neatly lined up at Ashford station and boarded a train to Dover - which was deserted when they arrived. The sealed envelope opened by Lieutenant Colonel

Ellison-Macartney told him he was expected to land at Calais and secure the town against 'a few German tanks' which had 'broken through towards the Channel Ports.' As he read his orders the men loaded their equipment onto the cross Channel ferry, the *City of Canterbury*.

Lieutenant Colonel Keller and most of 3RTR arrived in Dover at about the same time as the QVRs, but without their tanks which they were told were on a ship in Southampton and due to sail that night for Cherbourg. His orders informed him that there were seven light and four medium tanks in the Boulogne/Calais area.

The men of 3RTR boarded the *Maid of Orleans* with some Royal Engineers and some QVRs, and together with *The City of Canterbury* they sailed out of Dover in thick mist at 11 am, their tanks still in the hold of the *City of Christchurch* in Southampton. The men arrived safely at the Gare Maritime at 1.15 pm but had no idea where their tanks were. When they arrived on the quayside at Calais on the afternoon of 22 May it was utter chaos. There were numerous non-combatants and refugees everywhere trying to escape the advancing Germans. While his men began to unload, Keller went to find the Military Commander of Calais. This took him an hour and a half. He eventually found Colonel Holland in the Boulevard Leon Gambetta after being refused entry to the Hotel de Ville because he did not have an official BEF identity card. Colonel Holland, who had been appointed Commander on 20 May, advised him that his orders would come direct from Hazebrouck and that he should unload as quickly as possible in case of more air attacks.

Back at the quay the unloading of the equipment was painfully slow and compounded by constant interruptions from the Luftwaffe and most of it was done by the men themselves. Keller then discovered that all the tank guns were packed in mineral jelly which would take at least a day to clean and zero and that many parts for the vehicles, weapons and radios were missing. Smoking was forbidden as the quay was full of four-gallon cans of petrol. Then, with no sign of their tanks, the men of 3RTR were directed towards the dunes east of the Gare Maritime where they used their time to manually force bullets into the .5in machine-gun belts because the mechanical chargers had not arrived.

On arrival Colonel Ellison Macartney also went to find Colonel Holland who, although delighted to have some extra men that he was not expecting, was astonished to find that the QVRs, a motorcycle battalion, had been ordered to leave its motorcycles in England. Nevertheless, he still directed them to set up barricades on the six main roads into Calais to prevent any more refugees or enemy troops from entering the beleaguered town. To defend a perimeter of 30 km with less than 600 men and no transport was an enormous task. They were also to secure the submarine cable terminal at Sangatte and patrol the beaches to the east and west to prevent German aircraft landing at low tide.

At the quay things were also steadily deteriorating for the QVRs. Not only had they arrived without transport, they had also arrived without their 3-inch mortars. Only two thirds had their rifles and the only ammunition they had were some older 2-inch mortars and some smoke bombs in lieu of ammunition. Several fifth columnists and German snipers had managed to infiltrate the town with the constant stream of refugees fleeing the German advance and had begun firing intermittently at the disembarking men. The dockers immediately disappeared as soon as the snipers started firing leaving no one to unload their equipment. As some of the men took up positions and returned fire, others tried to unload what little equipment they did have. This took longer than expected because the cranes and other unloading equipment were no longer working, whether from sabotage or just bad luck wasn't clear.

Eventually the men finished unloading only to discover that there was no transport available at all to move the stores so everything had to be carried by hand to wherever they were needed. But by the time equipment and stores reached the advance posts on the outskirts of the town the barricades erected by the QVRs were already struggling to prevent the terrified civilian population from breaking through. In many cases they had already done so adding to the chaos and confusion but even worse as far as the QVRs were concerned, were the fleeing French soldiers, sometimes wounded, sometimes not, but all appearing dejected, dazed and demoralized which did nothing for their own morale.

Lieutenant Colonel Keller arrived back at the Gare Maritime at about 4 pm, the same time as *The Christchurch* appeared with their tanks, and immediately supervised the unloading which was painfully slow. At 5 pm he was given new orders by Lieutenant General Sir Douglas Brownrigg (Adjutant General of the BEF), who having evacuated the Rear GHQ of the BEF from Wimereux was on his way back to Dover. Brownrigg told Keller that there was only a small, lightly armoured German force in the area so his priority was to move into the harbour at the Foret de Boulogne, make contact with 20th (Guards) Brigade and secure the town. In some ways it was very fortunate that the unloading was so slow as it prevented Keller from following these orders. Even while he was speaking to Brownrigg 2 Panzer were attacking Boulogne and some of 1 Panzer were heading to their overnight positions in the Foret de Boulogne. Within three hours of the conversation with Brownrigg they had reached and occupied the Forêt de Boulogne. If Keller had followed orders his part in the battle would have been over before it began. However, he was initially convinced by Brownrigg's assertion of the position so went with his Adjutant, Captain George Moss, to reconnoitre the route to Boulogne and decide where to concentrate his forces. His eventual decision was to concentrate the main force at La Beussinge Farm and the rest in the Coquelles area.

When Keller returned back to the dockside he found it full of retreating troops from other regiments. The unloading of his tanks was hurried and haphazard and as soon as they were ready they were manned by whoever was available. This meant many Squadron Commanders did not get their own tanks or even their own crews and many tanks went into action with crews who had never trained together. Even worse some of those who had trained on cruiser tanks were ordered onto light tanks and vice versa. As day gradually turned to night confusion continued to reign. During the course of the night Keller received several contradictory orders from Gort's HQ, and also from Brownrigg, who was now safely in Dover.

Meanwhile, once they had finished unloading, the few remaining QVRs were sent north to the sand dunes to secure the area for the arrival of the rest of the Brigade. Although they could still hear the sound of intermittent fire fights from the town and see the untended fires raging in places, the dunes were very quiet and as night fell and the stars appeared in the cloudless sky the sound of nightingales drifted across from the nearby woods. Many would remember this as the calm before the storm.

Back in England it had taken much longer to break camp than anticipated and it was 11 am by the time the 300 open trucks were refuelled and loaded and ready to go. The men of the 1st Battalion the Rifle Brigade climbed in wearily to begin their long journey south. Most of the delay had been caused by the necessity to refuel the trucks. The official petrol pumps had run dry so the much-needed fuel had to be sourced from elsewhere, all of which had taken time. After the warmth of the day the night air was cool and although the new greatcoats provided the men with some protection, the movement of the trucks increased the wind-chill factor until they found themselves huddling together for warmth. When that failed they tried stamping their feet and rubbing their hands together to try and restore some circulation to their cold feet and hands.

The transport included some very ancient 30 cwt trucks, which to the men in the back seemed to travel at a maximum speed of about 12 mph. Driving up hills was even more laborious and on some of the steeper hills they could only manage about half that speed. However, the drivers soon made up for this by speeding downhill, much to the concern of those who were bouncing about unrestrained in the back, unable to do anything about it.

The quiet, dark country lanes provided little to look at other than the occasional red eyes of a fox or rabbit caught in the dim glow of the headlights of the truck. This did not happen very often because for part of the way they had to drive with the headlights off to prevent any possibility of showing lights to enemy aircraft. None of the drivers had maps so they had to rely on the occasional signpost to prevent them from getting lost. By now Ted, like many of his companions, was very tired and although he tried hard to doze, the movement of the truck as it went round bends, down hills at great speed or over potholes, kept shaking him awake.

'God, this is bloody miserable, I hope we're not going wherever it is that we're going, all the way by these back roads. Haven't they heard of main roads?' Chalky was one of Ted's best friends, but was well known for always finding something to moan about.

'Suppose it depends on where it is that we're going,' Ted responded abruptly, his normal good humour lost as he tried in vain to shield himself from the cold draughts circulating round the truck. He was so tired that even talking was becoming too much effort. Giving up on trying to sleep he took out his cigarettes and put one in his mouth. Cupping his hands round the matches, he tried several times to strike it. Every time he managed to get it to light, the wind blew it out and he had to start again. Taffy, who was watching him struggle, took the matches from him and, using Ted's hands to protect the match from the wind, eventually managed to get a strike. 'Self-interest' he said, waving away Ted's thanks. He pulled out his own cigarette and reaching across he used Ted's lit one to get his own started. Sitting back as far as he could to get out of the wind Ted drew heavily on his cigarette and said, 'Anybody got any ideas where we're going?' The question was casual enough, but underneath the nonchalance Ted had a feeling they were going overseas. He wasn't entirely sure how he felt about that, a mixture of fear and anticipation was probably the best way to describe it. After all that was what he had been trained to do and a part of him couldn't wait to put the things he had been taught into practice. The first units of the BEF had been sent over in September 1939 and had gradually been added to over the past few months. There were now several hundred thousand men in France and, although he had not had much contact with his father over the past few years, he knew his father was one of those troops from Britain. He wasn't sure exactly where he was, but he was attached to one of the supply units of the BEF so the chances were that he was already fighting the Germans.

'Perhaps we're going to Norway', Chalky said thoughtfully.

'No, I think we've blown that one. Hitler's already got his feet in the door there,' Taffy opened his eyes just long enough to make his contribution to the discussion.

'Apparently we're going to Southampton', a voice from the other end of the truck piped up

'How do you know?' Rob asked

'I heard a couple of the officers talking before we left', the disembodied voice responded. 'They were going to tell us once we were underway.'

'And after Southampton?' Ted asked

'Dunno', the voice replied. 'Don't think they knew. I think they'd just been told Southampton.'

A very young Ted with one of his friends and a dog.

'Right'. Ted looked at Chalky who was nearest and for once neither of them could think of anything else to say. It sounded as if they were definitely going overseas. Ted finished his cigarette and tossing it out into the dark, silent countryside he closed his eyes and found himself reliving the last few hectic months.

Much to his initial dismay, Ted had received his call up papers almost immediately war had been declared, with orders to report to Winchester on 15 September 1939. Winchester, Hampshire, was the Regimental home of the Rifle Brigade and the 60th Rifles. As a Londoner he had been sent to join the 1st Battalion the Rifle Brigade which recruited mainly from the London area. It had all happened so quickly there had been little time to think about it. At first he was not very enthusiastic. After all he was perfectly happy with his life as it was. He enjoyed his job, liked his workmates - Ted had worked at Green's Engineering on the production line making spiral staircases and fire escapes since leaving school at the age of fourteen, some six years earlier - and in general life was good. He was settled and content. Ted was a gentle, considerate and hard-working boy who attended church regularly and was a Sunday School teacher. He loved nature, knew killing was wrong and was not sure that he would really be able to kill someone, even if they were trying to kill him. However, as a young, fit twenty-year-old in a non-reserved occupation he had no choice in the matter. Reluctantly he had said goodbye to his colleagues who wished him well and had gone home to pack up the belongings he wanted to take with him. He then said goodbye to his Mum and his two brothers. His Mum had been really upset, although she had tried not to show it. But his brothers,

Crofton Park Baptist Church where Ted met Brenda. He was a Sunday School teacher there.

Cyril who was two years younger, and Bernard who was four years younger, were envious and couldn't wait for their turn. Ted had also said goodbye to his girlfriend, Brenda, who was in her second year training to be a nurse at Lambeth Hospital. He had met Brenda through the Crofton Park Baptist Church when he was a member of the Boys Brigade and she was a member of the Girls Brigade. This was the Baptist Church equivalent of the Scouts and Guides. They had become firm friends at first, sharing the same sense of humour, religious beliefs and outlook on life. As they got older, the friendship developed until they both knew they meant more to each other than just friends. The outbreak of war had only strengthened that feeling, yet it was tempered with the sudden realization that their future together was no longer certain.

It hardly seemed any time at all since that momentous broadcast by Chamberlain saying that they were at war with Germany yet, within two weeks Ted's life had changed irrevocably and there he was in Winchester, about to begin his training.

The thirteen weeks had passed so quickly that Ted could hardly believe it was Christmas already and time for his first leave. He had packed up his 'civvy' clothes which they were instructed to take home and then hurried to the Guard House where he had to pass inspection before being allowed out. From there he went out through the medieval West Gate, over the bridge and across the road to the station to catch the train home. He almost felt sad to be leaving Winchester with its feeling of timeless history and the cobbled square that sparked when their steel capped boots marched at rapid pace across them. After Christmas, he would go immediately to Tidworth on Salisbury Plain to complete his training to be a driver of a Bren-gun carrier.

Chapter 3

'Will You Marry Me?'

Christmas 1939 was a time of great happiness tinged with an indefinable sadness. Although Ted soon became used to wearing his uniform and carrying his rifle on base it felt strange to be in uniform at home. It was even stranger to have to carry his rifle and a little ammunition around with him wherever he went. Although he was happy to be reunited with his Mum, brothers and Brenda, there was an underlying feeling of sadness that things had already begun to change. Even worse he would only have a couple of days and it seemed that no sooner had he arrived then it was time to go back. Everywhere he looked there were people in uniforms. Sandbags protected all the public buildings and many gardens and private homes had already been turned over to vegetables. Some had an Anderson shelter dug in. He barely recognized his family's garden with the cumbersome shelter now taking pride of place, its entrance facing away from the house in order to minimize blast damage if the house was hit.

According to his Mum there were numerous strict specifications about building Anderson shelters and she and his brothers had spent ages making sure they didn't fall foul of any of the regulations. There had to be at least fifteen inches of earth on top and thirty inches at the sides, otherwise they would not provide effective protection against bombing. To conform to requirements the shelter had to be in place by 11 June 1940. Apparently, any that didn't conform could be removed and serious penalties imposed on the hapless individual involved. This seemed a bit excessive to Ted who was under the impression that one of the reasons they were going to war was to protect people's individual freedom.

Communal shelters also appeared in streets that didn't have gardens. Many businesses opened up their cellars so that staff had somewhere to shelter and in Bromley, Kent, the Chislehurst caves were opened up so people could shelter there.

However, the biggest threat so far seemed to be boredom. After the initial siren heralded the beginning of the war and the closure of cinemas, theatres and football grounds, things had gradually returned to normal as the government realized that the public needed entertainment to keep up their morale.

Since then there had been a few more false alarms, but other than sporadic bombing of seaside towns by a single aircraft or small groups, very little had happened. Although many people in the suburbs now had Anderson shelters or access to communal shelters, some preferred to stay in their homes and take shelter under the table or under the stairs. This would lead to many unnecessary deaths, yet some of the communal shelters were also to become death traps.

Although the obvious places to shelter in London were the underground stations this was initially discouraged by the government as it was frightened the population would disappear below ground and not come back out again. This fear stemmed from pre-war reports which exaggerated the number of casualties that might result from sustained bombing raids. These

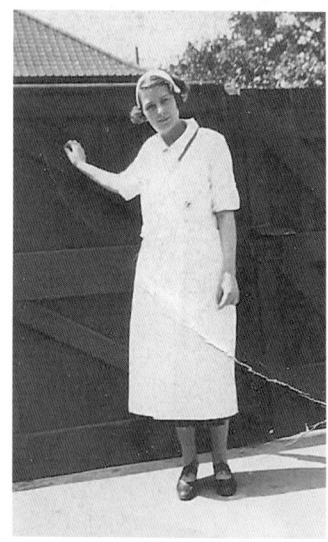

Brenda before the war.

reports, based on studies undertaken during the inter-war years, also discounted the number of people likely to be homeless and injured. This was to lead to severe shortages of accommodation and rescue centres because councils had completely underestimated the number of survivors who would become homeless.

However, for many the war just meant restrictions, an increase in prices and a shortage of goods. This was beginning to create divisions between the civilian population and those in the Armed Forces and Merchant Navy. But for Ted at least, Christmas was a time for forgetting divisions and spending time with those he loved, and in 1939 he had a particularly important reason for really looking forward to it.

Christmas dinner was a meal Ted always enjoyed and this year was no exception. Fortunately, rationing had not yet begun and his family were able to buy most of the traditional food they normally had, although there wasn't quite as much as there had been before the war. However, he was noticeably distracted throughout the meal and his Mum was quite concerned. Ted brushed off her questions with a rather nervous laugh and explained his distraction by saying he was disorientated by being at home again. The rest of the day passed quickly and Ted was relieved that his Mum didn't really have another chance to question him. When she did ask him again later, he pretended that it was just because he was not used to sitting around as he was always busy in the Army. He did have something on his mind, but he did not want to say anything yet, not until he had spoken to Brenda the next day.

Brenda as a baby with her parents, Mabel and Frederick, and two older brothers, Ron and Doug. Mabel died on 14 May 1923 and Frederick in March 1948.

As arranged, Brenda came round to Ted's Mum's house for dinner on Boxing Day. Because she had not seen Ted since September, she arrived early, eager to spend as much of the day with him as possible before he had to leave. But Ted seemed edgy and distant and quite unlike his normal self so Brenda asked him several times if everything was alright. He was definitely behaving strangely and she was worried he didn't want to go out with her anymore, but wasn't sure how to tell her. Feeling very nervous she nodded at his suggestion to go for a walk, got her coat from the hall stand and followed Ted out into the icy streets. He put his arm round her and pulled her close which made her feel slightly better. If he didn't want to be with her he would have kept his distance, not pulled her close to him. She wanted to ask him again if there was anything wrong, but sensed it was best to let him talk in his own time. They walked in companionable silence for a while. Brenda enjoyed the sensation of feeling him close to her, but she was too nervous to relax. They were walking in the direction of the river and as they approached it Ted spoke for the first time since they had left the house.

'Brenda, you know I love you don't you?'

She smiled nervously, this was it then. 'Yes I know Ted, I love you too.'

'Well I was thinking, we've known each other over four years now and as we've said we both love each other and … I though perhaps we should … That is it might be nice to …. Well perhaps … What would you think to us….Do you

31

think we … Maybe we could get engaged'. There, he'd said it! Even if it was after much stuttering and stammering and it hadn't quite come out how he'd intended. Brenda looked at him in astonishment, relief and happiness mingled together as she realized that he hadn't found someone else and he didn't want to leave her. 'Is that a proposal?' she asked anxiously. She had to make sure as she would hate to get it wrong. 'Yes', he said grinning, relieved that he had finally managed to do it. But he was still nervous in case she turned him down. 'Wasn't a very good one was it?!'

Brenda as a little girl.

'Well you should really get down on your knees and ask', she responded laughingly. 'But it is very cold and I wouldn't want you to get cold knees.' Then she shrieked, 'Ted!'

Much to the amused stares of the few people brave enough to be walking around, he knelt down on the frozen river bank and said much more coherently, 'Will you marry me?'

'Yes, yes, yes, of course I will', she said, and with great delight Ted swung her round in his arms and they kissed passionately, oblivious of the cold and damp and of the war that was soon to tear them apart. Releasing each other, they both spoke at once.

'I've been worried sick in case you turned me down.'

'You were acting so strangely I thought you were going to tell me you had found someone else.'

Laughing, they kissed again and then held each other close, wishing this moment could go on for ever and that they would never have to go back to the real world where Ted would return to camp and she would go back to work, their only contact being letters and the occasional phone call if they were lucky.

'When do you want to get married?' he asked

'I don't know'. Trying to be practical, although what she really wanted to say was 'now or tomorrow', Brenda carried on. 'We'll need time to organize it and we don't really know where you are going to be or what's going to happen so maybe we should think about some time in 1941, the summer maybe? Perhaps the war will be over then. What do you think?'

'I don't know if I can wait that long.' Ted looked at her seriously. 'But it makes sense I suppose. Oh, I nearly forgot,' he said grinning like an idiot and fumbling in his uniform pockets, 'I bought you this. It's a ring', he added unnecessarily as she opened the small box in delight. The ring was a beautiful solitaire diamond on a platinum base and it fitted perfectly. Brenda kept looking at it unable to believe she was engaged.

'Is it alright?' asked Ted anxiously as she continued to stare at it without speaking.

'Yes, it's just so beautiful. I just can't help looking at it. Oh Ted, I'm so happy and I love you so much.'

Relieved, he held her close again and then said reluctantly, 'I suppose we'd better go home or we'll be late for dinner.'

She linked her arm in his and in comfortable silence they walked back the way they had come.

'Hello Mum' said Ted as soon as they entered the house. But he didn't get the chance to finish before Brenda, showing off her ring, interrupted him excitedly. 'Ted's asked me to marry him.'

Then everyone was talking at once and congratulating them and it was only when

Ted, Cyril and Bernard as young men.

there was a moment's silence that a small voice said, 'So did you say yes then?'

Everyone laughed and Ted jokingly shook his fist at Bernard, his youngest brother. The rest of the day was spent in celebrating and after lunch they went round to Brenda's house where Ted formally asked Brenda's guardians Doris and Arthur Rudling, her aunt and uncle, for her hand in marriage. Brenda's mother had died from tuberculosis when Brenda was very young and as her father had been unable to look after her and her three brothers and go to work, Brenda had gone to live with her mother's sister and her husband. Her brothers had been raised in an orphanage and it was only recently she had been reunited with them.[5] Brenda's aunt and uncle were not surprised, having expected it for some time. They liked Ted and knew that he was honest, hard-working and reliable. Having given their permission, they added their congratulations and then withdrew discreetly leaving them on their own to say their goodbyes. It had been dark for some considerable time now and was getting late and Ted knew that he had better head home to get ready to go back to Winchester early the next morning, but he really didn't want to leave.

Brenda followed him to the door and down the stone steps into the street.

Brenda's brothers with Ada, Doug's wife.

Brenda's father, Frederick Ernest Burge.

Brenda's father with his two brothers.

Brenda's father in WW1.

An icy wind was blowing and it was freezing as they stood outside her house in Brockley. She put her arms round him and they held each other in a long embrace wishing the world would go away and leave them alone so they could stay like that forever. Eventually, knowing time was passing and that she would have to let go, Brenda pulled back so she could look straight into his eyes and said softly, 'You will look after yourself won't you?'

'Of course I will. Nothing's going to happen to me. I've got you to come back to and nothing's going to stop me doing that.' Ted looked and sounded so confident that Brenda found herself believing him.

'I really have to go sweetheart.' Reluctantly he withdrew from her arms and kissed her, gently at first, then with more passion until he pulled away smiling. 'Now I really have something to remember you by.' He smiled once more and walked away. Brenda stood watching, trying hard to stem the tears that threatened to engulf her. It wouldn't do to let his last sight of her to be one of her crying. She made a supreme effort and when he turned back at the corner for one final wave, his last view of her was of her waving with a big smile on her face. Whenever he closed his eyes after that and thought of her it was always that image that came to the surface.

Once Christmas was over Ted returned to Winchester and from there he was sent to Tidworth where he learned to drive a Bren-gun carrier. That had been one of the most enjoyable times of his training. Just thinking about it still made him smile. Surprisingly enough, although the carrier used tracks instead of wheels, it was not that difficult to learn to drive and it hadn't taken Ted any time at all to get used to it.

Although he hadn't seen Brenda since Christmas he had received several letters from her and some from his Mum and he had been so busy he hadn't realized just how much time had elapsed since he last saw them.

Things had not improved on the war front and at the beginning of May Neville Chamberlain was forced to resign as Prime Minister. Because they could not hold elections in wartime the new choice of leader had come down to two people. Lord Halifax had been the preferred choice, but he was closely connected to what was increasingly being called the 'Peace in our time' fiasco and the Labour Party had refused to endorse him. So, despite the catastrophic failure of the Norway campaign, on 10 May Winston Churchill had taken over as both Prime Minister and Minister of Defence. The fall of Norway and Denmark was swiftly followed by the collapse of Belgium, Luxembourg and the Netherlands, and now France was next in line.

When they received their orders earlier in the month some thought they were going to Norway and others thought it more likely that they would go to France. Instead they had been deployed to Needham Market to prepare for the possible invasion that everyone seemed to think was going to happen. But it had all been really quiet and at the ripe old age of twenty-one, Ted was quite looking forward to putting his training into action. However, as it was the first time he had been out of England, he would have liked the chance to have told Mum and Brenda where he was going so they didn't worry when they didn't hear from him. But he wasn't about to tell his mates that or he would never live it down!

To his relief the trucks pulled out of the country lanes onto the main road and the pace quickened. However, his relief was short lived because no sooner had they approached the outskirts of London, than it started to rain. Caught in the open trucks, they were all soon soaked to the skin and as the rain continued to cascade heavily, water trickled down their necks making them even colder. There wasn't even the consolation of being able to see anything. From 3 September 1939, all windows had to be covered after dark so that no chink of light showed. Shops very quickly sold out of blackout material so all sorts of improvizations had to be used - which didn't matter as long as you made sure no light showed after dark. It wasn't just house and shop windows that had to be covered. Vehicles had to have their lights dimmed and pointing downwards and streetlamps were filtered with a special screen that directed the light down. Despite kerb edges being painted white, the number of road accidents rose dramatically after the blackout came into force and well over half of them involved pedestrians, either bumping into each other or into cars. Men had even been encouraged to leave their shirt tails out so they could be seen in the blackout.

The number of cars on the road significantly decreased in 1939 and only those civilians for whom a car was essential were given a basic petrol ration that would allow them to drive a maximum of 1,800 miles a year. For those civilians who were not bothering to comply, there were always the ARP wardens or 'little Hitlers' as they were known, ready to enforce the regulations. Going out in the blackout had become a hazardous business. Even torches had been banned!

Staying in night after night wasn't much fun either. The electricity voltage was reduced in an attempt to cut down fuel which made it more difficult to read, and initially the BBC regional broadcasts were stopped to reduce airwave traffic. They had also withdrawn most of the more entertaining programmes and replaced many of them with heavily censored news broadcasts. However, in January this policy was overturned in the interest of raising morale and at last, more interesting programmes were broadcast again. Much to everyone's delight 'ITMA' returned on Thursday nights and became one of the most listened to programmes. It also gave rise to lots of great wartime catchphrases which everyone used with increasing frequency. ITMA stood for 'It's That Man Again' and originally started in July 1939 as a swipe at Hitler's territorial ambitions. Every time he was heard to be making more demands the comedy show aired with the familiar 'It's that man again'. It returned in January 1940 with Tommy Hanley and was one of the most popular programmes of the war. It was often said that if Hitler had invaded on a Thursday night he would have met no opposition at all because most of the country was listening to the radio.

For Ted and the others, deep in their own thoughts, these things were of no real importance any more. The blackout was just something else to be endured along with the rain and the cold. Their real unspoken concerns were solely about where they were going and what they were expected to do.

As the night wore slowly on the convoy gradually skirted round the northern suburbs of London and was then escorted out onto the Great West Road by the London police. For the most part the journey was silent as the men wrestled with their thoughts, most of which were focused on where they were going and whether they would soon be coming home to their loved ones. Like Ted, most of them thought that they were to embark on their first real engagement and although, like him, they were looking forward to putting their training into action, there was also a good deal of apprehension about what they could expect. They were also concerned about how they would react when under fire.

What if they froze or were unable to do what they had been taught? The fear of not performing properly was almost worse than the fear of being injured or killed. Having never been to war they could only imagine what it was like and their idea of war had come mainly from the films they saw in the picture houses. Most of these were about the Great War and although weaponry had moved on apace since then, blast damage and the injuries caused by shrapnel were the same. The first aid training they received at Winchester highlighted some of the horrors they could expect. There was also the constant fear of gas attacks, something else for which they had been trained. Some of them had relatives who had experienced the mustard gas attacks in the trenches of the Great War; others knew soldiers who had suffered from shell shock. This was the ultimate horror and something they could only pray they would not have to face.

So, with fear mingling with excitement, the trucks went ever southward towards Southampton carrying the troops and their officers to a fight that would ultimately result in battle honours that equalled, or even rivalled, those gained by past regiments. Also unbeknown to the men, these honours would not come easy. In four days they would lose over sixty per cent of their strength, their Commanding Officer would be mortally wounded, Brigadier Nicholson would die in a German POW camp and only a few of the wounded would be evacuated. The remaining survivors would spend the rest of the war, five long years, in POW camps in Poland.

Chapter 4

'Stick it in, twist it round and pull it out!' Tuesday 22 May 1940

It was still raining as they arrived at a transit camp three miles from Southampton docks at 1 pm on Tuesday 22 May. They didn't have much sleep on the long tiring journey and had only stopped twice. The first time was just after dawn on the Great West Road when they refuelled. At first they were relieved to have a break from all the jolting and jarring, but as they were told it was only to be a short stop most of the men decided that it wasn't worth trying to sleep. Much to their frustration the refuelling took much longer than anticipated and they missed the opportunity to grab a little sleep free from the constant bouncing around.

The dispatch riders who drove alongside were not as fussy. Many of them were so exhausted that they ignored the order to stay awake and fell asleep on their bikes in the pouring rain. Once the refuelling was finished they started up again and continued on their way. By now it was light, but it was still pouring with rain. There was no promise of the hot and sunny day to come and it was a dark and cloudy sky that greeted the tired, wet and thoroughly fed-up troops.

As the journey south continued the rain became heavier and more persistent and the men became more disgruntled. Finally, just when they were beginning to feel really aggrieved, they pulled up at Hartford Bridge Flats on the side of the A30, near Camberley, Surrey. Here they were allowed to get off the trucks, given an hour to stretch their legs and to cook themselves a hasty breakfast.

This vast expanse of land was to become RAF Hartford Bridge in 1942 where it would initially be the home to RAE6 Farnborough. It was used to conduct secret trials of military gliders and air-to-air searchlight trials. In April 1943 the first of two Photo Reconnaissance Squadrons would arrive, followed later in the autumn by three bomber squadrons including the Free French Lorraine Squadron that would spend considerable time trying to destroy the V-

1 ('doodlebug') launch sites being built in France. Mosquito and Spitfire fighters were also based there in 1944 as they hunted for German Reconnaissance planes and shot down 'doodlebugs'. It was also one of the trial sites for FIDO, the Fog Investigation Dispersal Operation. The airfield later changed its name to the RAE (Royal Aircraft Establishment) Blackbushe in December 1944 and in March 1945 it was handed over to RAF Transport Command who used it to ferry medical supplies to the Continent and also to bring home Canadian POWs at the end of the war. For a short time, it became a satellite airfield for London Airport.

For the tired, drenched men, their surroundings and its future activities were of little interest. Relieved to be off the extremely uncomfortable trucks they wasted no time in preparing some hot food on their petrol cookers. As the rain was still relentless, it was a testament to the efficiency of these cookers that they were able to do this. The petrol cookers were extremely lightweight and consisted simply of a cooking ring that sat on a fuel container. Although fuel containers were designed to use petrol they were also used with anything else that would burn including cardboard, twigs and various other materials.

Breakfast rations for Ted that morning comprised some porridge made from a block of sweetened oatmeal. This needed a considerable amount of time and effort to crumble or it would come up lumpy. The milk came from a 5oz tin of evaporated milk, which was also used to sweeten the rather coarse, service-blend ration of tea. Others heated up one of their breakfast cans which contained liver and bacon, ham and eggs or fish and eggs. Once they had eaten and had a hot cup of tea, they all felt slightly better and fortunately the rest of the journey was uneventful. It was still quite early so they passed few people on the road. Apart from the countryside there was little to look at and they soon became bored looking at a constant procession of fields. Because of the threat of invasion, the view would change dramatically when checkpoints were set up on bridges and cross roads and defensive trenches criss-crossed the countryside. However, in May 1940, these changes were still in their infancy. With little to occupy them apart from taking bets as to where they were going after Southampton, Ted's thoughts returned to his training, which now seemed like several lifetimes ago although he could still just about remember how he felt.

The first stage for the new recruits was to undergo the medical. Standing in line stripped to the waist with what seemed like hundreds of others, Ted had felt increasingly nervous. His initial reluctance when he had first received his call up papers had been replaced by a growing sense of excitement. Having talked himself into looking forward to his new life, he was having doubts again. But this time the doubts were not about if he really wanted to join the army, but whether he was suitable for this whole new life he was about to embark on. Looking round at his companions, he realized that they all felt the same. In some ways Ted found this comforting and started to relax. They were all new, no one knew any more than he did, so no one was expecting too much. What he had also failed to appreciate was that unless he was medically unfit, the Army would take him regardless. It was no longer a case of being the right material for the Army, it was simply the case that you were automatically the right material unless there was a good reason why you weren't.

He spent the days before his arrival reading up on the history of the Rifle Brigade and he had found it really interesting but, if anything, it made him even more nervous. The Rifle Brigade was formed in 1801 and had their Headquarters in Winchester. Their illustrious Regimental history included forming the rearguard at Corunna in 1809 and holding the crossroads at La Haye Sainte for a whole day during the Battle of Waterloo in 1815.

Ted before Calais.

What if he couldn't live up to their expectations? He had always been brought up to believe that if something was worth doing it was worth doing properly and the opportunity to be part of such a prestigious 'family' made it doubly important that he did his best. He sighed deeply, the queue seemed never ending and the longer he waited the more nervous he became. What if he wasn't fit enough? At least two of the men in front of him had walked out looking totally dejected, collected their belongings and left. His fears of not living up to the role were now replaced by fears that he might be rejected before he had even got through the door. Glancing at the man behind him he saw his own fears mirrored on his face and somehow this reassured him. Taking a deep breath he made a conscious effort to relax, after all, if he failed the medical he would just go home and take up his old life again. What on earth was he worrying about? Feeling better he concentrated on watching the activity around him and after what seemed an interminable wait he found himself at the front of the queue.

'Next.' The bored soldier standing by the door looked impatiently in his direction. Ted took yet another deep breath and stepped through the door.

Numerous questions were thrown at him: Name, age, place of birth, have you ever had....? This was followed by a long list of diseases Ted had barely heard of let alone experienced. The list seemed never-ending. Ted answered clearly and precisely while the doctor listened to his chest, checked his hearing, eyesight and blood pressure, weighed him, measured his height and, much to his embarrassment, asked him to cough while they checked the more private parts of his anatomy.

'Done. Go back outside and they'll send you to collect your uniform.' The doctor sounded totally bored and uninterested. Ted was so surprised that it was over and he had been accepted that he almost didn't hear the order. The doctor raised an eyebrow and Ted fled back triumphantly to the cold waiting room where he reclaimed his shirt and followed the others to the stores to collect his uniform. He had done it. The first hurdle had been overcome. He was in the Army.

Brigade insignia and Regimental shoulder flash.

The cobbles on the square glistened with rain as Ted ran swiftly across them. Having got this far he didn't want to give the wrong impression by getting lost on the way to the stores. He needn't have worried because there were soldiers waiting at various points to direct them and Ted reached the right building only to find yet another queue of men waiting to be given their kit. This was supposed to consist of two sets of battledress, web anklets, steel-capped boots and a steel helmet with a cover to prevent reflection and loops to hold twigs as camouflage. The battledress was a single-breasted, rough serge blouse with a stand-and-fall collar, a fly front, pleated breast patch pockets with a flap and a concealed button which was made of a vegetable compound and normally green. Wartime restrictions meant the normal Rifle Brigade black buttons were not available in the quantities needed so they, like every other regiment, had to make do with green buttons. The blouse was gathered into a waistband and fastened with a flat metal buckle on the right of centre. Trousers were straight with normal side and hip pockets, a large patch pocket with flap on the left thigh and a pleated pocket on the right front just below the waist. At the bottom of the trousers there was a tab and button so they could be fastened around the ankle for wear with black leather ankle boots and web anklets. The uniform was designed for ease of movement and for most of the items to be carried above the belt, leaving the legs free. The men were also equipped with thick socks and underwear. They would also be given anti-gas capes and gas masks, both of which weighed three and a half pounds, as well as ammunition pouches for a Bren gun or rifle and ammunition or grenades which weighed 10lb each. They were also issued with a water bottle, mess tin, knife, fork and spoon, emergency rations and a cup.

Each man was expected to carry a 10lb pack containing his double-breasted great coat, spare shirt, laces, comb, toothbrush, shaving outfit, socks and towel. As if that wasn't enough he was also expected to carry a 5lb haversack, a bayonet and scabbard that weighed one and three quarter pounds and of course his Lee Enfield rifle which weighed eight pounds ten and a half ounces. The

Rifle Brigade wartime battledress uniforms had chevrons and badges edged with rifle green and on the left arm was a divisional sign with a black cat proclaiming the men belonged to the famous City of London Brigade.

However, shortages often meant only overalls, boots, mess tin, water bottle, knife, fork, spoon and cup could be collected. After this, the men went to get their rifles which they had to be measured for so that the butt was the right length. They had to wait for the rest of the kit, which was allocated as soon as it arrived in the stores. For some of them this would take months and a number of men of the Regiment never received their whole kit. Emergency rations were kept centrally by the Colour Sergeant to be given out as and when necessary.

Fortunately for Ted they had his size in boots. The man in front was not so lucky. He had feet larger than the average and this meant that he would have to wait while they found some boots in his size.

As they were gradually loaded with their kit, Ted and the other recruits wondered how on earth they were going to manage to walk from the barracks to the drill shed, let alone train with this weight. Surprisingly this did not last long, and soon they found they could function perfectly well either with full kit or without it. In any case, as most of the kit was normally carried in the platoon truck it was only when in the field or on training exercises they had to carry it all. On that first day however, everything seemed very strange and, like many a recruit before and after him, Ted questioned what he was doing there and if he would ever settle in.

Once they had collected the available kit, they were taken to Mons Block which was four floors high. Ted found himself in a long room with thirty beds. Each bed space had a small cupboard in which the recruits were expected to put their kit and any personal belongings. These were normally photos, letters, writing materials, books and the civilian clothes they had arrived in. There was no room for anything bigger and recruits had been advised to leave all other possessions at home before reporting for duty. In the middle was a coke-burning stove which provided the only heating. The coke to fill the burner was near Long Block, which was about 200 yards away. Washing was done in the ablution rooms in the block that had rows of sinks with running cold water in the middle and rows of toilets on the outside. Ted and the others looked bemused at the basic facilities as they realized that privacy was obviously going to be a thing of the past.

The next few days were a blur of drill and lessons. Much of the training was done with the 60th Rifles and provided a good deal of friendly rivalry. The men marched from each session to the next at the rapid Rifle Brigade pace until marching and drill became second nature. If it was dry they drilled and trained in the open and when it was wet they continued their training in the drill shed, a large barn-type building with three walls, a roof and open frontage that was situated in the north-west corner of the barracks.

As their training progressed Ted and the others were taught how to use their bayonets effectively - 'Stick it in, twist it round and pull it out!' - and taught how to yell at the top of their lungs while they were doing it. They also learned how to kill with their bare hands as well as various other methods of unarmed combat. Map reading provided some of them with a chance to shine and with an invaluable skill that would stand them in good stead when escaping from German POW camps. First aid training was a more dampening experience as it brought home to them some of the injuries that they could find themselves dealing with in the field. This reminder of their mortality was uncomfortable at first, but with the resilience of youth was soon put aside as like most young people they considered themselves to be invincible.

Ted before he went to France.

On the indoor firing range they were taught how to fire 'five rounds, rapid fire' and how to maintain and clean the rifles and ammunition. When firing on the indoor firing range they used .22 rifles. When on the outdoor firing ranges at Chilcombe Range, on the outskirts of Winchester, they used 303s. They also practised taking the rifle apart and reassembling it in the dark.

Ted enjoyed the field exercises - even sleeping under groundsheets on the icy cold and damp ground in one of the coldest winters in living memory. Pipes froze, roads were sheets of ice and the weather alternated between frost, snow, sleet and rain, during which they took part in a War Office exercise. Under the strict, but fair tutelage of the platoon commander and his sergeant, Ted grew fit and strong. He learnt how to camouflage himself and his weapon, how to crawl for long distances on his stomach using only his knees and elbows or his knees and knuckles, and how to swim under water. He enjoyed the challenge of the assault courses and the exercises to storm the enemy's strongholds. He learnt how to spot snipers and the presence of enemy troops although he could still hear the training instructors' voice in his ears, 'There are no straight lines in the country Taylor!', after he missed the sniper silhouetted against a bush for the third time.

Ted quickly became accustomed to the blackout both in the barracks and in the town. Going out into the town meant going first through the Guard Room at the main gate to be checked and then out through the West Gate. The first pub outside the gate was called The West Gate and was a popular haunt when finances permitted. For those who didn't have much money, and a shilling and sixpence a day didn't go that far, there was a café above a cinema in Jewry Street where they could get 'milk and a dash.'

Once they had finished their continuation specialist training at Tidworth the men travelled to Bournemouth to begin their first war duties. This involved patrolling the lengthy coast, digging trenches and generally making sure the coast was safe. A, C and I Companies were all in separate villages and many found country life dull. B Company were the envy of the others as they were billeted on the outskirts of Bournemouth and were within easy reach of the cinema.

The sea defences they helped to construct consisted of three separate stages, a line of scaffolding erected onto concrete posts that spanned the whole length of the beach, concealed mines that also spanned the length of the beach and rolls of barbed wire spread in rows along the beach. Behind the wire were more mines and then concrete cubes intended to impede the progress of any tanks. Interspersed with these defences were large, deep trenches or tank traps as they were known. Behind these were more mines and then pillboxes from which gunners were able to cover the beach with machine-gun fire. Although these defences seemed impregnable to the untrained observer they were not meant to stop or even contain an invasion, but merely to delay its progress for sufficient time to allow other factors to come into play. There were a further two more defensive lines after the sea defences that were intended to stop the Germans.[6]

In April the men received their mobilization orders. These were expected to be completed in three days. Although the destination was never mentioned Ted was sure it must be Norway as the vehicles were all filled with a double ration of anti-freeze and the men issued with thick vests and pants. Three days of intense activity followed and on the evening of the third day the Colonel inspected each company and that was it. After a fortnight of 'standing by', magazines were unloaded and life returned to normal. However, because they were still fully mobilized, they had to leave the anti-freeze in the vehicles and as soon as the warm sunshine broke through the engines boiled!

Still lost in his thoughts Ted suddenly realized that the rain had decreased to a steady drizzle and the sun was trying to break through the thick layer of clouds. He looked round at the others and opened his mouth to comment, but most had their eyes closed and looked to be asleep. Sighing, he closed his eyes and tried to get some sleep as well, but the combination of the continual bumping and rocking of the truck and his own active mind defeated him and he gave up and stared sightlessly into the distance as the truck sped ever southward and the sun won its own battle with the rain.

The transit camp was busy when they arrived. The vehicles, the drivers and the dispatch riders went straight to the docks where their transport and equipment was to be loaded onto the ships. Ted and the others were delighted to be able to get off the uncomfortable trucks and stretch their legs. They were even more grateful to be given a nourishing meal of meat and vegetable stew.

The rain had stopped and as their uniforms quickly dried out in the sun, their spirits began to rise. While they waited for further orders the men took the opportunity to have a shave and a wash and looked forward to getting some sleep. As yet they had no idea how long they were going to be there, so they were reluctant to settle down to sleep in case they were woken immediately. With little to do some of the men took the opportunity to write letters to their wives and girlfriends. Others with more experience who had learnt the military skill of being able to sleep anywhere took the chance to get some much needed rest.

Ted finished his meal and then took his time washing and shaving. He had been feeling very tired when they had first arrived at the transit camp, but the food and the wash and shave had revitalized him somewhat. Feeling restless he wandered around chatting to his mates, trying to push thoughts of where they might be going or what they were going to be doing to the back of his mind

Three hours passed quickly and as 5 pm approached, the order came to fall in ready to move. The men grabbed their possessions, paraded and then marched the three miles with full kit towards Southampton. This was the final confirmation that their assumptions were correct and that they were going somewhere overseas. As they marched through Southampton, they were conscious that this might be the last time they saw an English town for a while and they looked round trying to remember everything so that they could imprint it on their minds. There were no cheering crowds and those who had fought in the last war couldn't help but compare the way they were treated this time to the incredible send-off they had received when going off to the trenches.

The evening was warm and balmy and there was not a breath of air. Over Southampton town and docks the barrage balloons floated lazily and as they marched to the docks they passed a cricket match. The sight reminded them of the game they had been playing when they had received their marching orders the previous evening. As the batsman hit a resounding six causing the ball to soar high over the boundary, the sound of applause from the spectators echoed round the ground. The six being added to the scoreboard was one of the last things they saw as they marched out of sight of the cricket pitch and the docks came into view.

It was now early evening and Ted and his friends boarded the *Royal Daffodil'*, a small flat-bottomed paddle steamer normally used as a ferry. Their vehicles and equipment were set to follow on the *Kohistan* and the *City of Canterbury*. Unbeknown to them, rather than leaving the Regiment to supervise the loading of their own equipment and transport as they normally did, some rather officious embarkation staff officers had removed most of the maps from their officers and taken charge of both their vehicles and their equipment. This lead to considerable confusion because weapons and kit that should have been

Royal Daffodil, *the flat-bottomed steamer that took Ted and his friends on their 'Weekend Trip'.*

loaded onto the personnel ship for use by the men and officers were loaded onto the vehicle ships *Kohistan* and the *City of Canterbury* instead. Furthermore, vehicles and equipment of different companies were mixed up which led to even more confusion on their arrival.

Ted was very proud of the fact that he was a driver of a Bren-gun carrier and he and Rob watched the confusion with a growing sense of unreality. The Bren-gun carrier looked rather like a small tank and was capable of speeds up to 40mph on good surfaces. Its real use though was its ability to travel easily over ploughed fields and rough countryside. The carrier had a crew of three. The gunner, who was in charge, sat beside the driver and the third man sat behind the gunner. Although the crew was normally exposed when travelling, if they came across enemy fire they could pull a lever which lowered the front seat so the gunner and driver were below the level or the front bullet-proof screens. The third man had room to crouch behind his own bullet-proof screen at the back. The petrol tanks were also protected making it a very practical serviceable machine that was very popular with those who used it.

The main role of the motorized regiments was to carry out patrols and overcome any obstacles that could impede the armoured advance. As well as intensive training in driving and the maintenance of vehicles and signals, they were also trained to clear woods and built-up areas, hold rivers, capture positions and take care of prisoners. Down to platoon and even section level they were designed to be as independent and self-supporting as possible. They carried their own ammunition, food, water and cooking equipment as well as an extensive tool kit, fire extinguishers and signalling lights, all things that were essential to a fast moving unit on the move. The week before they received their orders to go to Southampton, they had also been given a 3-inch mortar although they had never practised firing it and hadn't yet worked out how they would carry it on the Bren-gun carrier. Ted was proud of the importance of the role he had been detailed to perform and was looking forward to driving the carrier in a war situation.

However, the loaders were obviously in a hurry and treated the vehicles like scrap metal. When Ted and Chalky complained they were told they had to get the ships ready to sail as quickly as possible. Even more worrying as far as Ted was concerned, they had pumped out all the petrol from the trucks and Bren carriers and were storing it in very small jerry cans.

This was bad enough, but while they were being hurried aboard the *Royal Daffodil* by the same officious embarkation staff, they overheard a conversation between one of the officers and a loader. Obviously trying to make small talk the officer remarked that they were busy and that there were obviously a lot of ships sailing. The loader shook his head and replied in the negative. Not only were there very few ships sailing towards France, but in his opinion there would be a lot more of them coming home. As far as he was concerned they were going in the wrong direction.

Under the impression that there was only light enemy activity in the area which was why they were being deployed, Ted looked at Chalky who had also overheard this and saw his own concern mirrored in his face. The conversation was soon being repeated with embellishments, all round the ship, which hardly enhanced the mood of the men.

Expecting to be with their own company they were even more fed up when they discovered that no thought appeared to have been given to ensuring particular parts of the ship were allocated to individual companies. Consequently, Ted, Chalky, Rob and Taffy found themselves berthed on deck with some men of the 60th who were equally disorientated and fed up.

Finally, in convoy with the two vehicle ships, they set sail for Dover at 7.30 pm. However, they didn't get very far before they stopped and remained anchored at the end of Southampton water for some time. The decks were very crowded and uncomfortable and they were given very little to eat. Once they got underway again the sea was quite calm, but several of the men suffered from seasickness and had to either scramble to the rails to be sick over the side or throw up where they were. Ted was grateful his stomach was unaffected by either the sea or the men retching round him. He was exhausted after their long uncomfortable journey south and he would have loved to have been able to make himself comfortable enough to sleep.

As they continued underway, the sea remained calm and the instances of sea-sickness gradually lessened as the men either adjusted to the motion or had emptied their stomachs. Managing eventually to curl up nearer the rails Ted fell into a fitful doze only to wake up as they sailed into Dover at 6 am.

Chapter 5

'If I'd wanted to be a sailor I would have joined the Navy' Wednesday, 23 May 1940

'We left Southampton on 22 May 1940 and stopped in Dover on the 23rd for five hours before sailing for an unknown destination which turned out to be Calais.'[8]

The men had been woken at 5 am but the more experienced had immediately gone back to sleep, a wise decision as it was to be another hour before they sailed into Dover. Ted, disorientated through lack of sleep and having never been out of the country before, looked up at the shore and seeing all the coastal defences thought they had arrived in France. Seagulls circled lazily overhead, calling and shrieking as they looked for food and he could hear the water gently lapping against the hull. The sky was blue with hardly a cloud in sight and Ted was struck between the similarity between England and France. He'd expected it to look quite different but instead it looked just like Bournemouth. From his position on deck he could see Ariel masts on the top of the cliffs and on the beaches were enormous piles of scaffolding. Having spent time helping to erect sea defences in Bournemouth he assumed the French must have done the same in France.

To add to his confusion, in the far distance he could hear the sounds of gunfire and the muffled booms of heavy shelling. Ted held tight to his rifle and nervously waited for the order to disembark. It was only when a paper boy appeared above them on the cliffs announcing loudly in English that the Germans had overrun Holland that he realized they had, in fact, gone no further than Dover.

Relief that they were still in England soon turned to boredom and frustration as the troops waited to see what was going to happen next. They were also uncomfortable as they had embarked with enough of their kit to be ready for instant action and were not prepared for just sitting about. To add to their nervousness rumours were rife about the E boats and submarines patrolling the Channel and about mines protecting all the French ports. At 10.40 am, just when they were becoming really fed up and tempers were becoming frayed, the convoy sailed for Calais.

They were joined by the *Autocarrier* with the 229th Anti-Tank Battery on board. It had left Sheffield at 4.45 am on 21 May and arrived at Dover at 1.10 pm. Although scheduled to leave at 10.30 am on 22 May, their departure had been delayed because they had six wireless trucks on board that were meant for another unit. This meant there was no room for the whole of their battery so their commanding officer was eventually ordered to embark with only two of his troops and battery staff. The rest were due to follow within twelve hours. Because of this only eight of their twelve guns were loaded onto the ship and the rest never arrived at Calais at all.

But Ted and his friends knew nothing of this. They only knew they were tired, fed up and hungry. They had no idea where they were really going or why, although they had heard rumours and bets were still being taken as to their eventual destination.

Although Norway was still being mentioned, it was not now considered to be a realistic bet and most of those who *had* bet on it had come to the conclusion that they had probably lost their money. The northern ports of France were also not popular in terms of betting and most money was now centred on Cherbourg. One of the lads overheard the officers discussing their objectives and their conversation confirmed the erroneous view that a small mobile armoured unit was causing major problems behind the lines and it was their task to locate it and destroy it. This was exactly the task that Ted and his friends had been trained for, but as much as they would have liked to believe this, the conversation between the loader and the officer kept replaying itself in their minds. They were finally told their destination was to be Calais, but then realized the transport ships were not with them. This left them anxious about where their equipment was and when it would arrive at Calais.

For the first few months of the war Calais and the other northern channel ports had been of little military interest. Because the French initially refused to allow the British to use Calais, Dunkirk or Boulogne for fear of provoking the Germans, they had only been used to facilitate those members of the BEF who were going home to visit Britain on leave. Therefore the British supply lines stretched back to western France. Eventually, after considerable pressure by the British, the French relented but by the spring of 1940 only Boulogne was in use while the main supply routes still stretched back to the ports west of the Somme. Once the German campaign in the west started this changed, but by then it was too little too late.

The German breakthrough at Sedan on 14/15 May split the Allied armies in half. This was followed swiftly by the rapid advance of Guderian's panzers to

Abbeville on 20 May which effectively cut the supply lines. Calais, Boulogne and Dunkirk were now critically important, but even then the scale of the disaster was not readily apparent as communications and information to London were almost twenty-four hours behind. The first troops to land in Calais were charged with opening up a new supply line to the BEF which was still fighting near Lille and Arras, over fifty miles inland. There were also plans to evacuate the BEF through the three ports if necessary. The first elements of Calais Force, the Queen Victoria's Rifles and 3RTR had already arrived in the port on 22 May, but they were still concentrating on preparing to link up with the forces at Dunkirk and in creating new supply lines for the BEF.

By the morning of 23 May the Germans were much closer than at first thought and by mid-morning columns of German tanks from 1 Panzer were seen approaching from the south west. The QVRs sent out early-morning patrols to confirm the German positions but they never returned. Later in the morning Lieutenant Colonel Keller left Calais for St Omer which was more than twenty miles to the south-east. They were only five miles outside Calais at Guines when they ran into 1 Panzer Division who were approaching from Marquise and a short but extremely fierce battle took place. This first attack was successfully repulsed although the British tanks retreated to Coquelles, south-west of Calais and 1 Panzer moved on towards Dunkirk leaving X Panzer to take Calais.

The Rifle Brigade, however, were still completely unaware of the turn of events in France and as they travelled to Calais their orders were still simply to open up the supply lines to Dunkirk.

As they left Dover all troops were ordered below decks other than those who were to man the eight Bren guns on deck. For Ted and the other troops this was much more cramped and uncomfortable than being on deck. Doors and hatches were kept closed and the claustrophobic heat and constant throbbing of the engines added to their feelings of nausea. To add to their discomfort they weren't allowed to smoke below decks either.

For several hours, as the small convoy crossed the English Channel, the rest of the Rifle Brigade and the 60th remained in these cramped conditions. In an attempt to pass the time and ignore their surroundings several played cards, others wrote letters and the fortunate few who had learnt the military trick of being able to sleep anywhere, closed their eyes and slept soundly, much to the envy of their less experienced companions. But the cramped conditions were nothing compared to what was about to come:

'On the way over we were bombed by a German plane which did no damage and which was brought down by gunfire from the Archangel and we were torpedoed by depth charges that were dropped by our escorting destroyer.'

As they neared Calais the troops could hear gunfire and the sound of aircraft. Even below decks they could hear the muffled sounds of the explosions and every time a bomb was dropped in the sea they felt the ship pitch and roll in an alarming way.

The men looked at each other in alarm wondering what was going on above their heads and Ted began to wonder if they would survive the voyage and actually reach France.

'We'll 'ang out the washing on the Siegfried line … Seeing the unsettled mood one of the older more experienced sergeants had started singing. Although some of the soldiers looked at him in disbelief, others picked up on the refrain and joined in. The mood lightened slowly, especially as the more rude versions of other songs followed.

'Hitler has only got one ball … Himmler has similar and Goering has no balls at all …' This made them smile and although it didn't stop the bombs falling or completely stem the underlying unease, it did much to raise morale and even those who felt sick made an effort to join in.

The nearer Calais they got, the worse the bombing became. The continual screaming of the Stukas and Heinkels as they dive-bombed the convoy and the constant chatter of the machine guns from the gunners on deck became louder and louder. In an attempt to avoid the mines and the bombs the ship was also constantly changing direction which only added to the general nausea and unease.

Ted closed his eyes and offered up a silent prayer. It was one thing being able to fight back, but being stuck in this tin can listening to gunfire and explosions and not being in any position to do anything about it was not his idea of fun. He was a soldier, not a sailor and the sooner he was off this tub the better. Anything had to be better than this. Looking round at his friends he knew, from the expressions on their pale faces, that he was not the only one who felt like that.

Those on the deck at least had options and were in control of their own destiny. As things stood, if the ship took a direct hit, they would have no chance at all. It was bad enough being on deck with all that water around them but being stuck under the deck and not being able to see what was going on was a million times worse.

Just as they thought it could not get any worse the sound of a particularly loud explosion rocked the ship, closely followed by another. They could hear the machine guns firing frantically and the screaming sound of a plane diving. They found out afterwards that a Heinkel had dropped two bombs perilously close to the *Archangel*. Fortunately both had missed but the feeling of being a sitting target did not leave them until they were standing on the firm ground again.

Although Ted and the men below decks were finding it frustrating, the gunners who had been left on deck on air alarm stations were finding it even more so. Frustrated by their inability to hit the German bombers, the gunners took unnecessary risks. Their feelings of frustration were exacerbated by the knowledge that the gunners on the *Archangel* sailing close behind them, had successfully taken down a German plane earlier which crashed into the sea on their starboard bow showering them with spray.

Because they were coming out of the sun it was difficult to get a fix on the Stukas as they dive-bombed them until they were right over head, hence the increasing propensity to take risks. They were even more irritated by the behaviour of one of the corporals who kept wandering round the deck picking up the spent cartridges to see how many rounds they had fired.

The gunner whose gun it was that the corporal was monitoring, murmured in disbelief, 'Doesn't he know there's a bloody war on?' He looked anxiously upwards hoping to see a sight of the RAF. As if in answer to his prayers, a familiar sound was suddenly heard in the distance as two Hurricanes appeared in the sky above them and begun chasing the Stukas off. A spectacular display of aerobatics ensued as the Stukas and Hurricanes duelled high in the sky above the English Channel, their only witnesses the men of the convoy watching from their vantage point far below. Round and round they went gracefully, like two protagonists tied into some macabre dance to which only they knew the moves. To the men it appeared as if everything was in slow motion and they watched transfixed. Suddenly a plume of smoke appeared from one of the German planes followed swiftly by an explosion as the plane disintegrated into several pieces which fell slowly into the sea with a series of splashes. The gunners stood up from their gun emplacements and cheered, for once ignoring the Sergeant's admonishments to get down.

When they finished cheering they looked back up in time to see the second German plane heading back to the French coast with the Hurricane in close pursuit. The puff of smoke from its tail heralded its impeding end and even from there they could hear its dying engines as it whirled round and round plummeting and spiralling towards the sea. Something white appearing to shoot upwards caught their eyes and they could just make out the parachute as the pilot or one of his crew managed to escape the dying plane before it hit the sea and disappeared below the icy depths.

Dipping their wings in the customary victory wave the Hurricanes continued on their way back to the French coast. For the men above decks it had at last given them some hope and they swiftly recounted the details of the air fight to the waiting soldiers nearest the hatches. The information was quickly circulated amongst the others with several embellishments, but it helped to raise their spirits.

Their jubilation was short-lived though as the ship suddenly pitched and rolled alarmingly and the air around them echoed to the sound of enormous explosions, each louder than the one before. The ship rocked so much that they felt it would turn over completely.

As a brief gap between the explosions gave some relief from the pitching and rocking, the word quickly went round that a torpedo had just missed them and their escorting destroyer had been dropping depth charges to try and flush it out.

Ted was feeling thoroughly demoralized now. He hadn't expected it to be like this. It was nothing like the films he had seen. They were just sitting ducks here. If the ship went down they wouldn't stand a chance in full kit. Gradually, to his intense relief, the noise of the explosions faded into the distance and the movement of the ship became much less violent. Now the immediate danger had passed the tension amongst the men gradually dissipated and those nearest Ted resumed their card game. He watched with half his attention, the other half of him still praying that they at least survived to reach their destination and that it would be sooner rather than later. He didn't think he could stand to be trapped on the ship much longer.

Fortunately it seemed as if someone was listening to his prayers and the rest of the journey was reasonably uneventful. But it was still with intense relief they heard the ships engines begin to slow down and knew they were approaching the harbour. With the *Archangel* close behind them they nosed slowly into the berth that was reserved for them and prepared to disembark. Once ready, they followed the instructions to go ashore and got their first glimpse of Calais.

'On arriving at Calais harbour we found??? at ??? [9] so we circled and immediately set up defensive positions as we were told that Jerry was about three miles away. The town had almost been evacuated and was burning furiously in about eight or nine places.'

However, for the disembarking men their first sight of the town was not at all what they had expected. The docks were a shambles with untended fires in some of the buildings and civilians and soldiers milling about, seemingly aimlessly. They were also littered with abandoned kit from those non-combatants who were racing to get aboard the ships that the incoming troops were still vacating. Many on them looked battered and dishevelled which didn't provide the ideal welcome for the disembarking soldiers.

These first impressions were not helped when they looked out beyond the docks and towards the town itself. It appeared that several parts of the town were on fire. They could count at least eight or nine different places where smoke was rising and flames could be seen. There was broken glass everywhere and an air of desolation. As the men disembarked another Heinkel flew over dropping bombs and strafing anyone in the open. The loaders immediately ran for cover leaving the vehicles and equipment untended and unloaded. The cranes did not seem to be working either, although whether from bomb damage, lack of electricity or sabotage was unclear. Already exhausted from lack of sleep and their uncomfortable journey Ted, Chalky, Rob and Taffy looked at each other wearily. It was obviously going to be a long process. The whole place looked like something from Dante's *Inferno* and was nothing like the orderly scene they had expected. The sound of shelling, mortars and gunfire was ominously close and the acrid smell of cordite caught in the back of their throats making them cough.

Finding no one available to unload their equipment one of the sergeants then ordered them to do their own unloading. This caused plenty of grumbling from the tired men who with much cursing and complaining began the process of unloading at least some of their equipment. Other soldiers broke open the packs that had already been unloaded and doled out the linen bandoliers of .303SAA in clips of five rounds to anyone who wanted them.

With rounds of ammunition slung round their necks they looked more like bandits than soldiers and were soon almost bent double with the weight. There was still no sign of the transport ships and the tide was beginning to go out. Ted and the others looked anxiously at the ebbing tide. If it got much lower the ships wouldn't be able to get in at all. They could hardly be a motorized battalion if they had no transport and without transport their job would be that much harder.

In 1940 the town of Calais was still contained within a line of bastions and ramparts. Although these were modified after the Franco-Prussian War this work was more than sixty years old and Brigadier Nicholson soon realized it was not possible to defend the outer perimeter for any length of time. He therefore decided that the inner perimeter - which included the northern part of Calais - the old town, the docks and the Citadel was the best place to make his main stand. This was a shorter line to hold and much of it had the added advantage of including the protection of water lines provided by the canals that ran through Calais and in the docks as well.

Eventually, with no transport in sight and the tide gradually going out, the decision was made for the troops to make their way to their 'hide' areas in the dunes to wait for the transport there. These areas had already been mapped out earlier by the officers while they were on the ship, and while the KRRC (60th) went to the south edge of the Bassin des Chasses de l'ouest, the 1st Battalion, Rifle Brigade, were directed to take up a position in the sandhills between the north side of Bassin des Chasses and the sea, where they could keep a look out for their vehicle ships.

'Right lads fall in, keep alert and let's get dug in quickly.' The orders were welcome as the men became increasingly restless just standing around doing nothing. Feeling slightly more cheerful as it seemed they now had some purpose, they fell in and headed towards the dunes. But this feeling didn't last long as to get to the dunes in the north they needed to go through the Gare Maritime (railway station).

As the troops marched through the station they saw the remains of bombed-out trucks on the lines and more worryingly, lines of stretchers on the platforms. There were fires still raging in some of the buildings and a strange smell in the air. They looked more closely and saw that many of the stretchers were covered completely. It was obvious that those on stretchers were dead and for many men this was the first time they had seen one dead body let alone rows of them. But that was only half of it.

As they continued on their way to the dunes they were passed with increasing frequency by stretcher-bearers carrying the injured and wounded to the ships that would take them home to England. The moans and screams of the wounded and dying were almost worse than seeing the stretchers carrying the dead as they could hear the pain in their voices. Even more pitiful was the sound of those who were calling out for their mothers or for something to kill the pain. Others were just screaming, a continuous wave of unintelligible sounds conjuring up their worst nightmares; only this was real.

'Eyes front!' came the order but despite their discipline it was only half obeyed as the troops found it almost impossible not to look at the stretchers as they passed. 'Eyes front lads. They don't need you gawping at them do they?' This time the order had more effect and, trying to ignore the noise and the smell, they concentrated on looking ahead as they continued onto the dunes. Once there they dug themselves in. They still had very little equipment as all their tools were on the transport ships, but at least the sand was soft enough to allow them to use their bayonets to dig shell scrapes that were deep enough to afford them some cover. As if to hamper their efforts the heavens opened and yet again they were soaked by driving rain. Finally though, the trenches were dug and the rain eased off and they settled down to wait for their transport. By now there were serious concerns about their lack of transport. Other than the eight Bren guns the troops had and which had to be divided between them, they had very few armaments and without their vehicles and weapons there was very little they could do.

Unable to do anything else the men followed the Sergeant's advice to brew some tea. Having the chance to chat, smoke and make tea helped to relieve the tension. Those who were more experienced took the opportunity to get some sleep in the relative comfort of the dunes. Sipping their hot tea, eating their bully, biscuits and chocolate, and smoking the first cigarette since Dover that morning they relaxed for the first time since leaving England. Although they could hear shelling in the distance and the dock area was occasionally lit up with the flashes of mortar fire they felt much safer than on board the ships.

The excitement and stress of the past twenty-four hours were finally beginning to catch up with them and yawning loudly Ted said he was going to try and get some sleep while he could. The others agreed and after finishing their tea, emptying their dregs in the sand and smoking their cigarettes to the end, they dug themselves into their holes and closed their eyes. As a lifelong Baptist Ted always said his prayers before he slept and tonight was no exception. He had the feeling that tonight his prayers were needed more than ever, not only for himself and his family, but also for all his friends who were about to face the biggest challenge of their young lives. He prayed that not only would they be safe, but that they would all find the courage they needed to carry out whatever orders they were given with honour, bravery and dignity. As he was at last dozing off his thoughts returned to his brief conversation with the Sergeant as they had marched through the station

'What's that smell Sarg?' The somewhat sickly familiar smell had been puzzling Ted ever since they arrived.

'Burning bodies', the Sergeant replied grimly. Ted had swallowed nervously as they marched passed the dead and the dying, the words of the loader back in Southampton prophesizing that they were going in the wrong direction, even clearer in his head.

That feeling of foreboding was reinforced as they watched the speed in which other soldiers, officers and civilians boarded the *Maid of Orleans* that had carried the 3rd Royal Tank Regiment. They looked as if they really couldn't get away fast enough. The thought that it did look as if everyone was going in the other direction except them, was the last one Ted had before falling into an uneasy sleep.

Chapter 6

Too Close for Comfort
Thursday 24 May 1940

'The day passed without further incident and at midnight the section was called off to go up the Boulogne Road and shift an anti-tank gun so that we could make communications with the BEF at Boulogne and we had the help of three medium tanks as back-up we met just outside Calais' [10]

Brigadier Nicholson had been ordered to escort 350,000 rations to Dunkirk where the BEF were already on half rations. To aid in this operation, earlier in the day he had ordered the withdrawal of the 3rd Royal Tank Regiment back to Calais where they were to assemble after dark in the Parc Saint-Pierre opposite the Hotel de Ville. Here they would fill up with petrol ready to support elements of 1st Battalion the Rifle Brigade in their attempt to open up the road towards Dunkirk. They were then to make their way to the Pont Saint-Pierre, the bridge that straddled the Canal de Calais, where the Boulevard Lafayette and Boulevard de L'Egalite met, and wait for further orders.

Unaware he was surrounded, Brigadier Nicholson met with Lieutenant Colonel Keller at 11 pm at Pont Saint-Pierre to discuss the support needed to open the road to Gravelines. Unsure whether the road was still open it was decided to send a patrol consisting of one cruiser and three light tanks of B Squadron, 3rd Royal Tank Regiment under the command of Major Reeves along the Calais-Gravelines road to see if was clear. Major Reeves and his patrol had not gone far when they lost wireless contact with the tanks behind them. Unperturbed they carried on through three unguarded German roadblocks and lines of German tanks until they reached the safety of Gravelines. Somehow the Germans had mistaken them for their own tanks and therefore ignored them. However, although the men had reached the safety of the British in Gravelines, the radios were not working properly so they were unable to contact Lieutenant Colonel Keller to let him know about the roadblocks.

Having waited some time and still unsure whether the road was open or not, at 3 am Brigadier Nicholson made the decision to try again. This time he sent a composite force made up of one squadron of tanks and a company of the Rifle Brigade to find out. If it was still open, they would be able to escort the rations halfway to the BEF in Dunkirk.

Earlier, Ted, Chalky, Taffy and Rob had left the relative safety of their dugouts in the sand dunes with the rest of their company and made their way to the Dunkirk road where they had been told to await further orders. Moving as cautiously as possible they made their way carefully along the road. The shelling of the town was intensifying and the sky was lit up with the flashes of mortar fire and heavy artillery. The ground shook every time a heavy shell landed and the noise was deafening. By the time they arrived at their given point on the road between Le Beau-Marais and Marck, it was daylight so they pulled off onto the roadside under cover while the tanks went on ahead to recce the land. After several minutes, which seemed like hours to the waiting men, they returned and informed Brigadier Nicholson there was a strong German roadblock further up among the houses and allotments. Unable to bluff their way through in the same way Major Reeves had, it was decided that the Rifle Brigade should go on ahead and clear the way leaving the road open for the convoy to pass. Ted and Chalky were two of the twenty men chosen and heads down, rifles at the ready, they followed the others and the Major in the direction of the roadblock.

Progress was painfully slow as they hoped to get as close as possible before being seen. But they had not travelled far when they were spotted by the Germans who immediately let loose a barrage of artillery and mortar fire. Reacting automatically as the first rounds were fired, the men dived off the road to reach what little cover there was. Fortunately the guns hadn't yet got the range and the shells flew harmlessly overhead exploding with a furious noise that shook the ground and hurt their ear drums. After several minutes of inactivity it became apparent that it would not be too long before the gunners found the range and the British troops started taking hits. Major Hamilton-Russell made a decision and called them back. Keeping low they inched their way towards him and while the shells roared over their heads he looked at his map and considered their options.

They were ordered to split into two sections to form a pincer and come up behind the German position. As part of this pincer Ted and nine others were ordered up the railway line, but no sooner had they begun their perilous journey when the Germans spotted them and opened fire with a machine gun. Again the men dived for what little cover was available but it was too late. Ted felt something scrape his helmet and threw himself flat. 'That was bloody close', he said turning towards the man who he knew was behind him. To his horror he saw him lying a few feet away, blood pouring from a head wound. The bullet that had scraped his own helmet had ricocheted and killed him. But there was no time for Ted to take it in or to realize just how close he had come to death. All around him was noise and chaos. As well as the deafening sound of the bullets ricocheting and bouncing off the railway lines and the ground in front of them, there was the constant shouting of the men of both sides as they gave directions or warned of danger. Added to this was the almost unbearable screaming and shouting of the wounded. They had taken at least two other casualties and for a brief while Ted forgot his narrow escape and concentrated on firing angrily in the direction of the Germans. Somewhere to the front of him he could hear the incoherent murmuring and screaming of German casualties. Having advanced towards the British lines they were too badly wounded to get back to their own lines and their fellow Germans were unable to come forward far enough to reach them.

One of the more unpleasant things they had been taught in training now made sense to him. If you kill the enemy they are without one man. If you wound them, particularly in the stomach, it takes at least one other man, possible two, to look after him so the enemy has lost three possible combatants. Furthermore, they make a lot of noise which is demoralizing for other members of their company. He closed his ears to their screaming and moaning and tried to concentrate on the job in hand. The barrage continued, but they stayed where they were and doggedly returned fire, making sure every bullet counted. Taking casualties and seeing they were not to be moved, the Germans retaliated by sending over some small high-explosive mortar shells which fortunately did no damage, but came uncomfortably close.

For over four hours they held their positions and gradually advanced so that at last they had overrun their original objective by about 3,500 yards forcing the Germans back. Unaware of the situation on the rest of the front line they would probably have continued to advance but for the order to retire. This order came from Brigadier Nicholson who, upon receiving reports from other front line sites within and around the town, realized that if they stayed where they were they would be surrounded. Not realizing that they were in danger of being surrounded and feeling that they had the upper hand, the order to retire was not very well received. However, orders were orders and they had to be obeyed. Grumbling outwardly, but inwardly rather relieved that they had survived their first encounter with the enemy, they put down covering fire to enable them to get their wounded back. The man behind Ted who had been killed was not their only casualty, two other men had also been wounded, one quite badly and they needed to get him back to the main party who were still waiting at the original position. Carefully, making sure the Germans were unable to use their retreat to overrun them, what was left of the scouting party made it back. They were only just in time as the main party was preparing to withdraw. When the scouting party arrived back they realized their casualties were not the only ones. They saw one of their trucks alight and smouldering over by the bushes. The initial 3-inch mortar shells fired by the Germans that had soared harmlessly over their heads had exploded further back onto the main party. One had scored a direct hit onto the truck killing three men and wounding four others.

Realizing it was now futile to try and advance, aware he was probably already surrounded, and mindful of the small numbers of troops at his command Brigadier Nicholson made the decision to call it off and the men were pulled back to defend the outer perimeter of Calais. The two platoons taken from the 1st Battalion to make up this composite force were never to rejoin the rest who were kept in reserve in the dunes. Instead, they were to be deployed in small groups to strengthen other positions on the front line.

It was only as they made their way back under the continuous shelling and gun fire that the reality of what had just happened hit Ted. It was his first time under fire, and once the fight started he had no time to feel scared. Like the others he had initially felt buoyant he had survived, had performed well and had not frozen or in any other way disgraced himself. But reaction was now starting to kick in. He had been so close, another inch and it would have been him lying in a ditch in France, not the other man, whose only mistake had been to have the misfortune to be standing behind him. Looking round he saw that he wasn't the only one, some of the lads were shaking and at least two were crying.

Ted fixed his gaze firmly ahead and made himself concentrate on something else, then glancing round again at his companions he was almost surprised to see how dirty and tattered they looked. The man nearest him had patches of dried blood on his battledress and there were several rips in his trousers. Ted didn't know if he looked as bad. Glancing down at his own uniform he saw that he too had patches of dried blood, mud and the occasional tear where his trousers had caught on brambles. He sent up a silent thankful prayer that the blood wasn't his and that a bit of mud and a few rips in his uniform were all the damage he seemed to have suffered. He wished they could all have been as lucky. Shaking himself mentally, realizing there was no point in dwelling on things, he returned his attention to his surroundings and looked round with interest to see what had been happening while he had been gone.

While they had been fighting the rest of the Battalion had moved forward from the dunes and taken up positions further inland. In the distance they could see that the station yard was ablaze with cars, ambulances and ammunition lorries burning away and once again they were deafened, only this time it was by the thunderous noise of the ammunition exploding. It also looked like they had some more transport and weapons.

The *Kohistan* and *City of Canterbury* had eventually arrived at 3 pm but it was low water and there were no tugs to tow them into the avant-port (outer harbour) where they could be unloaded. Unable to dock they had sat outside the harbour in low water for an hour and a half until the tide turned and they were able to get in. Unloading finally started at 5 pm.

Unfortunately the German gunners had found the correct range, so bombing and heavy shelling continually interrupted the unloading. The British stevedores were already exhausted as they had spent the previous day unloading the 350,000 rations for the BEF, and the French stopped work every time the Germans started shelling or bombarding the docks. Thirty tons of petrol, which had been shipped in wooden crates, had to be unloaded first before they could even reach the transport. By the time it came to unload the Rifle Brigade equipment there was only one crane working and the stevedores and crane hands finished work at 10 pm. Nearly all the weapons, equipment and ammunition of both battalions were packed onto the vehicles and it was only with great difficulty that Captain T. R. Gordon-Duff was able to persuade the exhausted stevedores to return at 3 am the next morning.

To make matters worse, throughout the night and early morning, while Ted and the others were trying to break through to Dunkirk, conflicting orders were received about whether Calais was to be evacuated. But by 7.30 am it was widely assumed that the plan was to evacuate and the Transport Officer at the Gare Maritime ordered the holds of the *City of Canterbury* to be closed. Movement Control and the quay staff then announced they had orders from the War Office to return home. The ship would sail for England within the hour and therefore all unloading was to be immediately stopped. Unfortunately only half of the 1st Battalion's transport had been brought ashore and much of their equipment and ammunition was still on board. Major Allen, their second in command, was horrified as his orders clearly stated that the final evacuation would not occur for at least another thirty-six hours. They needed all their transport, equipment and ammunition to have any chance of holding out until then and for them to cover any withdrawal.

The Gare Maritime came under increasingly heavy shelling as the morning progressed. The decks of the *City of Canterbury* were by now covered with wounded, many of them carried there by drivers from the Rifle Brigade who were still waiting for their vehicles, and the bombardment was getting worse. The ship departed at 8.30 am without unloading the other half of the desperately needed equipment. The *Kohistan* remained until noon while all the non-fighting men were released to join her, then she too left under heavy shellfire. As no one was expecting her to be the final ship to leave there was no panic and many of the remaining men waved her out of the harbour fully expecting her to return to help in their evacuation at a later time.

On their return to Calais, Ted and the other members of the Rifle Brigade were split up to either cover roadblocks or to reinforce other companies. However, as it was some time since they last ate they were first given time to have some lunch. They sat down and hungrily consumed their emergency rations which consisted of bully beef and biscuits followed by chocolate and a drink of water. Although Ted was really thirsty he had been sure that he wouldn't be able to eat so he was surprised at just how hungry he was and despite the noise of the continual bombardment, how quickly he wolfed down his rations.

Earlier in the day, following the heavy shelling that had breached the outer perimeter in several places, the Germans had launched an attack from the south-west. This had put the positions held by the 60th Rifles in danger so orders were given to withdraw and take up new positions. While the 60th Rifles used the moat in the old town to mark their boundary the Rifle Brigade were ordered to set up their new positions behind the Marck Canal. Their position was to be bordered on the left by the Perimeter canal and on their right by the Calais Canal.

The situation was rapidly worsening. The men had no supporting artillery and only two remaining anti-tank guns. Due to a mix up with the demolition charges they were even unable to blow up the bridges that spanned the canals. On the evening of 23 May a naval vessel had pulled up beside the *Kohistan* and unloaded some anti-tank mines and one and a half tons of gelignite which was left on the quay together with a demolition party. After a brief look at the primers the demolition party had stated that they were unsuitable which meant that the gelignite was useless. However it was still too dangerous to leave it on the dock even though at that time the bombardment of the docks was not particularly serious. With little else to do the demolition party were then persuaded to remove it safely to the dunes to wait for the arrival of the correct primers. Unfortunately these never arrived.

But Ted and his companions were unaware of these details and were taking the opportunity to rest and finish their rations when the Major came over and issued them with their new orders. These were to support the QVRs who had taken heavy casualties and were currently pinned down by the canal. Ted and the others spent a few minutes familiarizing themselves with the area both on the map and through field glasses and then prepared to move out. The shelling was even heavier than before and as they made their way through the streets to the canal, the sky was continually lit up with brilliant flashes coming from the heavy mortar fire .

Although the bombing and continual raids by German aircraft were constant this was not their main concern. Advancing through built-up areas was always fraught with danger, especially as they had not been particularly trained for this type of warfare. But the tension in the air was heightened as they had been warned of the continuing activity of fifth columnists. These were believed to have been resident in the city prior to the attack or to have entered the city amongst the hordes of fleeing refugees who had swarmed into the city ahead of the German invasion looking for boats to England. Whereas some were there solely to keep the Germans informed of their positions, others were snipers. It was these the men were most concerned about as they carefully made their way through the city, past derelict buildings and those that were relatively unscathed. Not knowing the snipers were there until they fired, meant it was inevitably too late for at least one person.

As they made their way towards the canal their journey was punctuated every so often by swarms of German planes flying over dispensing death and destruction in equal measure. But, other than taking cover until the danger had passed, they had little effect on Ted and his friends who were almost becoming used to the constant bombardment.

The air was thick with dust and smoke but even if they hadn't known where the canal was they could have found it by following the sound of artillery and small arms fire which intensified as they got closer. Relatively unscathed they reached what was left of the Queen Vics who had been fighting for two days with very little equipment. Having had virtually no sleep since they had arrived and running short of food, water and ammunition they were more than pleased to see Ted and his colleagues approaching from the rear.

As the men of B Company crawled over to the men they were replacing, dust and smoke filled their lungs and obscured their view making it difficult to aim accurately. The Queen Vics looked dishevelled, their uniforms in tatters and covered in a mixture of mud, grease and dried blood. Ted wondered briefly if he looked the same, but he didn't have much time to think about it before he realized the predicament they were in. With no tools, sandbags or wire they were at a severe disadvantage. The east side of the canal had little cover to offer and he frantically dug into the earth with his bayonet to enlarge the shell scrape one of the Queen Vics had just vacated so he could at least get his backside down because he felt dangerously exposed.

He was joined almost immediately by a couple of other men who, after digging their own shell scrapes with as much haste as Ted, fired off some rounds in the direction of the Germans. Immediately the Germans returned fire and a particularly ferociously round of machine gun fire whistled dangerously close to their heads causing them to duck back down quickly. This exchange of gunfire continued for some time with the Germans getting closer with every succeeding barrage. Bullets rattled round their heads and ricocheted noisily off the surrounding banks, throwing up earth and stones that added to the general noise and confusion. It was apparent that they needed to find cover and quickly or they would be slaughtered.

Looking around they saw some potato sacks and decided that if they could reach them they could fill them with soil and use them as a defensive wall.

Ted counted to three and ran full pelt at a crouch back to the house where the sacks were and threw himself flat on the ground as bullets rattled round him, ricocheting off the ground and zinging off the roof tiles. Taking a deep breath he grabbed the sacks and then looked frantically round at the surrounding properties for some soil. There was nothing close to hand and he realized that the nearest soil was in the gardens on the other side of the road. There was no way he could reach them as there was no cover. He waited for a brief lull in the shelling and then, taking another big breath, ran as quickly as he could back to the canal and explained the situation.

Frantically looking around, the beleaguered riflemen then made the decision to try and get into the houses that backed onto the canal. They didn't know if they were empty or not but they were rapidly running out of choices. The German bombardment was intensifying and the continual shouting was making Ted's throat sore. That and the smoke was making him really thirsty but he dare not drink as he only had the one water bottle and the canal didn't look that appetizing - especially as he was sure that was an arm he saw floating in front of him.

Sighing heavily and muttering a silent prayer under his breath Ted repeated the half-crouching, zigzag run back to the houses behind them, concerned that the bullets he heard following him would find their mark. He was lucky and reached the house safely, but there his luck deserted him and despite frantic efforts with his rifle butt he was unable to break the sturdy locks on the doors. Giving it up as a bad job he headed back yet again to the canal. He was only just in time as the whining drone of a squadron of Stukas clearly heading in their direction could be heard. Hands covering their heads the men tried to make themselves as small as possible while the Stukas dive-bombed them repeatedly. The attack only lasted a short time but to the men of the Rifle Brigade it seemed like it would never end. Ted could no longer hear anything and he couldn't breathe properly. His lungs felt like they were full of dust and his throat ached from the acrid smoke and cordite that had replaced the oxygen in the air around him. Although his eyes were firmly shut they felt like they were full of grit and he had to fight hard to resist the urge to rub them. When they flew off it was several minutes before the thick, swirling smoke cleared and they realized that the attack was over. When Ted finally felt it was safe to remove his arms from over his head he was surprised to find that apart from damage to his hearing and breathing, which was probably temporary, he appeared to be uninjured.

As his hearing gradually returned he realized he could hear a crackling sound and that the smoke he could smell was different to that he had become used to. Turning round slowly, taking care to keep his head down, he looked back at the surrounding houses that he had been unable to break into just a short time ago. Those that were still standing were engulfed in thick black smoke and dust and had flames shooting several feet into the air. Ted saw people's possessions burning along with their furniture. As he watched, more walls crumbled and exposed glimpses of a peacetime life that seemed so long ago. He was grateful now that they had been unable to get in. If they had they would probably have been dead or, at the very least, badly injured.

He turned round and looked to either side and was relieved to see that his best friends were also unhurt although they were filthy and covered in soil, mud and something else that he belatedly realized was blood. But it seemed they were in the minority. Others hadn't been so lucky. Several riflemen had died in the attack, their life blood seeping slowly into the earth beneath. Others were no longer identifiable, torn apart by the ferocity of the bombings and explosions. Others had no marks at all on them, the blast damage having left no outside trace of the cause of their death.

Ted looked in disbelief at the carnage around him, struggling to take it in. Not far from where he was dug in he saw one of his friends who had talked about his wife and children only two days ago. At first glance Ted had thought him alive; it was only on closer inspection that he realized his body was only held together by his uniform. Ted tried to stem the rising bile and made himself look away. But all around were reminders of the murderous barrage. He tried to ignore the sight of the disembodied limbs and parts of bodies that he didn't recognize and focus on the living. But the dead were only one part of the scene that met his eyes. Other riflemen were severely injured. A few feet to the left one man was unsuccessfully trying to stem the bleeding on the man next to him whose leg had been severed at the knee. As Ted watched the man's life slowly drained away and his eyes stared sightlessly at him.

Ted was unable to take his eyes away for a moment and then his training kicked in. He swore loudly, picked up his rifle again and turned his attention back to the action which was rapidly becoming too close for comfort. There was no time to grieve, no time for anything other than to carry on fighting. Rumours were rife that the Germans didn't take prisoners, just shot them. Whether this was true or not they didn't know but the Poles who had escaped to Britain told tales of atrocities that made them all the more determined to fight to the death. If they were going to die anyway they might as well take some of the bastards with them. His angry thoughts were interrupted by a frantic shout saying the Stukas were returning

Ted didn't need the warning. They had all heard the dreaded droning of the Stukas and were already curling up into the foetal position in an attempt to make themselves invisible. But fortunately this time the Germans didn't bomb them or shoot at them. Instead they dropped leaflets urging them to surrender. Ted looked in disbelief at the leaflets cascading round his head and then slowly let out his breath. At least leaflets didn't kill. But the brief lull did not last long and Ted was sure that they were getting more accurate with every shell. He was also concerned that he was running extremely low on ammunition. It seemed the others were also rapidly running out too and so they were extremely grateful to be given the order to start falling back.

While one of the riflemen aimed the Bren gun in the direction of what appeared to be the main German onslaught and sprayed covering fire with what remained of the Bren gun ammunition, Ted and the others took the opportunity to crawl rapidly towards the relative protection of the few buildings that were still standing. Once there he and a couple of others fired and reloaded rapidly ensuring the Germans kept their heads down, while others threw hand grenades and fired what was left of the mortars into the enemy lines. The rifleman grabbed the now useless Bren gun and half running, half crouching, sped towards the buildings where they were waiting. He had just reached them when another squadron of Stukas flew over their heads strafing the ground where they had been entrenched only a few moments earlier.

The men continued in this vein, from house to house, street to street, covering each other and gradually withdrawing until they had retired back to a new position between two dock basins. Relatively safe for the moment they sat back and watched as directly above them the air was alive with the screams and whines of the Stukas and Hurricanes as they fought their own battle to the death in the skies over their heads. They could hear the rattle of their guns and see the puffs of smoke and they watched enthralled, their own position temporarily forgotten.

To their delight smoke appeared on one of the engines of a German plane. The fire spread rapidly and soon engulfed the aircraft in flames. It span wildly out of control and then exploded with a deafening roar showering the countryside with debris and burning fuel. It was swiftly followed by another German plane that whirled faster and faster out of control, screaming in its death agonies until it plummeted nose first into the ground. It exploded on impact sending a large cloud of dust and smoke into the air. The cheers of delight quickly turned to dismay as the demise of the two German planes was followed by the explosion of one of the Hurricanes and then to relief as they saw the tell-tale sign of a parachute as the pilot escaped just in time.

By 6 pm the Germans had broken through the outer perimeter and Brigadier Nicholson was forced to move his headquarters from the Boulevard Leon Gambetta to the Gare Maritime on the waterfront. The Royal Navy destroyers HMS *Wessex* and *Vimiera* continued to provide artillery support together with the Polish warship *Burza* until the *Wessex* was sunk and the *Vimiera* and *Burza* were damaged. HMS *Wolfhound* and HMS *Verity* also made trips to Calais carrying supplies of ammunition and on one trip brought Admiral J. F. Somerville who had a meeting with Brigadier Nicholson to ascertain the British position. Nicholson informed him that his men were desperately short of ammunition and that he only had two anti-tank guns and two light anti-aircraft guns left. The Admiral took this information back home and the Navy prepared plans to evacuate the Calais force. But Churchill was already coming to the conclusion that the troops at Calais would have to fight on for as long as possible to allow the BEF to reach Dunkirk. Realizing the implications of this, he did not make the final decision until the next day.

By the time Ted and his companions reached the rest of the Battalion and dug in for the night the sun was fast sinking in the west. They were exhausted from their experiences and conversation was limited. Not only had they witnessed the death of friends and comrades they had also inflicted their own casualties on the enemy and much as they might have wanted revenge for the deaths of their friends it was not easy to come to terms with killing another human being. As the sun gradually sank lower and lower they ate their rations, drank some water and smoked, for the most part in silence.

As it sank into the sea the sun added its own red hue to the skies over Calais which were already glowing red from the many uncontrolled fires still raging and the constant shelling from the advancing Germans. All around them smoke, clouds of dust and the ever-present smell of gunfire and cordite were now joined by the crackle of buildings as they burned and the sound of falling masonry as homes and businesses collapsed into piles of unrecognizable rubble. But the shelling now seemed to have faded into the distance and relieved that there seemed to be a temporary lull in the German onslaught, Ted gradually fell into a restless sleep, his dreams punctuated by the intermittent shelling and continuing small arms fire as his fellow defenders in other parts of Calais continued to hold off the advancing Germans.

Chapter 7

'Like Hell Let Loose on Earth'
Friday 25 May 1940

During 25 May X Panzer Division made a concerted attack on the defences on the inner perimeter. These were now made up of numerous separate posts which although able to provide supporting fire were essentially isolated. Despite this they managed to hold off the Germans for the whole day. In the middle of the afternoon Brigadier Nicholson moved his headquarters for the final time to the Citadel.

It had been relatively quiet overnight but, exhausted as they were, the men had not really been able to sleep. They were constantly on the alert and although there was a kind of still in the air they were very much aware it was like the calm before the storm. As dawn broke the fighting resumed and by sunrise the Rife Brigade were once again under a fierce artillery barrage.

The fighting was becoming desperate. By now they only had a few scout cars, light tanks and Bren-gun carriers to support them. Although Ted was away from the canals he could hear the fierce fighting in the distance. To his horror, from his position, he could also see the ominous sight of the German swastika flying high above the Hotel de Ville. The bell tower of the hotel was the equivalent of Big Ben and this meant German snipers had an unrestricted view of anyone moving near the three bridges that spanned the canals and waterways dividing the German and British front lines. It was only a matter of time before the Germans were able to smash through the roadblocks and barricades that formed part of the outer ring of defence.

Ted and a few others were given new orders to take cover in one of the buildings and fire at any Germans coming over the canal. The building in question had already been hit several times and part of it was exposed to the elements. They clambered over the rubble and headed for the stairs that still remained to give themselves some height. Before they managed to climb the stairs they spotted activity coming from the canal and took it in turns to launch some small arms and mortar fire in the general direction of the advancing

Germans. Their fire was eventually rewarded by the sight of German soldiers falling and then silence. Now the returning fire had stopped they resumed their climb. The bombing had loosened the plaster and as they climbed bits fell off the walls crashing on the ground beneath.

Rob's voice echoed down the stairs, 'I hope these stairs are safe'. This remark was greeted with hoots of laughter from the others as the irony of his comment struck them.

'We're in the middle of a war with Jerrys trying to kill us however they can and you're worried about whether the stairs are going to collapse!' Ted found this really amusing.

'Well I don't want to have an accident', Rob replied indignantly. 'What's it gonna look like to my family? Instead of "killed in action fighting bravely for his country" it will be, "he fell down the stairs!"'

They all laughed, glad to have some relief from the constant tension and carried on up the stairs and round the small bend at the top into what had once been the front room of someone's house. Torn curtains flapped in the open space where the window had been. Dust and debris covered what had probably once been an expensive sofa and chairs; a newspaper lay half open on a wooden table, its print obscured by dust, and a child's teddy bear lay in the middle of the floor. The sight was a poignant reminder of happier times.

Ted positioned himself to the side of the empty space which had once been the window. Leaning back against the wall he had a good view of the street in front of him. He carefully scanned the area, at first seeing nothing out of the ordinary. There seemed to be a lull in the fighting on the canal and for a short time it was reasonably quiet. Sounds of normal life could be heard which seemed even more bizarre given their surroundings. Taking advantage of the break in the fighting the people of Calais were taking the opportunity to get food and water and check on friends and relatives. Ted watched this 'normal' activity from his position in the open window and tired from lack of sleep, had to fight hard against allowing the silence to lull him into a false sense of security. But it was not to stay quiet for long.

The sound of a rifle shot from somewhere to the left caught his attention. The few civilians on the street below him disappeared almost instantly into the surrounding houses or doorways. Ted scanned the area and waited. Another shot rang out and a man fell face down into the street, blood pouring from his head. To Ted, from his vantage point, it was obvious that he was dead before he had hit the ground. He had been sheltering in a doorway a few houses down. Ted couldn't see anything. There was a long silence and then there was more firing. But the focus seemed to have changed and this time it seemed to have come from a warehouse further down the street and was aimed somewhere else. Perhaps there was more than one. He leant out cautiously to try and see who was firing and what they were firing at. Still unable to see anything he shouted to the others to see if the sniper was theirs. But no one knew and as they didn't have a radio with them there was no way of verifying it.

Realizing it was probably a German sniper Ted cursed the fact they did not have any radios. This meant that to warn the others one of them had to go back, putting themselves at risk of being shot.

As one of his friends took over Ted made his way rapidly but carefully back to the lines where they were dug in, using the buildings to try and avoid the barrage of artillery falling all round them.

'We've got a sniper over there further up the road Sarge', he shouted trying to make himself heard above the noise of shells exploding and guns firing from all sides.

'I'll send someone up to look.' The Sergeant was looking around to see who was closest as he spoke. Ted had barely had time to absorb that before there was the sound of a single shot and further back in the ranks a man fell to the ground with blood pouring from a ragged circular wound in the centre of his forehead.

'Sniper! Take cover!' There was no real need for the Sergeant to shout as other than those in shock everyone else had scattered. 'NOW, Bains. What are you waiting for? A bloody written invitation'. The sound of the Sergeant shouting brought Bains back to reality and he remembered his training. Crouched down in the way he had been taught he ran towards a stack of crates and threw himself behind them. The Sergeant continued to shout orders, sending three men to try and find the sniper and ordering others to send covering fire.

Ted joined the others in firing in the direction of the warehouse while the men ran full pelt towards it. The others waited, eyes scanning the horizon for any sign of movement. As they watched the distant sound of a Heinkel was getting louder by the minute.

'Keep you heads down'. The order was unnecessary as they were all sheltering as much as they could. As if in slow motion they watched the bombs begin to fall, one after the other in a line that got closer and closer. The noise was so loud their ear drums felt like they were going to burst. The ground shook as if it was moving and buildings crumbled in front of them leaving huge jagged scars on the skyline. Those who were able to muster any coherent thought revised their opinion of the bombs they had heard while on the *Royal Daffodil*. This was much, much worse.

The landscape was inexorably altered, craters, some the size of buildings, others smaller, appeared in front of them like the aftermath of a tantrum of some giant monster in a rage. Ash from the burned buildings and debris from the craters rained down on them mingled with bits of charred flesh, disconnected limbs and bits of cloth. Unable to process this horror the men's brains ignored the evidence of their eyes and they covered their heads with their hands as yet another wave of bombs dropped. These fell further away and the men opened their eyes again and looked anxiously towards the warehouse. To their relief and amazement it was still standing and appeared untouched. As the dust cleared they saw their comrades racing back across the open ground, heads down.

They had not found anything but at least they had survived the bombing. Ted made his way carefully back to the building where the others were still keeping watch. The firing from the warehouse had stopped as soon as the men had gone to investigate and the defenders on the canal were still holding their own.

Losses were frighteningly heavy and as the day wore on the shelling got worse and the Germans came gradually closer. It was now 10 am and the sun was climbing high into the cloudless, blue sky giving the promise of a hot day. The men were running short of food, water and ammunition and still the bombing and shelling continued. Thirsty and hot and needing some light relief from the horror in which they found themselves they joked about what they would like to drink. Ted was just about to add his own contribution when a shell landed in the street in front of them. The building shook violently, loosening more bricks and roof tiles that crashed loudly into the street below, narrowly missing Ted who was on the ground floor.

Another shell landed on the house next door reducing it to rubble. The building shook and hearing the foundations begin to groan the men made the decision to vacate the building before it collapsed around them. They ran rapidly down the stairs and out into the street, only just in time as it collapsed, showering them in yet more debris and throwing up clouds of smoke as bricks, tiles, wood and furniture hurtled to the ground followed by a loud rumbling as the building disintegrated. In the distance, through the haze of smoke and falling debris they could just make out figures heading purposefully towards them. Knowing it wasn't their own side they fired a couple of covering rounds in the general direction of the advancing Germans and headed rapidly back towards their lines.

The rest of the company were still under a heavy artillery barrage and with visibility down to a minimum the returning men had to be careful not to be hit by their own men. 'Don't shoot! It's me Ted', Ted shouted as loudly as he could, desperate to make sure he could be heard above the general noise and confusion. The last thing he needed was to be hit by one of his friends. With everyone shouting, the horrendous noise of shelling, buildings collapsing and the wounded calling out, it was a miracle that the Sergeant heard them at all.

'CEASE FIRE!'. There was a momentary lull while they threw themselves onto the floor safely behind their own lines. But their safety was short-lived as the cry of 'Sniper' rent the air seconds before the man next to Ted fell to the floor, blood pouring from the place where a second ago his eye had been.

The Sergeant singled out five men including Ted and sent them in the direction of a deserted factory a few hundred yards on the left of their position.

Ted and the others needed no further invitation and keeping low they headed towards the factory. But they had hardly covered any ground when another shot rang out narrowly missing one of them. Instantly they threw themselves flat while they tried to work out where the shot had come from. But in the silence that followed the only thing they could hear was their own breathing. There were no glints of light on metal to give the sniper away and after several minutes of remaining motionless they decided that one of them should edge carefully forward again in the hope of drawing the sniper into the open. It was a risky tactic but they had little alternative. If they did not take out the sniper he could keep them pinned down indefinitely, putting all their lives at risk from the advancing Germans. While the man who had volunteered got up slowly the other four watched for any tell-tale flash but there was nothing, all was quiet.

Having reached the factory without incident they split into two groups, one of two and the other of three, and started to search the building carefully. Inching along the walls and swinging round corners, rifles cocked, they gradually covered the whole of the factory but the sniper was long gone and they found nothing.

Annoyed that the sniper had eluded them they decided to search again. But again they found nothing and disappointed, they returned to what was left of their company who were now taking fire from two sides and struggling to hold their position. Back with the others they stepped into fill the gaps and took careful aim before firing. They were running very low on ammunition so every round was precious and every round had to count.

The rest of the Rifle Brigade had held their own for several hours and managed to inflict severe casualties on the German infantry. Eventually however, the sheer weight of numbers overwhelmed them and they had to withdraw to a new position between two dock basins. It was during this withdrawal that Lieutenant Colonel Hoskyns was fatally wounded. The Brigade also lost five officers and two platoon sergeants in the space of an hour. The situation across the part of Calais that remained in Allied hands was becoming increasingly chaotic and the defenders found returning fire more and more difficult. The situation was aggravated by the presence of thousands of civilians frantically looking for refuge from the bombardment. To make matters worse their numbers were swelled by about a thousand unarmed French and Belgium soldiers also looking for refuge from the heavy shelling that was continuing relentlessly.

The front line was fluid and moving rapidly. The fierce fighting had become hand-to-hand in the tightly packed streets. Soldiers used the doorways of suburban houses for cover as they lobbed grenades into the street. The battle raged on, the firing coming at them from every angle as they moved from house to house. Any civilians still resident in these properties were quickly and unceremoniously removed and their places taken by the exhausted defenders. The same applied to the vast numbers of unarmed French and Belgium troops who had also taken refuge in civilian houses while they waited for the surrender.

The shelling didn't discriminate between houses and factories, nor could it distinguish civilians from troops and the air was filled with the anguished sounds of the wounded and dying. The defenders found their vision obscured by the thick smoke and dust emanating from the burning and collapsing buildings and their lungs filled with the choking acrid smell of cordite. Telling friend from foe became more and more difficult, but it was not only their line of vision that was affected. The noise was tremendous and they were unable to hear anything above the sound of shelling and the noise of rubble and masonry crashing all around them. Their ammunition was rapidly diminishing and even the 20,000 rounds distributed from the extra supplies delivered by the Royal Navy the night before were starting to reduce rapidly. Even worse was the lack of water. The main water pipes had long since fractured leaving them with only the water they carried. Those who tried drinking wine and Champagne taken from nearby bombed-out businesses found that unfortunately it only increased their thirst.

Then, at 3 pm, the shelling suddenly stopped and an eerie silence replaced the bombardment. The silence was so unexpected that many of the men thought they had gone deaf. They looked at each other puzzled until the sound of falling bricks in the distance reassured them that their hearing was fine; the shelling had actually stopped. The Germans were again trying to persuade Brigadier Nicholson to surrender.

Under cover of a white flag the Germans had arrived at Pont Georges Cinq and were taken to the eastern gate of the Citadel via the Rue Royale. For a whole hour the guns remained silent and this brief lapse in the shelling gave them the opportunity for a well-needed break. For the exhausted men it meant time to eat some of their rations, have a long-awaited smoke and to regroup. They were also able to refill their water bottles from the little supplies that remained after being told to '… drink sparingly and make it last as this is the last of it and there's no knowing when we'll get some more'.

Ted sat back, closed his eyes and drew the smoke from his cigarette into his lungs. But as much as he was enjoying the cigarette and the break what he really wanted was at least two pints of cold water. His throat felt parched and he could not remember ever being this thirsty. He could also smell the stale sweat on his body and uniform and looking round he realized they all looked the same, dirty, unshaven and barely recognizable. Their uniforms were filthy and most had lost buttons, had rips and tears and were covered in a mixture of dirt, mud and sweat as well as the blood of their friends. Their boots had long since lost the shine the army were renowned for. Some men had lost their own boots and been forced to wear ones from those who no longer needed them.

'Still, at least we're still alive… just', Ted thought to himself – remembering all their friends who hadn't made it. The brief break in the fighting only lasted an hour which seemed like no time at all to the exhausted troops. The resumption of the fighting left them in no doubt that their current positions were rapidly becoming untenable and so it was with no surprise that their next orders were to pull back even further to the railway sheds, just as the Germans launched a further attack that exposed their left flank.

The Company was down to only fifty men and two officers. The Germans advanced with every minute and had the advantage of plenty of equipment. Despite this Ted and his men continued to make them fight for every square foot of land as they slowly withdrew back towards the railway sheds.

The hand-to-hand fighting continued unabated and Ted threw one of his three remaining grenades in to the street killing four advancing German infantrymen. Taking the opportunity to pull back to the corner of the street that led to the railway sheds the men moved as quickly as they could. The smoke was making it increasingly difficult to see where they were going, but eventually they reached the first shed safely. Using it as cover they were about to withdraw further when the man beside Ted suddenly stopped and pulled him back, gesturing wildly at the others who were following.

Ted spun round just in time to see a shape coming at him out of the thick clouds of smoke and dust thrown up in the last barrage. He didn't have time to take aim and just fired automatically. The German's head exploded in a mass of blood, brains and bones that spattered onto Ted's uniform. But there was no time to register this as another German came out of the dust and he needed to reload. By this time the men either side had also turned and both of them were firing frantically, unable to see if the Germans were still advancing on them because of the clouds of smoke and debris. The rest of the men had also opened fire and bullets were flying everywhere, ricocheting off walls and rattling across the roof tiles.

'Cease firing!' yelled one of the Corporals who had come forward to support them. 'They're dead! Cease firing!'

Slowly they lowered their rifles, suddenly aware of the comparative silence and resumed their slow retreat.

The rest of the withdrawal was uneventful and as most of the shelling was concentrated on other areas, the noise diminished. The wind had gradually grown stronger, fanning the flames and spreading the smoke through the town. Ted, Chalky, Rob and Taffy dug themselves a deep slit trench in the dunes and finished the rest of their emergency rations. They had very little water left and their ammunition was also dangerously low.

B Company now only had forty men and two Officers left and they only had one Bren gun. The Bren guns, like their rifles, had become easily clogged by the sand and needed constant cleaning. They also had only a few 3-inch mortar bombs left. Those who had survived unscathed so far considered themselves lucky; but for how much longer. Even the resilience of youth couldn't replace the feeling that it was only a matter of time. Unless reinforcements were sent they would only be able to hold out for a little while longer and it was beginning to look like they would not be evacuated either.

Relieved to be out from under the constant bombardment, even if it was only for a short time, they tried to get some sleep and to relax. What little talk there was centred on where the Navy had got to and when they would be evacuated.

At last, exhausted, hungry and thirsty, as one they closed their eyes and tried to block out the smoke and the sound of the flames as Calais continued to burn in front of them.

Although the bombardment had stopped, the flames and smoke of the burning buildings were fanned by the increasing strength of the wind. From a distance the whole of Calais appeared to be alight and the sky was glowing red from the fires that were raging unabated. The light given off by these fires was so bright that it could even be seen from the south coast of England.

Tired as he was Ted found it difficult to sleep and he lay there thinking about the last time he had seen Brenda. He could still see her smiling face as he turned the corner and if he tried hard enough he could remember the feeling of holding her in his arms and the taste of her lips on his. He smiled, as he recalled his last words that her kiss had given him something to remember. He wished they had been able to get married before he had been sent overseas. Now it was quiet, the fears he had successfully suppressed during the day while they were busy fighting, surfaced and he found himself contemplating if they were going to survive. What if he died without ever having made love to a woman? Suddenly the morals and beliefs he grew up with didn't seem so important. He and Brenda had not made love because they had been brought up to believe it was wrong to do anything like that before they were married. It had been quite difficult at times to restrain himself, but he had always fallen back on his religion. But he wasn't so sure now. Several of his friends had died today. Would it have been so terribly wrong for them to have made love to their girlfriends first? In the normal course of events he could understand that it wouldn't be right, but these weren't normal times. Sighing restlessly, he changed position slightly catching the man next to him with his foot. He was instantly awake, his rifle pointing at Ted who whispered quickly, 'Sorry mate'.

The man grunted and Ted watched enviously as he appeared to go back to sleep immediately. Ted lay with his eyes closed trying not to move and finally fell asleep, only to be woken out of quite a deep sleep around midnight by the sound of heavy guns again firing over their heads, only this time the shells were going the other way. Under cover of darkness the Navy had arrived and the destroyers sitting off the coast had begun to shell the German positions.

Seeing the destroyers off the coast and hearing them firing repeatedly on the Germans, had not only given them renewed hope, it had also fuelled the rumours that they were going to be evacuated. Unfortunately for them, the only people being evacuated were the wounded from the tunnel under Bastion 1 who were taken off on a hospital carrier. Once emptied, the tunnel didn't remain empty for long and some fifty or sixty other men, whose wounds were also quite serious, quickly took the places that the other injured troops had vacated. Reports filtering through from the rest of the city confirmed that this was just the tip of the iceberg. It transpired much later that some of those who were wounded had refused to leave their posts and that many had carried on fighting until they were captured. It was only on the long march into captivity that the Germans pulled them out and made them get medical treatment.

The cheer that had gone up from Ted and his friends when the destroyers had started firing, soon turned to horror as they too came under bombardment when some of the shells fell short. Unable to dig themselves in any further they had no option but to try and sit it out. But worse was to come. The initial bombardment had kept the German shelling to a minimum, but not for long. The Germans now sent over Heinkels and Stukas to bomb the destroyers and the Germans gunners also retaliated. For the entrenched men, exhausted, hungry and thirsty, the German retaliation sounded, '… like hell let loose on earth for the region of about two hours or so.'

In Britain at 9 pm Churchill, Eden and General Ironside made the final decision not to evacuate the Calais force. This was one of the first really hard decisions Churchill recalls having to make and he recorded feeling physically sick as he resigned the men to their fate. The following signal was sent to Brigadier Nicholson that night although there are doubts as to whether he ever received it:

'Every hour you continue to exist is of the greatest help to the BEF. Government has therefore decided you must continue to fight. Have greatest possible admiration for your splendid stand. Evacuation will not (*repeat* not) take place, and craft required for above purposes are to return to Dover. *Verity* and *Windsor* to cover Commander Mine-sweeping and his retirement.'

Despite this decision Admiral Ramsey did decide to make a small flotilla available just in case the circumstances changed and the decision was reversed. On the night of 25/26 this small fleet made its way into the harbour and rescued the wounded and those survivors of the Royal Marine detachment that had been sent to protect the naval demolition crews.

Like Ted, the rest of the men in the sand dunes had no idea of the decisions that had been taken so, when the shelling stopped and daylight came, they looked out to sea only to see that the destroyers had gone. There was to be no evacuation; they were on their own.

Chapter 8

The End of the Line
Saturday 26 May

For the men of B Company, dug deep into the dunes opposite Calais railway station, each day seemed very much like the last. Their faces were pale and drawn and covered with stubble and their eyes felt gritty and were red-rimmed from lack of sleep. Their uniforms were almost unrecognisable, torn, tattered and filthy from the three days of almost continuous fighting. Their throats were dry and sore from the cordite and the smoke and flames of the city that was burning all round them and their heads were pounding from a combination of dehydration and the noise from the constant bombardment. They were dangerously low on water, a situation made worse by having to listen to the gentle lapping of the water on the shoreline behind them in the infrequent lulls in the shelling. In the distance, in the sky between Calais and Dover, a four-hour aerial battle had just begun and the fires burning in Calais were so fierce that they could be seen in Kent. But the men of the Rifle Brigade were not aware of any of this. They didn't believe anything could be worse than what they had already experienced and nothing could prepare Ted for the horror that was about to overtake him.

From their trenches they could hear the steady advance of the Germans as they gradually overran the British positions in the town, coming ever closer with every bombardment. The men braced themselves as they waited for the next attack, knowing there was nowhere else to withdraw to. With their backs to the sea there was nowhere else to go. This had to be their last stand.

It was just coming up to 8.30 am and, as they lay there eating the last of their bully beef and biscuits, they saw and heard another wave of Stukas and Heinkels heading towards them. Ted counted them and was horrified to reach 114 before putting his arms over his head and trying to bury himself even more. The planes attacked in formation. Grouped in threes they took it in turns to dive-bomb, dropping a mixture of high explosive and incendiaries which left huge craters and showered the men in sand and grit. This was accompanied by the rattling of machine guns, a sound which could barely be heard above the noise of the shelling, but the effects of which could be seen as the bullets whistled across the dunes spraying sand skyward. For the men trying to dig even deeper into the dunes each bomb seemed to come closer and closer and as each one landed, Ted recalled, how they thought 'the end had come'. Although it only lasted about half an hour, for the beleaguered troops the bombing and shooting seemed unending.

After the initial barrage the men fired back. They were aware of the pressing need to conserve their precious ammunition, but they needed to do something other than just lay there and take it. Their persistence paid off and it was not long before they heard a victorious shout. 'Got ya, you bastard'.

Even above the shelling and machine-gun firing there was no hiding the delight in the rifleman's voice as his determined firing struck its target. Carefully aiming his Bren gun he managed to hit the fuel tank of one of the Stukas. Its death- scream intensified, even out-shrieking its fellow attackers. It whirled round and round out of control until it exploded on impact as it dived headfirst into the wet sand near the shore. There was a ragged cheer from the few who were still alive, Ted included, before they turned their attention back to staying alive. But time was no longer on their side and it was under cover of this murderous bombardment that the Germans began dropping parachutists further along the beach.

Alerted by the shouts from the other men, Ted lifted his head up and saw the approaching Germans. Aiming carefully so as to make each bullet count he started shooting at the Germans as they spread out on the beach in an attempt to advance on their positions. To start with it was a fairly simple matter to shoot each German as soon as he showed himself and they were able to hold them off without too much difficulty. As each German fell, shouts of encouragement could be heard from those who were still alive. This raised their spirits and gave them some hope, a hope that was also buoyed by the mistaken rumours that were still persisting, that the navy would be evacuating them later in the day, if only they could hold out.

Because of the general confusion of battle and the difficulties of communication now that the radios had stopped working, not all had heard Brigadier Nicholson's orders only hours earlier. These were that Calais was to be held to the last man and that other than the wounded there would be no other evacuations. Because of this, rumours of evacuation continued to persist right up until the end with many of those who were forced to surrender still believing that it was only because the Navy had been late they had not been evacuated.

But for Ted time was rapidly running out. Like the other remaining members of the Rifle Brigade he continued to fight doggedly but as the day wore on it became more difficult and gradually the sheer weight of numbers and the lack of food, water and more importantly ammunition, took its toll.

Ted was almost unrecognizable, his face and body caked in a mixture of sand, grime and dried blood. The concern in his voice was echoed by the others who were also aware that they could not hold out much longer. With very little ammunition and no water their chances of survival were rapidly diminishing but they continued to keep firing, astonishing the Germans with their dogged persistence and causing them heavy casualties. If the situation had remained the same they might have been able to hold out for longer, but this was not to be. By lunchtime the Germans managed to get a large trench mortar into position directly in front of them. Their deeply dug trenches afforded them little or no protection against this latest threat. Unlike the shelling from the field guns, which bad as it had been, had often sailed harmlessly over them, the trench mortars' ability to fire mortars that climbed almost vertically and then dropped directly onto them meant there was nowhere for them to hide.

Ted was unable to hear his friends or even see them now. It would not have seemed possibly an hour ago but the noise had intensified even more and the smoke, sand and debris from the explosions was made even worse by the thick black smoke drifting their way from the oil refinery that was burning in the distance. His throat was so dry from the lack of water and congested from the cordite and smoke that he was having trouble swallowing. He tried hard to return fire but with minimal visibility and very little ammunition there wasn't much he could do. Frustrated beyond measure he was just pondering what else he could do when the world tilted sideways, the noise diminished and everything seemed suddenly to be happening in slow motion.

The explosion had thrown Ted right across the trench. Slowly picking himself up and shaking his head to try to clear the ringing in his ears, he turned to shout at Chalky who had been nearest to him. But he couldn't see him. Frantically flapping his arms to clear the smoke and ignoring the sound of more incoming mortars, he spotted something towards the edge of what was left of their trench. Crawling towards it his brain was at first unable to register what he was seeing. Shocked to the core, he realized that the mortar that had thrown him to the other end of the trench and left him with little more than ringing ears had hit Chalky and literally blown him to pieces. There was nothing left other than his head on the side of the trench. It still wore Chalky's helmet with the chin strap missing. Ted sank to his knees unable to take in the horror of what he was seeing. How long he knelt there he had no idea. He only knew that he couldn't move.

He was vaguely aware of an insistent voice in his ear yelling at him, but he still couldn't move. Realizing his words were having no effect, the corporal shouted at Rob to take Ted and get out of there. But Rob was also in shock so he shouted again knowing that if they didn't move now they would be overrun.

Somehow Rob managed to pull himself together enough to grab Ted and they moved as quickly as possible towards the railway station. The corporal and the few remaining riflemen quickly joined them, but the German gunners had their range and were firing straight at them with their machine guns. It was impossible to run through the sand which was so fine that they kept sinking into it so progress was agonisingly slow.

Ted was positioned between Taffy and the corporal who had pulled him clear of the trench and the three of them were struggling through some particularly deep sand when Ted stumbled and missed his footing just as a murderous barrage sprayed them all in a hail of machine-gun bullets. Spread-eagled, his mouth full of sand, he swiftly picked himself up. Aware that his friends were lying next to him and not moving, he looked to either side of him and then froze. The bullets had hit them with such ferocity that they had severed their heads from their shoulders and would have done the same to him if he hadn't stumbled at that particular minute. As he knelt there staring in disbelief he felt someone grab his arm and, offering no resistance, he allowed himself to be propelled along the dunes till they reached the edge of the road. His brain felt numb and he was unable to think clearly.

Fortunately for him Rob shoved him down just as another barrage sailed dangerously close to them.

'Ted! Ted!' shouted Rob again, trying desperately to shake Ted out of the trance he was in. Ted slowly registered his friend and then the danger of the situation they were in.

'Somehow we need to get over that and bloody quick', he said, pointing to the high concrete wall surrounding the station. His words were almost drowned by another hail of bullets which sailed by so close the men could feel the rush of air above their heads. By now they had been joined by the remaining men who were all that was left of their Company. Together they ran full pelt down the road towards the station. But the German gunners had found their range and they had little chance as the machine guns sprayed bullets that were, recalled Ted, 'to knock them down like ninepins'. Men fell to their left and to their right, and Ted realized Rob was right - the only way out of their range was to somehow get to the other side of the wall. However, the wall was about ten feet and much too high to leap over, and they were unlikely to have enough time to climb it.

'We'll never get over it', shouted Ted in despair. Rob was relieved that Ted seemed to have recovered, but he had to agree that scaling the wall did seem an impossible task. By now the Germans were slowly gaining ground and the men's numbers diminished rapidly. 'One chap did make a tremendous leap and got across, rifle as well, but I am sure he couldn't do it again if he tried a hundred times.' Ted was right. Despite their desperate efforts the others couldn't manage it.

Realizing their only chance was to break a hole in the wall, Ted and Rob hammered frantically at the concrete with their rifle butts. Although they really didn't think they had any chance they had run out of options so it was either try that or wait until they were overrun or mowed down. But fear lent them a strength they didn't know they had and miraculously somehow they broke through.

With relief the few remaining riflemen crawled through and made a dive for the pits under the railway wagons. Using the wagons as cover they crawled the length of the station until they reached Bastion 1, a fort on the edge of the harbour facing out to sea. It was here they found what was left of the battalion who were desperately trying to get some guns to work that the French had put out of action before leaving.

They moved quickly to assist the other riflemen in their frantic quest to mend the guns, but unfortunately they were totally beyond repair and they were fast running out of time. For half an hour they tried to fix the guns while maintaining their position in line with the clock tower on the roof of the station.

But the only covering fire available was one Vickers machine gun that was manned by a party of Royal Marines. They had arrived in HMS *Verity* just after midnight on 25 May and were first tasked with defending the Citadel with the French Marines. The party of Royal Marines originally consisted of eighty-one men and four officers. By the afternoon, the fighting intensified and one platoon and the machine-gun section were sent to help reinforce the Army front line. The heavy bombing and shelling of the Citadel soon rendered their position untenable so Captain Courtice ordered them to withdraw to the jetty. Crossing the blazing drawbridge and fighting their way across town under heavy artillery fire, the bombs and bullets from snipers hidden in the houses took its toll. By the time the men reached the remnants of the Rifle Brigade in the sand dunes they had been reduced to one officer and just sixteen men.

Back in Bastion 1, exhausted and dehydrated, the men fought on doggedly. Their determination not to surrender was buoyed up by rumours of evacuation. Glancing at their watches as the promised time for this came and nothing happened, their hopes gradually faded and many came to believe that the Navy had let them down.

As the afternoon wore on they finally ran out of ammunition. But rather than give up, they threw both empty and full wine bottles, bricks, rubble, anything that they could get their hands on, and which they could use as a weapon. The onslaught continued unabated until the Germans realised the men no longer had any weapons with which to fight and again asked them to surrender. At 3.30 pm on 26 May 1940, after three days of almost continuous fighting, the few remaining riflemen of the 1st Battalion, The Rifle Brigade, reluctantly did so.

The victorious Germans swarmed over their positions in their field-grey army uniforms waving revolvers and rifles and shouting orders at them in a language they didn't understand. Militarily defeated, but with their heads unbowed and a justifiable pride in what they had managed to accomplish with so little, the men threw down their now useless weapons and raised their hands. After searching them and taking many of their personal possessions, the Germans marched them out to a holding area where they joined hundreds of other prisoners of war. At this point they were not segregated so they were also joined by several hundred French and Belgium soldiers.

Over 800 French soldiers and sailors had remained in Calais and fought bravely alongside their allies despite orders from the French to withdraw. On 24 May there was a fierce artillery fight between the guns of the 10th Panzer Division on the high ground at Coquelles and those coastal guns of Fort Lapin, the Bastion de L'Estran and Bastion 2, which could be turned inland. However, they were soon short of ammunition, the Bastion de L'Estran having fired 683 rounds out of their stock of 895 by 10 am. It was becoming increasingly difficult to bear down on the enemy targets as the Germans encircled the town, so the officers gave orders for the guns to be spiked and to evacuate the Bastions. These naval crews then marched down to the harbour, joined on the way by numerous French soldiers. Here, many were seen sitting on their suitcases, waiting for the tugs that the French Navy would send to evacuate them. They were later joined by the gunners from Bastion 2 and the Bastion de L'Estran.

But Carlos de Lambertye, the French Naval Commander at Fort Risban, was aware that if the Bastions and Forts on the seafront were all abandoned the Germans would be able to surround and capture the Citadel by the end of the day. He persuaded many to stay and fight - men are who are still honoured in Calais today as the 'Volunteers of Calais'. Unfortunately, many others who could have swelled the Allied force hid in cellars and air raid shelters waiting for the fighting to stop. They could easily be identified by their clean uniforms and the suitcases and bags they carried.

Exhausted, dazed and more than a little scared, Ted and Rob joined the other men seated on the floor, put their hands on their heads and looked round nervously.

Now the fighting was over the adrenaline that had kept them going despite the lack of sleep, food and water, stopped flowing and the exhaustion of the past three days caught up with them. But, unsure what was to happen to them, and remembering the stories circulating about the behaviour of the German armies on the Polish battlefields, the men were reluctant to rest. Instead, they watched warily as the Germans stood guard over them.

The Germans who had accepted their surrender were not too bad and many even congratulated them on their fighting ability, but there was no guarantee that this would continue. Wearily they sat for some time, hands still on their heads, watching the activity going on around. Then they were suddenly confronted by a soldier shouting loudly at them. After several tense moments in which the German's temper rose as they failed to understand what he was shouting, understanding suddenly dawned on Ted that they were being told to take off their belts and bootlaces.

Exhausted from the fighting it took Ted took several minutes before he realized that it was a precaution to stop them escaping. As they had made no attempt to count them at this point it seemed unlikely that they would know if any had gone missing so this seemed rather pointless to Ted. But as the German was threatening to hit them with his rifle butt it didn't seem like a very good idea to argue and Ted and Rob quickly obeyed. The German stopped yelling, then nodded, and looked round at the soldiers nearest to them and gestured again to encourage them to do the same.

Deciding it was best not to antagonize their captors too much, the men continued to remove their shoelaces in silence. When they finished they handed them over to the German soldier who was now quite calm. To their surprise some of the Germans were quite friendly. Some, like their earlier colleagues, even congratulated them on their fierce fighting. But Ted recalled how others taunted them with phrases such as, 'For you Tommy, the war is over. You will never see England again. We shall put you all to work in the salt mines.'

One younger guard stood menacingly over one of the prisoners and said loudly in broken English, 'If you'd like to write a letter to your girlfriend I'll post it next week when I'm on guard outside Buckingham Palace.' As the guard pointed his rifle at the prisoner threateningly he was shocked when the soldier suddenly grabbed the end of the barrel and said loudly, 'You've got a dirty barrel there mate. Wouldn't get away with that in England.'

The German soldier pulled the rifle out of reach and cursed angrily. Roars of laughter went round those who were close enough to have heard the exchange. Ted, like the others, laughed, but underneath their show of bravado they were all scared. No one knew what was going to happen to them and there was no way of knowing how long they would remain prisoners, or even whether the Germans wouldn't just shoot them where they sat.

Knowing that Britain was only twenty-two miles away, a short hop across the Channel, only made the whole thing worse and although they watched carefully for the opportunity to escape, the men asked themselves when, and even if, they would see their homes again. As the day came to a close and the light faded, they were joined by more and more of their fellow defenders as one position after another fell to the Germans. The city was still racked by heavy shelling and gunfire but it was slowly diminishing as the Germans gradually gained the upper hand. There were now thousands of prisoners and the Germans were struggling to contain them. Although they were still sitting with their hands on their heads and had been yelled at repeatedly not to try and escape, there were so many of them that the Germans shouted at them not to move at all.

Uncomfortable and unable to relax, the men were almost relieved when the German soldiers made them all stand up and fall into ranks of four. The men fell in wearily and marched in the direction the Germans were pointing. Ted yawned loudly. He was totally exhausted and would have liked nothing better than to lie down and fall asleep. He was so hungry and thirsty that his fears about what was going to happen to them had been replaced by fear the Germans might not have enough food to feed so many prisoners.

The Germans were determined to get them out of Calais. They were still expecting the British to land more troops and if there was a counter attack by the BEF they could be vulnerable from the rear by the very prisoners who were behind their own lines. So they were lined up with NCOs (non-commissioned officers) and other ranks at the front of the column with the officers at the rear. As they marched out of Calais they passed some of their own food dumps. Encouraged by the NCOs some of them dived out of the ranks and quickly grabbed some food before the Germans shouted at them to move on. Ted and Rob managed to grab a couple of emergency ration packs each before they were encouraged back in the lines at the point of German rifle butts.

Their guards marched them relentlessly until they came to Marquise, nineteen kilometres outside Calais, and herded them into fields. The men were not given any food or water and Ted was grateful they had managed to steal something from the food dump. Deciding they might need to make what little they had last several days, Ted and Rob only ate some biscuits and after secreting the remainder amongst their clothes, tried to get comfortable by leaning against the hedge. However, Ted found that the twigs kept digging in his neck and although he was so completely worn out that he could have sworn that nothing would've kept him awake, the twigs were doing exactly that.

Now he had eaten something and his hunger had receded a little bit, he worried more about what was going to happen to them, with the threat of being sent down a salt mine replaying itself over and over in his mind. But even this was not enough to keep him awake for any length of time and soon he was fast asleep despite the twigs.

Using what was left of his pack as a pillow, Rob carefully lay down. There was very little room but it seemed most of the men were so tired that a little jostling and nudging was hardly going to bother them. Others sat silently staring into space as they relived the horrors of the past few days and mourned those who hadn't survived. As they sat there and as Ted and Rob slept, the sounds of gunfire gradually receded and faded away until an eerie silence took its place.

It was this sudden silence that woke most of the men up. Although they were over ten miles away from the fighting they were still able to hear it, even though it became more like background noise in the distance. Now even that stopped. There was no more bombing, no more shelling, no more artillery or mortar fire, just silence. The only faint noise to reach them through the still night air was the crackling of unattended fires and the crashing of falling masonry. The night sky was still glowing red and the smoke was drifting lazily across the horizon, but the silence said it all. Calais had fallen. The Germans had reached the coast. They were free to redirect the rest of their tanks towards Dunkirk and to try and prevent the evacuation of the BEF that was already underway. Although they did not know it, the defenders of Calais had bought Britain valuable time and their sacrifice meant others were free to fight another day.

The Calais Force had continued to fight for most of 26 May despite the lack of ammunition, food and water. The initial German attack in the morning failed but by the afternoon the lack of ammunition began to tell. The Germans then brought their medium tanks into the battle and by 4 pm they had captured the harbour area. They followed this by a successful infantry attack on the Citadel and captured Brigadier Nicholson.

Even then the fighting continued as British troops battled on, retreating into the Quartier du Courgain, the fisherman's quarter, where they held out until 9 pm. As darkness fell they were ordered to break up into small groups and to try and make their way out of the beleaguered town. But by then it was too late and there was little chance of escape so the majority were captured by the Germans.

The last British ship to enter the harbour in Calais was the yacht *Gulzar* which crept in just after midnight and remained until 1 am on 27 May. She succeeded in picking up fifty men from the end of the breakwater and then made her way home safely to Britain.

As Ted sat silently watching the exultant Germans celebrating, others mourned their dead. The memories of their friends were far too raw and too painful for many of them to discuss what they had seen and experienced. Ted found himself thinking about those who had died in the first couple of days. He couldn't face thinking about Taffy or Chalky, not yet. He knew he was lucky to have survived so far, but he didn't know what the future held. He also felt guilty. Why him and not the others? Why him and not those with children? It didn't make any sense and for once his religious beliefs seemed to dessert him. His head was hurting from dehydration and from drinking wine when the water had run out. Trying to fathom the reasons for his survival was just adding to the pain.

But what really bothered Ted was that his family and Brenda didn't even know where he was. They thought he was safely digging ditches in Suffolk. When they did hear he was in France they wouldn't know that he had survived the fighting and was still alive. He couldn't bear the thought of them not knowing he was alright. Somehow he would have to find a way of letting them know he was safe.

Chapter 9

The Signal Pad
Sunday 27 May

The night passed slowly and Ted only slept fitfully. He was too concerned about what was to happen to them to sleep properly. Even thinking about Brenda couldn't stop his mind from racing over and over the events of the past few days. He was also missing his friends and unable to come to terms with what had happened to them. Every time he closed his eyes all he saw was Chalky's helmet sitting forlornly on the side of the trench or Taffy's headless body lying prone in the sand. He could still hear the noise of the mortars and the machine-gun fire ringing in his ears, and although it was quiet now every time he dozed off he would wake up suddenly. His brain was frantically trying to process the events of the past three days. In his sleep they manifested themselves and reappeared in nightmare sequences of limbs and heads flying round him in all directions and the smell of burning bodies filled the air, but it wasn't his friends, it was his family he could see.

As Ted moved restlessly and shouted out something unintelligible, Rob woke him, worried he would draw the attention of the guards.

Disorientated, Ted looked around and then remembered where he was. He realized he must have been dreaming and shook his head to try and clear the vivid details of the last thing he had been dreaming about. Glancing down he saw that his hands were shaking and needing to think about something else he said. 'Seen anyone else from the battalion?'

Rob shook his head. 'No, just us, but there are so many soldiers here it's a bit difficult to see. It'll probably be better in daylight. We can't be the only ones.'

After the horrendous fighting Ted wasn't convinced and he turned his attention back to what would happen to them. The only good thing about their march from Calais was that it presumably meant the Germans were not just going to shoot them. Having had some sleep his natural optimism was beginning to return and he assumed they would probably be shipped off to a POW camp. He was still worrying about how his family would know where he was, but other than suggesting they would probably be allowed to write letters, Rob was unable to help. As he was about to say something else they were shouted at by one of the other men who was trying to sleep.

'Sorry mate', said Ted and Rob in unison. In the silence that followed they both tried to get some sleep but they had overcome their initial fatigue and their brains were too active. Ted was also too worried about the nightmares to really try very hard. They were both relieved when dawn broke and the sun started to appear on the horizon behind them, bathing them in its red glow.

'Raus, raus'. The sound of the Germans waking them was to become only too familiar but now it sounded raw and foreign and grated on their ears. The German order was followed by 'filthy English pigs', and various other uncomplimentary words which Ted tried to ignore. Prodded and poked by rifle butts and continually shouted at, the men roused themselves and slowly stood up. They were lined up into ranks of four again and then told to march. They had no idea where they were going but the familiar activity provided a small measure of comfort, at least at first.

The Germans had not yet separated out the nationalities so Ted was surrounded by French, Belgians and others who he thought might be Moroccan. Despite the night in the fields, those French who had hidden in Calais rather than fighting, were still easy to identify with their clean uniforms and back packs full of food, water, cigarettes and anything else that they had the foresight and time to pack. Thinking about those who had died and those who were wounded, Ted and the others felt disgusted by the sight of these Frenchmen flaunting their supplies.

As the sun steadily rose in the sky, their German guards marched the men mercilessly without a break and they started to feel the strain. They had been wearing the same clothes for over a week and had not been able to wash or shave for nearly as long. Some of them had not had anything to drink for nearly twenty-four hours and felt dizzy. Many had not eaten for the same length of time and were also starting to feel the effects. The Germans who were guarding them had no time for their captives. Anyone falling over was kicked and hit with rifle butts until they got back up and into line again. If they didn't get up in time they were shot. The first time it happened Ted and Rob looked at each other in total disbelief. But even worse was to come. As they marched onwards in the heat with no food and water they all became steadily weaker. Having seen the Germans shooting those who dropped out, the men's fear had become a great motivator and most of them kept moving however bad they felt. But eventually the weaker members succumbed and it was in total horror that Ted watched the Germans casually shoot another soldier for trying to help someone who had stumbled.

Feeling as if he was in some never-ending nightmare Ted put one foot in front of the other and tried to concentrate his mind on something else, anything other than thinking about the atrocities going on around him. In the few French villages they went through the streets were lined with people looking sullen and defiant. Children stood silently behind their parents, shocked and traumatized. Some of the French women brought out buckets of water for them to drink from but the Germans kicked them over, threatened the women with their rifles and beat anyone who tried to get near the water. The screams of the children as their mothers were hit by rifles, echoed in the troops' ears as they were marched inexorably on through village after village that bore the scars of the war. On and on they went along roads with huge craters in and past buildings that were either completely destroyed or were dangerously tottering piles of rubble.

As the day wore on the sun disappeared behind thick clouds and it started to rain. Just as Ted thought he could not go another step they came to another town called Desvres and they were herded into the football stadium. Relieved, they fell onto the wet and muddy ground, too tired even to feel hungry or thirsty anymore.

Ted tried to ignore the pains in his stomach caused by hunger and lack of water and attempted to rest. He had the feeling that the Germans were going to keep the men hungry and thirsty as a way of subduing them. The Germans obviously couldn't care less about whether they survived or not and would use any excuse to kill them off. At this rate it wouldn't be too long before discipline broke down and the men would be fighting amongst themselves for the scarce water supplies. 'So much for the Geneva Convention on how to treat prisoners,' Ted cynically thought. 'Obviously the Germans haven't read it.'

The Germans quickly recognized the animosity between the English and French and lost no time in adding to it by treating each nationality differently. They made a point of being friendly towards the French while verbally and physically castigating the English. When they stopped they allowed the French to make fires and cook the food they had with them, but as soon as the English soldiers tried to do the same they were beaten with rifles. Despite the fact they were supposed to be allies, those Frenchmen lucky enough to have food and water - some of it looted from the BEF - refused to share any of it with the English forces, instead flaunting it and laughing in their faces.

Trying to concentrate on something different other than the lack of food and the growing animosity around him, Ted thought about how he could let his Mum and Brenda know he was all right. If he could think of a way of getting a message out it would be a way of defying the Germans and would also reassure his Mum that for the moment at least, he was still alive. He also wanted to let Brenda know that he had kept his promise; that he was safe and he was coming back to her. He found his eyes closing and he drifted off only to be woken by the sound of a fight not far from where he was laying.

'What's going on?' he asked Rob who was watching intently.

Rob explained that one of the French soldiers had tried to sell some Cadbury's chocolate and Players' cigarettes to some of the British soldiers. As it had obviously been stolen from the BEF stores the British troops decided to 'liberate' it. The fight did not last long and as the Germans waded in and restored order in their normal fashion with rifle butts, punches and blows mainly aimed at the British soldiers. Ted saw at least one person who did not get up again. On closer inspection he could just about identify a French uniform and in normal circumstances he would have felt sorry for him and even tried to help. But these weren't normal circumstances and to try and sell food and cigarettes to starving men, especially when they had quite obviously come from those starving men's own supplies, was the height of stupidity. Like the others Ted was too exhausted, too weak, too hungry, thirsty and demoralized to have any real compassion. He felt only anger that as they were all supposed to be on the same side they should be working together, rather than stealing from each other. Sighing heavily he lay down again and tried to get some sleep, his only thought that he wished he'd managed to get some chocolate or at least a cigarette.

All too soon the break was over and the Germans lined the troops up again and they were marched on. The rain was coming down in torrents, adding to the fatigue and exhaustion that was now almost normal. Marching was almost impossible, given their weakened state, and Ted tried to focus on how to get word back to England that he was still alive. They walked for the most part in silence as they were too tired, thirsty and hungry to speak and anyway they had nothing to talk about. Their whole existence was reduced to concentrating on surviving the Germans' attempts to starve them to death. From time to time rumours spread through the lines that the Germans were just marching them somewhere to shoot them, but as there was little they could do most just ignored them and hoped that they were wrong.

The troops lost count of the number of isolated houses and tiny settlements they marched passed as the day wore slowly on. But as they walked through one small hamlet Ted spotted a discarded signal pad by the road. Checking no one was looking he quickly picked it up and put it in his pocket. He wasn't sure why he did it but he thought it might come in useful as toilet paper or something. His heart was pounding and he waited for the Germans to pounce on him. But nothing happened and as they continued walking an idea came to him. He still had his pencil. He could write a message to his Mum on this signal pad and use the safety pin from his field dressing to seal it. He could then give it to someone in one of the villages and trust that they would try and get it home for him. It was a gamble but he didn't really have anything to lose. If it was thrown away he hadn't lost anything and if he was lucky the message would get home so at least people would know he had survived the fall of Calais.

He would have to wait until the men stopped to write it as it was too difficult and dangerous while they were moving. The column of POWs was growing all the time and there were now thousands of men being marched four abreast, the other ranks at the front and the officers at the back. The column was closely guarded by a German lorry about every fifty yards in between the men. The lorry was armed with machine guns mounted at the front and back and the guards watched them continually. Armed German sentries also drove up and down the length of the column on motor bikes making sure no one slipped out of the line and tried to escape. Anyone who did try to escape was liable to be shot so those who did attempt it usually did so at night when there was slightly more chance of success.

Feeling happier now he had something other than food and hunger to focus on, Ted tried to look round at his surroundings with interest. The countryside looked very similar to England. There were fields with crops growing in them, trees with blossom and hedges with insects and small animals. Since the shelling ceased he could even hear birds singing again. His thoughts went back to Brenda and what she was doing. She would probably be at work. He had lost track of the days so maybe it was a Sunday. If it was, then she might be at church. He wondered if she knew where he was. Mind you, *he* didn't know where he was other than the fact that he was in France. The news at home was pretty heavily censored so they probably had no idea what was going on. He was in the army and *he* hadn't known what was going on. France had been a complete shock to him.

Although there had been rumours of invasion and the news wasn't very good, Ted would never have guessed they would be so badly beaten so soon. He wondered whether the Germans had captured the whole of the BEF. If they had it would all be over surely. Maybe England had already surrendered. As soon as that thought entered his head he realized that if England had surrendered, the Germans would have told them. But things obviously weren't going very well and if they didn't get better soon the Germans might invade and if that happened what would happen to his Mum, his brothers and Brenda. Shaking his head he decided there was no point going on with these thoughts. He couldn't do anything about what was happening in England and at the moment he had enough problems of his own. He would concentrate instead on the one thing he could do.

Now he had a plan it seemed like an interminably long time before they stopped again. As the afternoon headed towards evening Ted became anxious about whether they were going to march all night too. He had hoped to stop for a while, long enough for him to write a quick message, and then walk on. It would be much easier to hand over the message in the half light of evening than the bright light of the day. He knew the most dangerous time would be when he

This is identical to the signal pad Ted used to send his message home on. Unfortunately the original was lost.

was handing it over. If seen, there was a fair chance the Germans would shoot both him and the person he had handed it to. He certainly didn't want to be responsible for the death of someone else and, come to think of it, he didn't really want to be shot either for something as inconsequential to the Germans as a written message to his Mum. Although it was important to him, it wasn't going to make an awful lot of difference to the war effort.

As if an unseen presence was listening to his thoughts, the column suddenly ground to an unexpected halt. The order only needed to be given once and the men sank to the ground grateful to be able to have a rest, however brief.

'Christ I'm knackered', said Rob. Breathing heavily Ted looked at him. His tired face was now also showing signs of sunburn from the constant exposure to the sun while they walked.

Ted nodded in agreement, almost too tired to speak but then having regained his breath, explained about the signals pad and what he intended to do. Rob looked concerned, but despite his misgivings agreed to keep watch in case a guard spotted him.

Ted took out the signals pad, leant on his AB 64 (The Army Book 64, his Soldier's Service and Pay book), and wrote quickly. He had already thought about what he was going to say so once he had the paper under his pencil it didn't take him long to write the note:

'Dear Mum, I just wanted to let you know that I am alive. We were captured when Calais surrendered and we're going to some POW camp. I don't know where yet. I'm not wounded so don't worry about me. I'll be home soon. The war can't last forever. Give my love to Bren and ask her to wait for me. Your loving son Ted.'

He folded it up carefully and wrote the address on the other side. He had barely finished writing when Rob nudged him as a German soldier was approaching, rifle cradled in his arms, scrutinising the lines. This soldier was quite young, about their age and had a pleasant face. He nodded at Ted, who had looked up just in time to make eye contact, and then carried on walking past. Ted realized he had been holding his breath and releasing it slowly he took out his field dressing and removed the safety pin. Checking that no one was watching he pinned the note together so the address was on the outside and hastily put it back in his pocket.

Relieved that he was halfway there, he closed his eyes and tried to get some sleep, but it was too late. The Germans were on the move again and the guards were busy shouting at the men to get up. Those who didn't move quickly enough were kicked and threatened with rifles and at least one man was shot, the sound echoing down the road to where Ted and Rob were hastily getting to their feet. It could no longer be called a march; they were much too tired for that. Walking was about all they could manage and even that was too much for some of them. The British soldiers who fell by the wayside continued to be shot out of hand. This was becoming more frequent. Anyone trying to help them was either beaten by the guards or shot as well. The threat of brutality was never far from the surface and the use of casual violence was increasing.

As they approached yet another small village later that day, a disturbance broke out further back in the ranks of the masses of POWs and the column came to an abrupt halt. Ted had no idea what had caused it but that didn't matter. What was important was that it gave him the opportunity to hand over his scribbled message to a stranger in the sullen, watching crowd.

Making sure no one could see, he took the note from his pocket and scanned the crowd looking for someone to hand it to. He spotted a young man whose face clearly expressed his outrage and hatred of what he was witnessing and Ted made an instant decision. Once again checking that no one was paying him any attention, he handed the note to the man praying that he would have the good sense to hide it straight away and not stand there looking at it. Fortunately the man acted swiftly and the last Ted saw of his note was the young man slipping it into his pocket. His heart was pounding so hard that he thought it would jump out of his throat. He waited with bated breath for the inevitable shout and subsequent rifle shot but nothing happened. The whole transaction had taken less than a minute and attention was still focused on the continuing disturbance further back. Ted looked straight ahead, not daring to look at the young man for fear of drawing attention to them and waited for the order to march on. The wait seemed to go on forever, but eventually the order came and the young man soon disappeared out of sight as the road wound round a bend and the men were back out into the French countryside again. The night was fast drawing in and Ted felt a flush of success. He had done it. He had put one over on the Germans and now it was out of his hands, literally. It was in the hands of someone he hoped was a patriotic Frenchman and from there it was in the lap of the gods.

Chapter 10

Meanwhile . . .

Although the British government was unaware until Monday 27 May that Calais had fallen, Operation Dynamo, the operation to bring home the troops from Dunkirk, had begun at 3 pm on Sunday 26 May and went right through to 9 am on Tuesday 4 June. A total of 338, 226 troops were evacuated and the peak of the evacuation was on 31 May when 68,014 troops landed at Dover. Most of these weary troops were evacuated to Kent and Southern Railways were given the task of moving the troops on as quickly as possible when they landed to make room for the next arrivals. This was an enormous logistical operation as not only did they need to estimate how many trains were needed, they also had no idea which of the seven possible ports would be used and how many men would be coming through each one.

These seven ports were Sheerness, Margate, Ramsgate, Folkestone and Dover in Kent, and Newhaven and Southampton in Hampshire. After much discussion it was decided that as Dover was the port likely to be used by the most ships it should be allocated 327 trains. Sheerness was allocated seventeen trains, Margate, seventy-five, Ramsgate eighty-two and Folkestone sixty-four. Southern Railways managed to provide most of the 2,000 or so locomotives and carriages that were used, and the remainder were borrowed from the GWS (Great Western Railway), LMS and LNER.

The only large quays at Dover were the eight used by the cross Channel steamers. At the height of the evacuation these often had between sixteen and twenty ships moored up, sometimes as many as two or three deep. As well as this, the remaining forty to fifty mooring buoys were also busy as they were used by ships collecting stores and making minor repairs. There was no time for resting; most ships moored up, unloaded their precious cargo, refuelled at the mooring buoy where the oil tanker *War Sepoy* was berthed, and then returned to Dunkirk. As well as the destroyers and oil-burning steamers, 665 small pleasure boats and other crafts helped with the evacuation.

Dover's New Customs shed was used as a mortuary while the Old Customs shed was made into a clothing store because many of the men's uniforms were

Brenda as a nurse during the war.

Wartime picture of Brenda on the hospital roof.

Brenda on the children's ward during the war.

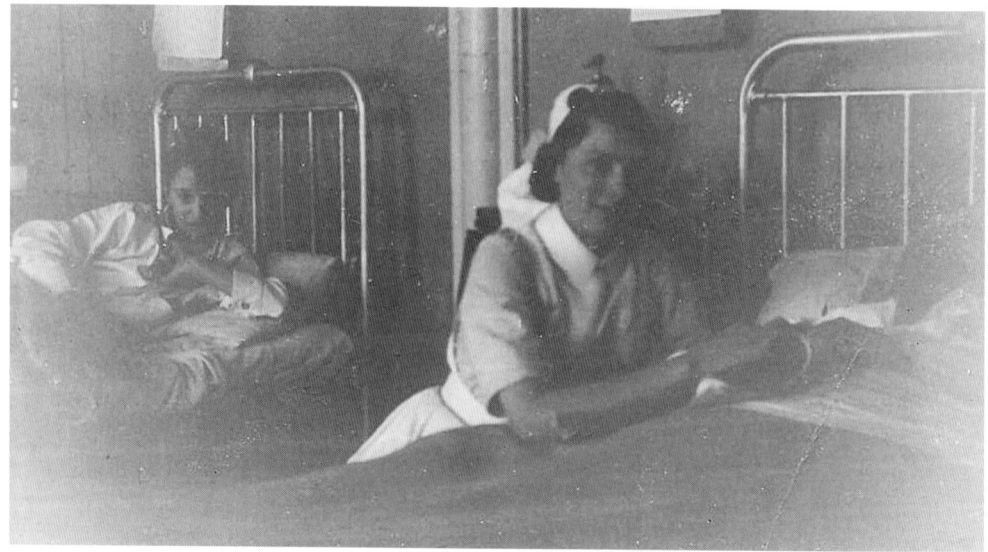

in tatters. Some men were virtually naked apart from a blanket. Many of the ships that berthed had dogs on board who had attached themselves to the troops and these were collected each day by a special lorry. Collection centres were set up anywhere and everywhere to collect food and clothing, and volunteers were recruited to transport it all to the stations to be given out.

A large barn was set up at Headcorn station and 145,000 troops from 207 trains were given food which was supplied by the army and prepared and distributed by volunteers. Additional provision was made at Paddock Wood so that the trains alternated and made eight-minute stops. There were often not enough cups to go round so as the train prepared to draw away from the stations there were calls to 'sling them out', and the cups were thrown on the platforms and collected by the volunteers ready for the next train.

The Defence of Calais delayed the 10th Panzer Division from joining the 1st Panzer Division for several days. The success of the evacuation was owed in no small part, not only to those who provided the rearguard at Dunkirk and who held the Germans while the evacuation took place, but also to those of the 30th Brigade in Calais.

The successful evacuation of so many from Dunkirk was a triumph and without it there is little doubt Britain would have found it difficult to carry on fighting. However there were significant losses and 68,111 men were either killed, classed as missing or taken prisoner. In addition, the BEF lost 679 out of their 704 tanks and half a million tons of military stores and ammunition. It also lost 2,472 guns, 63,879 motor vehicles and 20,548 motorcycles. During the evacuation the RAF lost 474 aircraft and 243 ships were sunk, of which six were destroyers.

On 31 May, with the threat of invasion now a real possibility, the laborious task of taking down all signposts in Britain and removing all milestones commenced. The names of all railway stations, streets and villages were also obliterated. The war was about to move into the next phase. Dunkirk had finally united the military and civilians behind one common objective - to defend Britain from invasion and to defeat Hitler. Britain was now fighting for its very existence.

Back in England other members of the Rifle Brigade had no real idea of what had happened in Calais.

'During this time rumour after rumour about the Battalion reached us, but it was not until the Prime Minister's speech in the House of Commons that we heard the first authentic news – when he told of the historic defence of Calais. Colonel Hoskyns, who had been wounded, was sent to Tunbridge Wells, and 'Coote' saw him there. Two days later he came to a nursing home at Winchester, and three days later he was dead.

To most of us this was our first great personal loss in this war. Though he was wounded on the first day of the fight, the amazing deeds of the Battalion at Calais were due in no small way to him, as he had commanded and trained the Battalion since October 1938.'[10]

On 2 June the Rifle Brigade received a message from Field-Marshal HRH, The Duke of Connaught, KG, KT, Colonel in Chief:

Bagshot Park
2nd June 1940

'I am prouder that I can say of the manner in which the Battalion I once commanded acquitted themselves in the Defence of Calais. In the glorious record of the Regiment there is little, if anything, that has been finer than the part they took in this action.

The defence contributed enormously to the successful evacuation of the Births Expeditionary Force from Dunkirk.

The superb conduct of all ranks in an operation attended by the greatest difficulty was worthy of the highest traditions of the Regiment.

England is proud of this magnificent action, and as an old Commander of the Battalion, I am equally proud. I am sure that this glorious passage in the history of the Regiment will live in the history of the Army.

My sympathy goes out to all the relations and friends of those who fell.

Arthur, Colonel in Chief'

Many of the families and friends of those who had fallen or been captured had no idea their relatives were even in France, let alone Calais. Brenda only found out by accident when she noticed that some of the wounded men she was nursing in the hastily erected casualty stations wore the Black Cat insignia on their arms and the RB insignia on their shoulders. Other family members had a long wait to find out what had happened to their loved ones as many did not hear until late September that they had been captured and were in POW camps.

On 3 June the Comptroller to the Field Marshal, The Colonel in Chief, received a letter from the Private Secretary to his Majesty, The King.

'My dear General
The King asks that you will thank the Duke of Connaught very much for letting him see a copy of the letter written to you by the Commanding Officer of the Battalion of The Rifle Brigade, giving an account of the exploits at Calais.

The heroic resistance of these Rifle Battalions undoubtedly made a great contribution towards the successful evacuation of the British Expeditionary Force from Dunkirk by holding up a large number of enemy motorised units.

It makes a truly wonderful story and one of which the King agrees that the Colonels-in-Chief have every reason to be proud.

Yours sincerely

A.H.L. Hardinge' [11]

Although the BEF evacuation from Dunkirk is the most well-known, it was not the only evacuation from France. The second BEF evacuation took place between 15 and 25 June through the ports in the north-west of France. The two operations to bring out the troops were called Operation Ariel and Operation Cycle and between them they managed to rescue 191,870 men. Of these, 141,171 were British, 18,246 were French, 24,352 were Polish, 4,938 were Czechs and 163 were Belgians. They also brought out 310 artillery guns, 2,292 vehicles, 1,800 tons of stores and a small number of tanks. The final evacuations from France took place from the south coast of France between 24-26 June where another 10,000 troops, mostly Poles and Czechs, together with about the same number of civilians, escaped to Gibraltar.

In the meantime, for France things deteriorated rapidly and on 5 June the Germans launched the second phase of their attack, outflanked the Maginot Line and attacked the rest of France. On 10 June Italy declared war on France although it did little other than make the declaration. That same day the French government fled Paris and set off on the long journey first to Tours and then to Bordeaux where on 12 June General Weygand declared Paris an open city. On 14 June the Germans occupied Paris and, by midday the swastika had replaced the Tricolore on the Hotel de Ville. The Germans continued to consolidate their position by advancing on Cherbourg and the Breton Peninsula at Brest. They also seized the Atlantic coast as far south as Bordeaux. By now they had also crossed the Loire and encircled the armies who had abandoned the forts of the eastern side of the Maginot Line. On 22 June the Second Army Group surrendered, and on 25 June France capitulated. Britain stood alone.

Chapter 11

'The Weekend Trippers'

For Ted the interminable march across Europe continued. The Germans were unable to use trains to transport the prisoners because the Allies had blown up the railway lines and bridges so had no option but to march them to Cambrai. For the prisoners each day was very much like the previous day and each day became a constant battle to survive. They had no idea where they were going or even if the Germans intended to march them all the way to Germany. Morale sank lower and lower as worry and uncertainty added to their hardship. As the days passed escape became less and less of a realistic option as most were becoming too weak to even consider it, and the constant preoccupation with trying to find enough food and water to survive became their sole motivating force. They existed mainly on a diet of weak ersatz[12], coffee, raw vegetables and water provided by the French.

The guards were no longer frontline soldiers; they had been replaced by the Waffen SS in their black uniforms with their death's head insignia. They changed about every five to ten miles and although some were friendly, others were aggressive and trigger-happy. Some allowed the French to give the prisoners food and water, others ordered them to provide food, and some tried to prevent them offering the prisoners anything. Starving, the men sometimes took the opportunity to break out of the ranks and raid empty houses as they passed. Some of the guards turned a blind eye to this, especially if they were French prisoners, but others continued the pattern of brutality that had begun so soon after their capture. Anyone leaving the ranks or helping those who were too weak to keep up were shot out of hand.

Every day invariably started the same way with the guttural 'Raus, raus', as the German guards roused the men from their sleep at dawn with the encouragement of rifle butts and kicks. The rest of the day was a constant trek through village after village and town after town. To the exhausted men their names were often unpronounceable and their inhabitants indistinguishable from those in the previous towns and villages. In between were great swathes of countryside linked by lanes, canals, rivers and in some cases, quite large roads.

The prisoners were passed at regular intervals by victorious German troops heading in the other direction in their transport trucks and various other vehicles, covering them with dust. Many ignored them but some leered, gloated and laughed, and although they couldn't understand the jeering comments the meaning was clear enough. Some Germans took photos which the men found even more demeaning.

The days were mostly hot with clear blue skies and few clouds to provide any relief. The roads were dry and dusty and as the men marched the dust caught in their throats making them cough. The occasional rain was initially greeted by ragged cheers as it provided them with water and flattened the dust, but its continual fall just drenched them adding to their increasing discomfort. Their uniforms steadily deteriorated leaving them feeling scruffy and dishevelled, and their boots, normally so well looked after, cracked and let in water. They were marched from dawn to dusk, stops were infrequent and when they did stop they were given barely enough water to get them to the next stop.

After a couple of days Ted and his fellow troops were separated from the French, Dutch and Belgium soldiers and joined by other British prisoners, remnants of the BEF who had been cut off from their units and picked up in various places on their attempted flight towards Dunkirk. Most of the men were delighted by this, relieved to be free of the French POWs whose attitude to captivity was beyond their comprehension and which had been responsible for several fights. Although they had lost the first battle there was still an invincible belief amongst the British that they would win eventually so they could not understand the defeatist attitude of the French who seemed only too happy to have surrendered.

These new arrivals mixed in with the marching column and two men fell in beside Ted and Rob. They waited until the guards were out of earshot and then struck up conversation, introducing themselves as Sandy and Pete from the Royal Sussex Regiment, captured at St Roche.

'Ted Taylor and Frank Roberts Rifle Brigade.' Ted did the honours, relieved to have something else to think about. 'Captured at Calais'

'How long you been over here then?' Much to their delight Sandy offered them each a cigarette.

'Don't know, what's the date today?' asked Ted drawing deeply on the first cigarette he had had for a while.

'29 May I think', Sandy answered.

'I think we got here on the 23 May', said Ted.

'Oh, just *weekend trippers* then', replied Sandy with a laugh. 'Hardly worth coming was it?'

Ted, Rob and Jim were about to object when they realized Sandy was only joking. It was a joke Ted would always remember and was the reason for the title of the original book.

The day wore slowly on and the men walked on wearily, only their strength of character and the fear of being shot motivating them to keep putting one foot in front of another. As the sun sunk lower in the sky they did not know when, or even if, they were going to stop. The last place they had passed through had been Lacres and that had been several hours earlier. They were exhausted and even the open fields with no shelter were beginning to look inviting. The night stops so far had all been in fields and they had tried to find spaces nearest the hedges as they at least provided some shelter from the wind. But there was no escape from the damp.

Whereas the days were hot the nights were still cool, and although it was mainly dry, the fields were still covered in early morning dew which soaked through the men's clothes leaving them damp and uncomfortable. The lack of any bedding with which to cover themselves left them feeling cold however much they curled up, and not being able to get warm meant they were also unable to sleep despite their constant exhaustion. The only advantage of sleeping in the fields was that they had managed to find the odd carrot or potato there to eat which, although raw, took the edge of their hunger. The downside of eating raw vegetables was that it upset their stomachs and many were now suffering from chronic diarrhoea which made their lives even more miserable. The guards were totally unsympathetic and would not let the troops leave the lines meaning many soiled themselves, the ultimate humiliation for these proud men. The smell of their unwashed bodies mingled with the smell of sweat and faeces much to the delight of the Germans who repeatedly taunted them about the state they were in.

But for once it looked as if they might find overnight shelter. As they approached another built-up area Ted busied himself with trying to memorize the name on the signpost. He had decided to do this quite early on in their march eastwards. He wasn't sure whether it would come in useful or not, but if they did manage to escape it would help if they knew which way to go and being able to recognize place names was absolutely necessary.

Hesdin was a small historic town built on the confluence of the rivers Canche and Ternoise, and dispirited and tired as they were the men couldn't help notice the large Town Hall with its impressive belfry that overlooked the main square. There were few people about and those who were watched sullenly in silence or looked away not wanting the Germans to see the resentment on their faces. The guards hurried the men along the cobbled streets and across several bridges over the fast- flowing rivers, past the equally impressive sixteenth-century Church of Notre Dame and back out into the countryside again.

In the distance they noticed a large chateau set back from the road. The guards herded them off the road and along a private track towards it. On either side of the road there were neatly-tended fields and in the distance they could see a couple of farm workers, although they couldn't quite make out whether they were planting crops or picking them. The guards continued to march them along the road until they came to an even smaller track leading off to the left towards some buildings which resembled large barns. The chateau was still a long way off and the men soon arrived in what appeared to be in some kind of farming area. The guards marched them across a large, concreted yard until they came to the big barn-type buildings that turned out to be stables. The guards pushed open the doors and herded them in gesturing to the stalls. Ted glanced warily at the others before allowing himself to be shepherded in.

Reaching the end Ted pushed open the door of the last stall and after one more look at the others who nodded, he went in. The stall felt warm after the cool evening air and the straw looked inviting after several nights of sleeping in trenches and fields. They were joined by some other soldiers and a sergeant who sat down heavily on the straw and closed his eyes, the strain of the past few days showing on his face.

Deciding that if the sergeant thought they were safe they probably didn't need to worry, Ted, Rob and their new friends also sorted themselves out some space and sitting down on the thick covering of straw they began to relax. They were all exhausted from the strain of not knowing what was going to happen to them, coupled with the lack of food and water and the long march. Although the straw was not particularly clean they didn't care, they were filthy anyway so the condition of the straw was irrelevant. At least it was warm and much more comfortable than sleeping on open ground. They all closed their eyes and one by one drifted into sleep. However, their rest was short-lived as after a couple of hours they heard the main doors open. Much to Ted's disbelief the faint fragrance of herbs and vegetables drifted across his nostrils, for once blocking out the awful stench of their own bodies.

'Hot food?' he asked, unable to believe his senses, but sure enough the guards had brought in several large tureens which they placed near the door. Even from the back they could smell the stew and see the steam rising from the containers.

For Ted and Rob it was the first hot meal they had had since leaving England on 22 May and although there wasn't much and it was very thin with a few vegetables, few potatoes and no meat, it was hot and flavoursome and took the edge of their hunger. Resting his back against one of the stable doors and feeling better than he had for a couple of days, Ted closed his eyes, feeling almost human again. His feet were hurting but he was wary of taking his boots off, not only because of what he might find, but also because he couldn't afford to have them stolen while he slept. Deciding he could always use them to lay his head on Ted carefully eased them off.

Ignoring the comments and complaints the others carefully followed his example and eased their boots off too. Much to Ted's relief his feet weren't too bad. He only had one large blister and that was on his heel. The one on his toe that had been really bad a couple of nights before was already starting to harden up so another day or two and it wouldn't hurt quite so much. It was nearly dark but he wanted to try and make some notes on his signals pad so that when he had an opportunity he could write it up properly. He knew that if he didn't write some sort of summary he would forget it all or wouldn't know on what day things had happened or where they were on certain days. He didn't know why it was so important to him to keep a record; he just felt that he should.

He started by writing down some points of the action in Calais together with the day they had occurred. Once he had done that he decided to try and write down some of the names of the villages they had passed through. Although he

All Ted's diary pages were written in pencil in tiny writing.

didn't know where they were going yet he could add that afterwards. The biggest problem was that he had no idea how to spell them so he would just have to write down how they sounded. Ted only had time to write down a few names before the light faded completely.

Deciding against leaving his boots off he put them back on and then, putting the pad away safely in his top pocket, he curled up into the straw trying not to disturb anyone else and closed his eyes. Experience had shown him that although he was physically tired at night his brain was still active so he found it hard to sleep. Eventually, out of sheer frustration he had developed his own relaxation method. As soon as he closed his eyes he would visualize Brenda lying next to him with her arms around him. He would then imagine she was asleep and that he was curled up, safe in her arms. As he drifted off he would see her smiling face and taste her lips on his. And if he really concentrated hard he could remember how her body felt when he held her close to him.

The night passed uneventfully and like the others he had to be prodded and shouted at several times before he was able to wake up properly as yet another early morning greeted them. Groaning and grumbling the men fell in and without anything to eat or drink they left the comparative comfort of the stable and began the slog to the next town, Frevent, where the inhabitants watched sullenly as they walked through. Although Ted had long since lost interest in where they were and just wanted to arrive so they could stop walking, he was taken aback by the sight of all the lines of neatly- tended graves in the cemetery on the eastern side of the town.

St Hilaire Cemetery was the burial place for many of the casualties from the clearing stations and hospitals who had been based there during the Great War. Looking at the graves reminded the men of their friends who were not with them and who had already died in this conflict. Although most conversation had pretty much dried up anyway as they concentrated on keeping alive, walking past the cemetery seemed only to reinforce the futility of war and for the most part they walked in silence, lost in their own thoughts, usually of their loved ones and home.

And as they walked further and further into captivity they passed yet more German columns marching towards the coast and the guards changed again.

Exhaustion, lack of food and water and the strain of not knowing where they were going or what was going to happen to them, was making them all bad-tempered and argumentative. Frequent arguments broke and after a while Ted learnt to ignore them, but as the day wore slowly on he was suddenly aware of the sound of raised voices coming from behind them. He turned towards the direction the noise was coming from just as a couple of shots rang out. Although they could not see exactly what was going on they could make an educated guess as they had seen it happen before. They had just passed an abandoned house set back several yards from the road. While a couple of the men had distracted the guards two others had taken the opportunity to dive out of the ranks and into the house to forage for food. They had obviously succeeded in finding something, but when they returned with it a fight must have broken out. The noise had been the fight and the Germans raising their rifles. Fortunately this time the Germans had only fired into the air but as they strode towards the scene of the incident they saw one of the more aggressive German guards, his rifle raised. A heated argument then ensued between him and the two guards who had first arrived on the scene. Unable to resist it the troops nearest were cheering quietly every time the friendlier soldiers said something and booing when the aggressive guard spoke. Although they were unable to understand the argument it was apparent that the two younger guards were being chastized for allowing the men to leave the ranks. Judging that the scene was about to turn nasty, especially as the aggressive guard now realized that the men were booing him, an RQMS swiftly intervened by shouting at them to fall in at the double.

The discipline that had been drummed into them throughout their training and beyond kicked in and they all obeyed instantly. Once the men had reformed into a line the Germans were completely confused because they had no idea who had caused the problem in the first place. Having taken control, the RQMS continued by assuring the Germans that there was to be no further trouble and before they could respond, gave the order to 'quick march'.

Despite their exhaustion the men quickly grasped the situation and marched swiftly and orderly away leaving the Germans with no option but to follow them.

Ted whistled softly through his teeth, relieved that the imminent danger had passed. In the back of his mind was the thought that it took very little for the Germans to shoot them. They seemed to have little regard for human life and as they assumed they had won the war they could more or less do as they pleased. He digested this thought in silence as they continued to march. He had not thought about it like that before. But now he had done, he had a feeling that he was probably right, which did not bode very well for their future treatment.

That night was spent in the fields outside Doullens. Again the men managed to scavenge some more carrots, turnips and potatoes which they ate raw before falling into yet another restless, uneasy sleep. The damp grass made an uncomfortable bed and the dampness seeped through their uniforms so that when they woke they felt as if all their clothes were wringing wet. Taking their time to get started angered the guards who shouted aggressively at them and threatened them with their rifles. Sighing heavily they struggled out of the fields and back to the winding country road they had been walking on the previous evening.

There was no early morning n and the sky was filled with depressing dark clouds that showered them in moisture, adding to their discomfort. The earth turned to mud which stuck to their boots making it even harder to walk. Ted had to concentrate hard to avoid slipping and sliding on the treacherous sludge that was all that was left of the field. Unfortunately, because of their position near the end of the column, he and the others encountered what had already been churned up by those in front.

The rain continued to fall, churning up the mud even more and making it harder for the men in their weakened state to walk through. Several men fell over but were lucky enough to be helped to their feet by the others before the Germans noticed. It was with a sense of relief that they reached the road again. The road was bordered on both sides by thick hedges behind which were quite densely-planted trees that shielded the road from the light but didn't stop the rain from drenching the troops. Those who still had their cups held them out as they walked, trying to salvage some water from the relentless drizzle that threatened to soak right through to their skins.

The rain alternated between light rain and heavy downpours that soaked them completely. The guards, wearing great cloaks that protected them from the worst of the rain, marched them on regardless of their discomfort. There was no stop for lunch, only one to change the guards, and the Germans ate their rations as they walked. The prisoners were not offered anything and had no option but to ignore the continuous rumbling of their stomachs and the ensuing pains. This lack of food and water was beginning to affect the way their bodies worked and many had not been to the toilet for several days. Others were suffering from dysentery and the further they marched the more intolerant the Germans became towards those leaving the main body of men. Although the fear of ridicule had long since disappeared, the fear of being shot purely because they needed to fulfil a bodily function only added to the men's growing despair and humiliation.

The morning wore slowly on and just as the prisoners were thinking about whether it would ever stop raining it gradually eased. Ted glanced up at the sky and realized that at last it was becoming brighter and that in the distance there was some blue sky. The May sun was hot and quickly burned some holes in the clouds. As the breaks got larger more of the sun's strength shone through. The temperature went up and the men's uniforms sent up clouds of steam into the sky as they dried out. The mud on their boots also dried and fell off, littering the road with large clumps that were broken up by the troops who followed on behind. But the warmth of the sun on their backs gradually lifted their spirits and they felt better.

The men walked on until they reached Bapaume, a small town synonymous with the Great War. Bapaume had been the objective of the opening attack by the British in the Battle of the Somme. It had taken from 1 July 1916 until 17

March 1917 to cover the 19km from Albert to Bapaume, and the race to be first to occupy Bapaume was won by the Australian Imperial Forces (The 30th Battalion New South Wales) on 17 March 1917. Shortly after the Australian Forces' arrival there a German delayed-action mine had obliterated the town hall. The town suffered other severe damage in the Great War with many of its building completely destroyed. This meant that most of the town had been rebuilt after the end of the war.

But the weary men were not really interested in its history; they were more concerned about whether they might be lucky enough to be given somewhere out of the wet fields to sleep and, more importantly perhaps, some food. That was all they could think about at the moment and the hungrier they became the more their minds focused on food. So urgent was their body's need for food, water and rest, that even their need to know their eventual destination and their future, became much less important. They no longer noticed how dirty they were or that they were all now sporting beards of varying lengths. Even the itching as a result of the lice infestations that had begun a couple of days earlier had become almost normal and they hardly noticed it. No longer interested in where they were, the men wearily marched through the town not even bothering to acknowledge the odd smile or sign of the cross they got from the locals who watched them pass. As they came towards the outer edge on the far side of the town they were beginning to despair of ever stopping when, much to their relief, the Germans suddenly called a halt and after much shouting and gesturing at the locals, requisitioned the use of the church hall.

After sleeping in fields and trenches the floor of the church hall was a luxury and in some ways was even more comfortable than the stable.

Ted and Rob followed Sandy and Peter and found themselves a space at the back. The proximity of so many bodies immediately raised the temperature and their uniforms, which hadn't entirely dried out, began to steam again filling the air with a stale, musty smell which mingled with the other noxious smells coming from their soiled clothes and unwashed bodies. But as they all smelt the same, no one really noticed anymore and if they did they were so relieved to be inside a building that they were not going to spoil the moment by complaining.

Easing off their outer garments the men sat down with their backs against the wall and closed their eyes. All Ted needed now was some food and, as if in answer to his prayer, a guard appeared and handed out pieces of bread. He shouted at the men and pointed in the direction of the door where they noticed a large urn. There was a mad scramble which resulted in the guards screaming wildly at them in German and gesturing angrily with their rifles, followed by a shot in the air. In the confined space of the hall the shot ricocheted around, bouncing off the walls and making all the men throw themselves flat on the floor. It also deafened them. Although they didn't understand the words the Germans were shouting, the meaning was quite clear and they all lay where they had thrown themselves.

In the ensuing silence the NCOs reasserted authority and gave orders for their prisoners to form orderly queues. There was a lot of grumbling but the men complied. Their patience was rewarded when they reached the front they were given a small portion of stew. It was only the second hot meal Ted and Rob had eaten since they had left England and it tasted absolutely wonderful. Unlike the stew they had eaten in the stable it was thicker and there was more of it. Ravenously hungry they tried hard to savour every mouthful and make it last. When they had finished Pete produced some crumpled cigarettes which they shared out. Lighting up they closed their eyes and reflected just how little it now took to make them happy.

Ted pulled out the only picture he had of Brenda and smiled at it. Although it was tatty and worn, just looking at it was enough to lift his spirits. He couldn't imagine how awful it must be not to have someone waiting for you, someone to dream about, to make you want to carry on even when you felt like giving up. He carefully replaced the photo, took out his pad and pencil and started to write about Calais. He wrote as small as possible as he had no idea when they would get any more paper. He tried hard to convey the events since their arrival while they were still fresh in his mind. But he found it difficult to find the words to adequately describe the horrific things he had seen and experienced. Still, the most important thing was to document it so that he had it for future reference. He would write to Brenda and his Mum properly once he was at whatever camp he was put in. Thinking about writing to them reminded him of his note. He wondered where it was now and whether it was on its way or had just ended up in a dustbin somewhere. He thought about the people he had given it to. Were they safely tucked up in bed now or were they trying to flee the Germans like the thousands of other refugees they had seen? Yawning he turned his attention back to his diary but the light had now faded and he was no longer able to really see what he was doing so he put the pad away and lay down. With a full stomach he had no trouble falling asleep and for once, feeling warm, he slept without waking, unaware of the dreams that filled his sleeping subconscious: dreams of Brenda, his Mum, brothers and the family that he had passed his note to days earlier. He did not wake until the next morning when the guards came round shouting and yelling.

Chapter 12

Out of the Frying Pan
June

The morning of 1 June dawned bright and sunny and as they walked through the morning the men noticed the landscape gradually changing. The fields became more compact and they passed more properties. They were obviously coming to some kind of small town. The road signs proclaimed the place to be Cambrai and they wondered if they were going to stop there.

'Oh, oh. Kraut alert', said Ted softly as one of the German guards dropped in beside them. Much to their surprise he offered them each a cigarette which, after a slight hesitation, they accepted with alacrity.

'So, you like football?' asked the guard in broken English

'Yeah mate, love it', replied Ted, curious as to where this conversation was going. Personally he hated football but lying to a German didn't count as lying and if it got them a couple of cigarettes what was the harm.

'I support Manchester United', the German continued. 'And you?'

Ted was stumped for a moment and then replied, 'Arsenal. Yeah you know, I really support the Woolwich Arsenal.' The other men turned their faces away quickly so the guard wouldn't see or hear their stifled laughter. They knew that Ted was not alluding to the football team, but to the Woolwich arsenal where the munitions were made. Fortunately the guard seemed not to understand and after introducing himself as 'Hans' by pointing at himself, he immediately launched into a mixture of English and German which Ted presumed was about football. Feeling a bit mean, especially when the German offered them another cigarette, he did his best to find something to discuss but being genuinely uninterested in the game was relieved when the others joined in.

At about 1.30 pm, when the men had walked through several narrow streets and past a large imposing building in the centre of the town, they were herded down more streets by the Germans towards some kind of large empty goods yard where, to their delight, they were offered bread and warm stew. It was slightly thicker than the meal of the previous evening and Ted was sure he could even see meat in his portion. However, when he looked closely he realized that the potatoes were beginning to go rotten and the bread had patches of mould on it. But he was starving so he ignored the appearance of the food and wolfed it down, praying he wouldn't regret it later. With his stomach feeling reasonably full - although he really didn't want to think too much about what he had eaten - and enjoying the warmth of the early summer sunshine, Ted felt much better. He took his boots off with a sigh of relief and putting them safely behind him he leaned back, resting carefully on them and closed his eyes. 'When I get home I'm never walking anywhere again', he muttered to himself.

Much to their surprise the men were left alone for the rest of the day and as evening fell they settled down in the goods yard to sleep, relieved that they were no longer being marched across Europe.

The next morning, to their delight, they were given water to wash in. It felt wonderful on their skin after their several days of fighting and then walking and sleeping rough. Ted looked at the water he had washed his face and hands in. It was filthy but like the others he took the opportunity to clean his feet and then wash his socks and put them on the grass beside him. This chance to wash revitalized them and the prisoners were even more pleased to discover they were now to be left alone to laze about for the rest of the day. The evening meal was again a weak stew and having survived it and having spent the day resting they all felt slightly better.

The following day, 3 June, the men were divided up into work parties to repair some of the damage done to the town by the Allied bombing. Although the work was hard it was better than marching relentlessly, and at the end of the day they were given double their stew ration.

Relaxing in the evening after their meal Ted speculated out loud about whether this was it and that perhaps this was where they would stay until the war was finished or they were able to return home. But the general consensus was that it was just a break and that they should make the most of it. Ted nodded in agreement as it did make sense, but privately hoped he was wrong. He was already really homesick and although he was glad he had some good friends - it would have been unbearable without them - he was really missing Brenda. When they had said goodbye at Christmas he thought it would only be a few weeks before they saw each other again. It had already been several months and now he couldn't even write to her. Feeling despondent he decided to try and catch up with his diary before it became too dark. When asked what he was doing he explained that he was writing a diary so that he could tell people what had happened to them and how they had been treated. To his surprise most of the others thought it was a waste of time saying that no one would be interested. The more cynical among them made the point that governments always treat those who fight for them as heroes when the war is on but soon forget them and any promises made that they would always be remembered and looked after by a grateful nation, once the danger was passed. Despite this, Ted decided to write anyway and as the snores of the sleeping men surrounded him he wrote well into the night until the light faded and he could no longer see.

The morning of 4 June arrived all too soon and the sun climbed steadily. The guards roused their prisoners and without food or drink they were marched back out onto the road.

That day seemed to set a pattern and for the next three days they were walked from sunrise to sunset without a break. The men were again reduced to sleeping in fields and scavenging for raw vegetables. One day they were also given small loaves of black bread which had already started to go green, to share between six or seven of them. Wondering how they could possibly survive much more of this they were relieved on the evening of the third day to be given the order to stop. They had just approached another town which the signposts proclaimed to be Beauraing.

Beauraing was in the French-speaking part of southern Belgium and its main claim to fame was that between 29 November and 3 January 1933, five young people reported thirty-three apparitions of the Virgin Mary. These apparitions had been accepted by the Catholic Church and Beauraing became a place of pilgrimage. But neither Ted nor the other men were the slightest bit interested in the history of their latest stop. Completely exhausted, dehydrated, and with many having dysentery from eating the mouldy bread and rotten vegetables, all they were concerned about was whether they would have rest, food and water. Their uniforms were now hanging off them, not only from the general wear and tear of their enforced march, but because they had lost so much weight. Several men had dropped out of the lines and had not reappeared. Looking at Rob's face properly for the first time in several days Ted suddenly realized just how gaunt his friend was and wondered if he looked as bad. A glance at the others confirmed his worse fears. Their appearance was dreadful. Not only were they filthy and dishevelled, with several days' growth from not being able to shave, their faces looked worn and strained and they all seemed to have aged several years.

Ted was suddenly struck with a terrible fear that they would never be treated any better and that the Germans would just keep walking them continuously until they dropped down dead, one by one. Perhaps those who had dropped out of the lines and been shot were the lucky ones. At least they were no longer in pain and no longer suffering. He shook himself to dispel the black clouds of depression that were threatening to overwhelm him. He knew that if he gave in mentally he wouldn't survive and he had so much to live for, so much to go back to. He took a deep breath and walked on, head high as he tried to ignore his aching feet and stomach and the pains in just about every part of his body.

The guards marched the men through the town and then stopped them in a large goods yard not far from the station. They could see the puffs of white smoke floating gently skyward as the trains arrived and departed and they could hear the sounds of the engines as they went about their business. Ted's spirits soared as the thought struck him that they might be going the rest of the way by train. No more walking. Anything had to be better than that.

They sat down heavily on the floor and were quickly joined by the others. They were given water but no food but they were so exhausted that for once they fell asleep despite their empty stomachs. The morning came all too quickly and again they were woken early. The sun was already high in the sky and it promised to be a very hot day.

The guards roused them and marched them down to the station. Ted stood on the platform and looked around. He was worried about where they were going and if he was ever really going to get home. His earlier euphoria at the prospect of not having to walk any further was replaced by the realization that if they were going by train they would be even further away from home, making it even harder to escape. Standing there with the sun beating down and the sweat pouring off him, watching the clouds of white smoke pouring from the approaching engine, Ted realized that he needed all his strength if he was going to survive. It was there and then he made the decision that the Germans were not going to beat him, no matter what they did. Ted silently vowed to himself that he was going home. He had promised Brenda that he would come back to her and he didn't break his promises.

Feeling better for having made the decision he stood silently with the others and watched as the train pulled slowly into the station. The thought that at least they weren't going to have to walk was now quickly replaced with utter dismay as he saw that it was just a goods train. There were no carriages, just cattle trucks. The train eased to a standstill and the guards hustled them into the trucks using their bayonets and rifle butts.

Each cattle truck held about sixty men. There was no food and no water and as the sun shone inexorably down Ted had serious doubts as to whether he was going to be able to keep his promise. The train remained stationary for several hours which made it even hotter and just when they thought they could not bear it any more they heard the sound of the engine beginning to fire up. As the train moved they heard the tolling of the clock in Beauraing announcing that it was 7 pm. As the train eased out of the station the men could at last feel a gentle breeze coming in through the open space near the top and through the badly-fitted slats in the side of the wooden panels. The train built up speed and the air cooled considerably which made the journey marginally more comfortable.

Ted removed his boots despite the protests of the others, but after a few moments virtually everyone had done the same. The smell of their unwashed bodies mixed with the sweat from the heat and the odour from their boots permeated the wagon, but they were all really past caring and no one was complaining. Most of the men were trying to sleep so Ted closed his eyes as well. But he had a really bad headache caused by dehydration as well as stomach ache from lack of food. He couldn't settle and eventually gave up. Staring ahead at the walls of the wagon he looked up at the open gap where the breeze, that had now strengthened, was freely circulating and cleansing the air. The rhythm of the train was strangely soothing and despite his unsuccessful attempts to fall asleep earlier he found himself gradually being lulled into a doze.

After several hours the Germans opened the hatch above them and threw down some more mouldy bread. To start with they were so thirsty that most of them really didn't want any food but they knew they had to eat to keep themselves alive. Each loaf had to be shared between six men, which meant very little each, but it was better than nothing. They were also relieved to be given some water which went some way to easing their immediate discomfort. As the night wore on and the heat was replaced by the chill of the evening air they all gradually fell asleep.

Throughout the night, as the exhausted men slept, the train continued eastwards across Belgium and into Luxembourg until it crossed the German border and came to a stop at Igel, near Dortmund. Here they were allowed to get out while the train they had been on headed back towards France.

Standing on the platform Ted looked round. There were swastikas proclaiming German superiority everywhere. The guards counted the men and then, when they had finished, they counted again. On the third count Ted felt faint and it was only his strength of will and the occasional hoarse joke from the others that kept him standing up. His throat was so dry that it hurt to speak and his lips were cracked and sore. He tried frantically to think of something else, anything other than the pain and exhaustion, and then it was over. The Germans had finished their counting and satisfied themselves that no one had escaped - although Ted was sure they had no idea of how many prisoners there were anyway. He thought idly whether the guards had to account for those who had callously been shot on the way. Then the troops were on the move again. If anything, Ted's feet hurt even more now that he had rested them and he winced with every step as they were marched across the station past jeering station staff and civilians towards another stationary goods train and herded onto it. Relief that they were able to stretch their legs soon turned to dismay when the men realized they had exchanged one prison for another. It was made worse by the fact that all the civilians they saw were Germans. Whereas the French had tried to help by giving them food and water, the German civilians just jeered at them, some even spitting, while others just laughed.

After what seemed like several hours the train left the station and headed

114

out on the short journey to Trier where, once again, the men were made to get off. Although it was a different station it might just as well have been the previous one as everywhere they looked they were surrounded by German flags and swastikas. The station staff threw empty bottles at them, narrowly missing Ted who ducked and remarked loudly that it was a shame it wasn't full. This produced some more laughter but underneath his show of bravado Ted, like the others, was shaken by the overt hostility. Although he tried not to let it affect him it was hard not to feel humiliated. They had come to France to fight for their country, had been defeated and were now being treated little better than slaves. He tried to shake off his depression as the Germans went through the now familiar counting routine.

Eventually the Germans were satisfied they hadn't lost anybody and the men were herded out of the station and through the streets of the main town. These were full of unfriendly civilians who jeered and called out at them, mocking their uneven stagger and their filthy, dishevelled and exhausted state. Those nearest spat at them and some threw stones. Knowing it would be suicidal to retaliate the prisoners put their heads down and concentrated on just staying upright. They couldn't understand most of what was shouted, but the meaning was clear and in their weakened state they had trouble making the last few yards up the hill towards an old cavalry barracks. This led to even more catcalls and jeers.

The barracks were quite old but were bordered by barbed wire and had watchtowers at all the corners. It made a depressing sight. But once inside the men were given some water and food. Much to their surprise they were also given razors and water and allowed to shave. This was the first time many of them had shaved since leaving England and when they finished a lot of the men were almost unrecognizable which led to some good-humoured banter which did at least put them in better spirits. After shaving they then queued up for the weak vegetable stew that was becoming a normal part of their diet. They were almost conditioned to looking forward to it and even though there was not much of it, it was at least hot and this time the contents did not look rotten. The men were surprised there was also bread which for once wasn't mouldy and although it had to be shared out it made this one of the more substantial meals they had been given since their capture. Unfortunately the stew was very salty and not long after they had finished eating it they were very thirsty.

The guards brought round some water but when several of the British sergeants saw the men about to drink it all in one go, they advised caution, pointing out that given their treatment so far they had no idea when they would be given any more so they should conserve as much as possible.

These words were prophetic and would come back to Ted later, but for now they all watched with a certain amount of interest as other captured troops appeared in the camp and were sent to join them. Although there were several hundred prisoners milling around, the men couldn't resist trying to find lost friends and members of their own units. But unable to move easily because of the sheer numbers, they eventually gave it up as it was rather like looking for a needle in a haystack.

The next morning they were again counted several times and marched back down through the streets past more jeering, contemptuous civilians, to the station where they were joined by yet more troops.

There was not much room on the crowded platform and the newcomers were encouraged, with the help of prods from rifle butts and bayonets, to mix in with those already sitting down.

After a couple of hours another train puffed slowly into the station and pulled up at the platform next to them. The guards walked down the line of men prodding and shouting at them to get up. The doors of the cattle wagons were pulled open and they were herded on, again sixty or more to each wagon. Once inside nothing happened. The men spread out as best they could, which given the limited space was almost impossible, and tried to make themselves comfortable.

The heat was unbearable and the salty stew they had eaten earlier only added to their discomfort. As they sat there sweltering they heard another train pull in opposite them. Rob and Ted managed to squeeze their way to the tiny opening at the top. Seeing that the train was also a goods train with cattle trucks crammed with people they wondered if they were more captured troops. After a few moments Ted called out to them. There was no answer at first so he tried again. To his surprise the voice that answered was female and sounded quite young. He was even more surprised when the disembodied voice went on to explain that they were not captured soldiers, but were Jewish people going to Poland to start a new life. Ted couldn't really think of anything to say so he explained who they were and wished them good luck. The girl responded by wishing them good luck too and then they heard the sound of the guards hammering on the wooden slats of her train and harsh words being shouted in German. Ted was about to say something else when a burly guard stuck his face up against the small gap and shouted something which made Ted jump and take a step back.

The others asked Ted what had been said and when he explained several looked bemused as to why Jewish people should be on trains similar to theirs if they weren't combatants. It took one of the newcomers to explain just how dangerous it was to be Jewish in the Third Reich and how there were rumours of camps where Jews were really badly treated and did not come out of. Ted looked horrified and thought about the young girl he had just spoken to. He was anxious about what would happen to her and her family. Thinking of families inevitably made Brenda and his Mum come to mind and as he closed his eyes he concentrated on thinking about happier times. He wondered fleetingly if his note had reached them, then smiled. It was unlikely of course. It was much more probable that it ended up in a dustbin or on a bonfire somewhere.

Conversation amongst the men returned to where they had been captured. Having not heard any news since his own capture, Ted was amazed to hear about the Dunkirk evacuation and even more gratified to hear that Churchill had made a speech about the Calais Force in Parliament, praising their heroism.

Ted felt slightly better although it sounded like it had been a close-run thing. What if the Germans invaded? Would there be enough troops left to defend Britain?

He was about to ask some more when he realized that his informant, like most of the other men, was fast asleep. Sighing, he closed his eyes again and tried to sleep. The heat in the truck was stifling and the air was stuffy and Ted no longer felt any cool air circulating. He undid another button in an attempt to cool down and thought about what Brenda and his Mum might be doing and whether they had been notified by the army that he was a prisoner. He wondered if they were missing him. Although he knew they probably were, the thought that they might not be was almost too much to bear and he had to make himself think of something else.

Every quarter of an hour the clock in the station chimed so at least he knew what the time was and gradually the suffocating heat of the day merged with the cooler air of the evening. Eventually at 9.30 pm (he knew because he heard the clock striking the half-hour in the station), the train left Trier for the two-day journey to Thorn (Torun) in Poland.

If the men had been uncomfortable before it was nothing to the way they felt now. The train rattled along throughout the night, slowing down through the built-up areas of the city before speeding up as it came out into the open countryside. To start with it wasn't too bad. Cool air circulated through the truck and as the men were exhausted, most of them slept anyway. Relieved not to be walking and thankful that their feet would have a chance to recover from the dreadful pounding they had taken over the previous days, most of the men dozed or chatted quietly with those around them. Ted also found it quite easy to sleep once the train picked up speed and so it was with a start that he woke up when the truck went noisily over a level crossing. He opened his eyes and saw Rob trying to peer through the open space near the top of the truck.

With some difficulty, as there was little room to manoeuvre without treading on someone, Ted got to his feet and joined Rob in looking out onto miles of open countryside. The sun was shining brightly overhead having risen from the direction in which they were heading. In the distance Ted saw a large forest, and every now and then the sun would reflect the glint of water leading him to assume there must be lakes or ponds nestling in amongst the green fields. The two men stood there for a while and watched as the fields, roads, isolated farm houses and the occasional person sped past oblivious of them and their journey.

The scene made Ted even more depressed as he realized that, serene and relaxing as the view was, every mile was taking him further and further away from those he loved.

Sitting back down he took the opportunity to take off his boots again. His socks were now full of holes - in fact they were mainly holes with bits of material in between. Sighing, he tried to decide whether there was much point leaving them on or whether it would be better to take them off all together. That was, of course, if he could actually take them off. Apart from the brief wash a couple of days earlier his socks had been stuck on his feet for nearly three weeks. His uniform felt almost as bad but at least it hadn't gone into holes completely yet. Would they ever be given clean clothes? Or would the Germans just leave them until their uniforms fell off them? Ted closed his eyes again and tried frantically to find something good about his situation. He eventually decided that at least they weren't walking.

The truck was beginning to warm up as the sun climbed higher in the sky and as the temperature went up the men's hunger was replaced by a raging thirst. They could hear the German guard above their heads moving about and stretching his limbs. Even more depressing was that they could see his shadow clearly above them drinking and eating which only reinforced their own discomfort. To start with they tried to keep their spirits up by singing. This worked well for a while especially as it had the added bonus of irritating the guards perched precariously on top of the trucks. By now the soldiers in other trucks had also joined in which was even more annoying to the guards who thumped on the roof in an attempt to stop them.

But as the day wore on it slowly dawned on them that the Germans were not intending to give them any food or water and they gradually sank into silence, trying to save what little strength they had.

The day wore on slowly with the men becoming more and more dehydrated and by the evening several were feeling dizzy and starting to become confused. With no toilets and no stops they had no option but to relieve themselves where they sat, the smell of urine and faeces mingling with the smell of sweat making the intense heat even more unbearable. Eventually the evening became night and to their intense relief the temperature gradually dropped. However, the sweat on their bodies also cooled down and made them shiver. As he tried to get comfortable so that he could at least sleep for a while, Ted found his thoughts wandering back over his life.

He had been born in Peckham on 31 October 1919 to Louisa and Henry Taylor. His father was a driver with the Royal Artillery in the Great War. His parents had married during the First World War in August 1917. He was christened Henry Edward George but to avoid mixing him up with his father, he had always been known as Ted. His brothers had been born soon after. His childhood had been reasonably uneventful although his parents separated when he was older which was never talked about because it was something that 'just wasn't done' even though it was a lot more common than people realized.

As far as he was concerned Ted's life had really started when he moved to Crofton Park and got involved in the local Baptist church. It was then he had met many of his close friends and, of course, Brenda. Leaving school had also been good as he had loved working at Greens and made many friends there. Sighing, Ted wondered how many of them would survive the war and whether he would ever return there. Even if he did, would life ever be the same? Mentally he shook himself. He was starting to get depressed again and that wasn't helpful. He tried to concentrate on Brenda and the lovely smile on her face the last time he saw her. Holding that image he managed to gradually fall into a restless sleep as the cattle trucks headed eastwards taking him ever further from those he loved.

Chapter 13

Stalag XXA

As the dawn broke and the sun shone through the badly made wagons Ted made an effort to get up and look out. The landscape had now changed considerably; gone were the gentle rolling countryside and rich agricultural lands of Germany. The landscape was much bleaker and showed the scars of recent battles. Although there were workers in some of the fields their dress indicated a much greater degree of poverty. As ridiculous as it seemed, to Ted they also appeared beaten and dejected, unlike the workers they had seen in the German fields who looked fit and healthy. Rob joined him and they watched in silence as the fields gave way to roads bearing German tanks and troops, and then to a small town. The train sped through the bleak station without stopping, but there was enough time for them to see the bomb craters in the roads and surrounding countryside where the fierce fighting in September 1939 had scarred the landscapes.

Seeing the evidence of German occupation stamped on the town immediately focused Ted's thoughts back to those he had left behind and he wondered out loud whether the Germans would ever succeed in their threat to invade Britain. Despite their discomfort and the appalling conditions, those who were still conscious immediately discounted this, absolutely certain that Britain was able to repel any invasion. Ted hoped they were right as it was bad enough being stuck here so far from home, but having seen the way their enemy behaved he couldn't bear the thought of them lording it over his friends and family at home.

He sat back down, closed his eyes and tried to imagine he was somewhere cold; anywhere but here. Being trapped on the ship had been bad enough, and then, when he was stuck in the thick of the fighting he had thought there couldn't be anything worse. But this was slow torture. Although there was less imminent danger this was almost worse because he had no idea how much longer he was going to have to endure it. Maybe the Germans were just going to leave them on these trucks until they all died of dehydration and starvation. His head started to feel strange with that odd kind of muzzy feeling he could vaguely remember feeling as a child when he was ill. Thinking coherently was becoming more and more difficult and after a while he could no longer remember why he was trying to think anyway, so he gave up and like many others drifted into a kind of semi-conscious state. Every now and then he would open his eyes and look round, but unable to work out where he was he would close them again and give himself up gratefully to his dreams which were much more pleasant than his current situation.

By the late afternoon of the second day, with no food or water in temperatures of nearly 100 degrees, there was little noise from any of the trucks. Most of the men were either too weak or confused to do anything other than just sit or lie in the small amount of space available to them, or were unconscious. Some of the men had died.

Ted wasn't sure whether it was the movement of the train slowing down or the loud chiming of a clock striking 7 pm that woke him up. But he was suddenly aware of the doors opening and people shouting at him to get out, at least he assumed that was what they were saying. Still dazed and acting purely on reflex, he managed to stagger to his feet and half climbed, half fell out onto the platform. All around him other men were doing the same, some unable to stand and being dragged out by their friends. He felt hands pulling him upright from his crouched position and saw Harry looking down at him with concern etched across his pale and drawn features

'You alright mate?' asked Harry, his voice gruff and hoarse and sounding nothing like normal.

Ted could only nod as his own voice wouldn't work and his brain was almost unable to form the words. His mouth felt swollen and his lips were so dry that the skin was peeling off them. They stood there for what seemed an interminable time and he was vaguely aware that they were being counted. If he hadn't felt so ill the idea that any of them could have escaped would have made him laugh, but his brain was hardly able to function and it took all his strength to just stay upright. After what seemed like hours, but was probably only about half an hour, the counting finished and the men were shouted at to walk.

After their enforced inaction, lack of water and food, they had trouble making their joints and limbs work and most were only able to stagger along, holding onto each other in what was often a vain attempt to stay upright. The guards were no more tolerant of them falling over than the ones on the march had been and it was only the sight of the rifle butts and boots being used on those unlucky enough to fall that kept most of the troops going.

Just when Ted thought there was no way he could take another step, a large fort standing proudly on a hill came into view. He looked up at the hill and thought that this was it. He could never walk up that. He knew his friends were thinking the same and he seriously considered just stopping. Surely being beaten to death had to be better than this slow drawn-out torture.

POW Ted (second from the left at the back).

Directly in front of them at the bottom of the hill was a large building which he later learned had been a Gazerna – dance hall. To Ted's unutterable relief the men were halted as the Germans counted them again before directing them into it. After the heat of the trucks the air in the building felt cool and Ted breathed a sigh of relief. Unable to go another step farther he collapsed onto the straw that covered the ground and in his weakened state he was almost unaware of the others slowly doing the same.

In the distance he heard shouting but he was no longer interested and it was only with a supreme effort that Ted responded as someone gave him water. At first his lips were so parched that it just trickled down his chin, but the person was patient and kept trickling small amounts into his mouth. He suddenly realized he was being given water, and opening his eyes, made a feeble grab for the bottle. The man gently pushed Ted's hand away and made him sip slowly. As the water gradually revived his body Ted opened his eyes properly and found himself looking into the eyes of a German guard. Unlike the previous guards this one had no animosity in his face and allowed Ted to sip the water until he had had enough.

Feeling slightly more human, Ted looked round to see that his friends also looked considerably better than they had just a couple of hours ago. Like him, they were still filthy, starving and weak but they were alive. Relieved to find his friends were still with him, Ted closed his eyes for a moment. He still felt dreadful but the water had revived him and at least his brain was working properly again. As they sat there the door opened again and to their amazement the guards appeared with large tureens of weak soup and coffee. Those who were able to stand formed an orderly queue, while those who were still too weak to stand were fed where they lay. To Ted's surprise and relief they were given a reasonably sized portion of soup, a small piece of bread and some coffee. When they had finished - most having eaten so little for so long that they were unable to eat it all - the men were left to sleep.

Now he felt full Ted was more interested in his surroundings and he looked round him with curiosity. His throat was no longer sore and his voice was much less hoarse as he asked if the others knew where they were. The general opinion was that they were in Poland in a place called Thorn (Torun) which was located in the Polish Corridor south of Danzig (Gdansk) on the banks of the Vistula river.

They were, in fact, in part of the camp known as Stalag XXA which was a sub-camp of the concentration camp in Sztutowicz. It was not a single camp and contained as many as 20,000 men at its peak and consisted of a number of defensive forts and a series of satellite working camps. The number of these working camps fluctuated throughout the war but in the summer of 1944 there were 190 within the Stalag XXA administration area. The Thorn Complex POWs often started in one of the larger camps, i.e. Fort 11 & 13, and were then assigned to working camps. After their work was completed, they would be reassigned after returning to one of the larger base camps.

But for Ted all this was to come. At that moment, as he closed his eyes, he hoped that the worst part was now over, and falling into a deep sleep, his last conscious thought was that he was glad he had not given in and would live another day.

The men's treatment over the next couple of days was much better than any they had received so far. This was mainly because Lieutenant Meikle, the German officer in charge of this part of the camp, had lost an arm in the Great War and was nursed back to health by the British after being taken prisoner. Having been treated well himself he saw no reason to treat the men badly, even if they were the enemy.

So the next three days were spent recuperating in the old dance hall where they were fed weak barley soup, small amounts of bread and ersatz coffee. As the prisoners did little other than laze around, their strength slowly returned.

After three days the Germans decided the men were fit enough to move so they were lined up again and made to walk up the hill to the main fort. Resting had given them some of their strength back but the effort of climbing the hill showed them just how weak and depleted they were, and they really struggled as the guards yelled at them to walk faster. It seemed that the decent treatment was now at an end as the guards resumed their beating of those who fell over or stumbled. Ted began to doubt whether surviving the train journey had been the right thing to do if this was an indication of how they would be treated in future. But the human instinct for survival kept him going and although each step was purgatory, and each breath felt as if his chest would burst, something inside him wouldn't give up. Drawing on an inner strength he had no idea was there, he made his feet take one step after another and somehow made it to the top.

'Halt'. The order came just in time and while he stood there swaying dizzily, Ted tried to focus on his surroundings. In front of them in the grounds of the fort were rows and rows of marquees to which they were directed. The hope that his journey was at an end gave him just enough strength to stagger into one of the marquees where he collapsed on the straw that covered the ground. Drifting in and out of consciousness he had no idea how long he lay there but it seemed hardly any time at all. Almost beyond pain, he was only dimly aware of a German soldier shouting and hitting him with his rifle butt and kicking him with his heavy, highly-polished boots.

Ted managed to drag himself to his feet and followed the others back outside where they were counted yet again. Ted felt as if he was in some surreal nightmare in which people did strange things that appeared perfectly reasonable while you were asleep and only looked ridiculous when you woke up. Did they really think any of them would have been able to escape in the condition they

Ted's processing form on his arrival at Stalag XXA.

were in? Or maybe it was because they actually had no idea just how many prisoners they had. Ted was too tired and weak to think any more and in a vain attempt to distract himself so that he could remain upright just a bit longer, he tried to take an interest in his surroundings.

The fort and the marquees were completely surrounded by a double row of barbed wire fences at least ten feet high with watchtowers at various intervals. In each of the watchtowers were armed guards with machine guns and rifles. Everywhere he looked there were guards with dogs, large vicious-looking German Shepherd dogs that barked incessantly and snapped at anyone who swayed or staggered in their direction. From the loud speakers came a never-ending stream of German military music punctuated intermittently by the staccato shouting of Hitler or an imitator shouting out how the Germans were invincible and that winning the war was inevitable. The broadcasts always finished by emphasizing that the British were defeated and should succumb to the German Super Race. Had they but known it, this had completely the opposite effect to the one the Germans intended. Rather than indoctrinate and demoralize the men it reinforced exactly why they were fighting. Like the others, Ted eventually managed to tune out from the raucous music deciding that even concentrating on the aches and pains in his body was preferable to listening to such garbage.

After they had been counted several more times, the men were herded out of the hot sunshine into the cool of the main fort where they were allowed to wash and shave and were then given clean clothes to put on. Not having had the opportunity to change their clothes since they had arrived in France, they were surprised at how much being dressed in clean clothes raised their morale. Shaving also caused a certain amount of amusement as they had been beginning to forget what they all looked like underneath the beards and facial hair.

Once they had shaved and put on their clean clothes, they were asked innumerable questions about where they were born and for their full names and even their mothers' maiden names. Once the Germans were satisfied, the prisoners were given their POW numbers. Ted's number was 8471 and he was given a metal disc with it on and told that he must wear it at all times. To ensure they didn't lose it, most of the men tied it onto the British Army dog tags they already wore round their necks. Ted did the same. Then they were marched along another corridor where they were made to strip to the waist and queue up. Eventually, they stood in front of an orderly who plunged a large hypodermic needle into their chests without warning. Like many of the others, Ted fainted as the blunt needle went in, not so much from the pain but because he was still very weak and the needle came as a shock to the system.

He came round in the corridor outside and, with the help of a couple of other men who were also looking very unsteady, he made his way back to his friends.

They were already lying on their straw palisades in the cellar they had been allocated to sleep in and were looking just as weak and pale as Ted.

The following day they were all given their Red Cross cards and issued with blankets, a towel, pants and shorts. Over the next few days they were given a variety of other items including a toothbrush and toothpaste, shaving soap, washing soap, and razor blades, which they were told had to last them a fortnight. The men were also given a comb, bootlaces, handkerchiefs, socks and a needle and cotton.

They later received some Red Cross rations which they were told they would be given once a fortnight. These consisted of a tin of milk, a tin of jam or syrup, a bar of plain chocolate and some date cake or bread pudding. They were also allowed a book once a fortnight. The prisoners were given permission to keep their pencils and anything they had that went with bread (as they had been starving for several days this was greeted with a certain amount of wry amusement) as long as it was wrapped in plain paper. No newspapers were allowed. 'Can't possibly imagine why!' Ted remarked grinning. He was feeling much better now that he had clean clothes and there was the prospect of a piece of cake, even if it did have to last him a fortnight.

The days followed a similar pattern, beginning with the early morning roll call when they were made to stand on the parade ground as the Germans counted them several times. The men could never understand why it took them so long and why they did it several times. For some reason the numbers on the guards' lists never seemed to tally with the number of prisoners. The interminable waiting eventually led to catcalls and jeers as the prisoners became more and more fed up at having to stand there, especially as they couldn't go and collect their breakfast until the count had finished.

Breakfast consisted of ersatz coffee which was barely drinkable, but which provided the hardened smokers with some grounds that they could dry out and smoke. Others used leaves from the odd tree that had somehow survived within the grounds of the fort which again, they dried out and smoked. Although they tasted disgusting it was better than nothing and smoking at least took away some of the hunger pains, if only for a short time. Hunger was a real problem and was the only real topic of conversation. The lack of food meant fainting became a common occurrence. Usually someone would check the man was still alive and then leave him to recover in his own time. Once recovered, the individual would get up and carry on with what he had been doing. Occasionally however, he forgot what he had been planning to do and just went back to his place on the straw and lay there until the next meal was due.

Lunch was yet another bowl of watery soup that may or may not contain a small piece of potato depending on how lucky you were. If a man ate really quickly and was lucky, he could occasionally queue again, but that only happened rarely as most did not have the energy to rush anywhere. This was normally followed by a return to the straw where the prisoners waited until the next roll call and more interminable counts. Then came the main meal of the day which consisted of a black bread loaf shared between six people. This often caused many disagreements as the men tried to agree the best and fairest way to divide it. They normally stuck rigidly to the group that comprised their own friends, known as a 'combine', as this was the best way to ensure they received their fair share. These 'combines' were men who looked after the members of their group. If one was sick they would try and get medical help for him or if one got into trouble and was locked up in solitary confinement, the other members of the group would often smuggle food into him.

But although the point of belonging to a 'combine' was to ensure you received your fair share, there was an unspoken rule that the person who took the bread from the guard did not disappear from sight. However much you trusted the men in your 'combine', starvation caused people to act in ways they would never have normally considered and fights would often break out between groups.

There were also occasional attempts to steal bread from the trucks and many conversations about the best way to do this. But as the trucks were always ringed by armed guards with large German Shepherd dogs that snapped and snarled at anyone approaching too close, these attempts were by and large unsuccessful.

The worst times were at night as the men lay there unable to sleep. Not only were they permanently hungry they were also alive with lice and often spent hours picking them off their bodies to get some respite from the constant scratching and itching that plagued them.

But it seemed their prayers in that respect were now about to be answered as after roll call one morning they were lined up and herded onto trucks. They were not told where they were going so there was a certain amount of joking to cover up their concern.

Chapter 14

France Surrenders

After a short journey the men arrived in Danzig and were taken to a large building that looked like a hospital. They were made to strip and their clothes were taken away from them. They were given some sandstone, which seemed to be a substitute for soap, taken to some showers and subjected to scalding hot water. When they had finished, they were made to queue up and were then shaved. The barbers had been instructed to remove all the hair from the prisoners' bodies including their heads, and were none too careful how they did this as the guards continually harassed them to go faster. Having escaped with only minor cuts and abrasions, Ted was horrified to see several deep cuts on Rob's body that were bleeding quite profusely. They were then given back their clothes which were still damp and smelled of the strong disinfectant that had been used to delouse them. Even so, the relief from the itching and the knowledge that they were clean, raised the men's spirits quite a bit and for the first time since they had arrived in the fort most of them slept well.

On 16 June Ted wrote home to his Mum for the first time. He had not done so before because he did not want to write a letter full of misery, and the journey had been so awful he had not felt able to report anything good. He had also used any energy and spare time to write down what was happening to him. But now, feeling more rested and slightly better fed, Ted felt able to write in a more positive way. He had listened carefully as the men were told that everything would be read and anything not considered suitable would be censored. More worrying, was that they would only be allowed to write one letter every month and a postcard in between. This meant having to learn the art of writing quite small - but not so small that the censors wouldn't pass it - and using every part of the paper so they could get as much as possible on to the limited space.

Not having written anything for a while, Ted spent ages wondering how to start. He couldn't afford to make a mistake as he would not be able to write another letter until next month. Frowning with concentration he began the letter slowly. He had no way of knowing if that hastily-written note had ever reached his mother, so he would have to assume it hadn't. This at least meant he could

Germans issued POWs with money to spend in the camps.

start by saying that he was safe, uninjured and in a Prisoner of War camp. Having made a start, he found it quite easy to continue and before long had covered both sides of the page. He reluctantly finished and handed it to the German guards. Curious to know how long it was likely to be before it arrived, he tried asking the guards, but any enquiry was either met with incomprehension or a shrug. 'There is a war on you know!' or even, from the more aggressive guards, 'We'll deliver them personally for you when we arrive in England.'

'Great', thought Ted, starting to get demoralized. 'The way they're talking, the note I gave to that Frenchman probably has more chance of getting there than this letter.' Shrugging philosophically, he realized that he had done everything now that he could to let his Mum know that he was safe, and reluctantly he made his way back to his place on the straw.

On 19 June the men had their photos taken yet again, but this time the cards proclaiming their POW numbers were held in front of them, rather than being tied round their necks. 'You've already done this', Ted muttered under his breath, finding the whole process intensely humiliating.

'It's so Red Cross can tell your relatives that you are prisoner', the nearest guard responded in excellent English, much to Ted's surprise. He wasn't so much surprised by the fact that the German spoke reasonable English, but by the civil tone in which he had answered. Encouraged by the German's lack of animosity Ted tried to find out when this was likely to be. However, the German didn't understand, leading Ted to assume he had been taught the phrase parrot-fashion in case the prisoners complained. But he persevered and eventually, after a certain amount of miming, he thought the German understood. But the guard only shrugged and shook his head.

The next day the bread ration was reduced to one loaf between nine men. This was met with unanimous disapproval despite the guard's explanation that now the men were fit they didn't need as much food, especially as they weren't doing anything.

'So what do we have to do to get extra then?' Ted asked in frustration. But the guard didn't understand and walked away leaving the men complaining bitterly, not to mention going to bed even more hungry than normal. It was another POW who informed them they needed to 'volunteer' for the working parties. As part of the Geneva Convention, all prisoners under the rank of Sergeant who were fit enough were allowed to be put to work for their captors, providing the work did not contribute to the enemy's war effort. The man said that they should then check the list that was put on the notice board each night and it would tell them where they were destined to go. However, he warned them that they shouldn't expect too much as the increase in rations wasn't exactly worth writing home about, but they would get paid - not that there was much to buy of course. Ted looked thoroughly confused so the man added that it also gave them a chance to speak to the locals and sometimes barter for extra food.

Shrugging, Ted and the others went to find one of the guards and 'volunteered' for the work parties the next day. They were given a form and asked to put down their POW number and the trade or work they had done before joining the army. Not sure what he should put on his, Ted had a quick look at the others. Amused, he quickly looked away as Sandy had put down his name as Adolf Hitler, house painter and, Ted was relieved to see, a wrong number. He couldn't think of anything to put down so he put down 'carpenter' figuring it might be an easier job. After some confusion the men understood that they would be called in the morning and after that, should check the lists at night.

On 21 June they were woken early and Ted, Rob, Pete and Sandy were picked for a work party. The forms they had filled in did not seem to have been used as Ted was given a job as a labourer even though he argued noisily and at length that he was a carpenter.

The first project they were employed on was building a new lido in the town, and the next two days were spent doing the back-breaking work to prepare the ground for its construction. It was hard, physical work with the only bonus being the increase in their daily rations - an extra bowl of watery soup and some extra ersatz coffee. However, there was also the opportunity to mix with the local people that meant the possibility of scrounging or trading for extra rations and away from the camp it was also possible to bribe the guards. On the second day Ted managed to get into conversation with one of the more friendly guards and after much bartering traded his watch for an easier job as a carpenter. This was a good decision as it meant that once the Germans accepted him in this job he would possibly be offered work as a carpenter in future, rather than the more back-breaking labouring work.

June 23 was another hot, airless day and all the men were relieved that it was a Sunday so there were no work parties. At 10 am the men paraded for the inevitable roll call and numerous counts, and then assembled for an open-air church service. It seemed ages to Ted since he had attended a church service, and to start with, he couldn't remember when the last one had been. As he stood there trying to remember, it came back to him that it had been on 26 May, the day they had surrendered. It was also the day he had lost his friends.

Ted had tried very hard over the previous weeks to avoid remembering how they had died, especially Chalky, but the singing and prayers rekindled memories and try as he might he couldn't shake them off. To his horror he felt his eyes begin to fill with tears. Angrily he shook them away and tried surreptitiously to wipe his eyes with the back of his hand. No one seemed to have noticed, or if they had they weren't paying attention, but his nose was running and he searched frantically in his pockets for something to wipe it on. Unable to find anything, he had no option but to sniff. Unfortunately, he chose the moment when there was silence as everyone had their heads bowed and were saying their own private prayers. To Ted the sniff sounded like an explosion and he looked round to see if anyone had noticed. But it seemed he wasn't the only one, and as he began to relax he heard the sound of other stifled sniffs and realized that others too were crying silently. Feeling relieved that he wasn't the only one, Ted also felt rather uncomfortable as he, like most of his generation, had been brought up with the belief that real men didn't cry - certainly not English men. He normally enjoyed his church services but he was glad when this one was over as the effort of trying not to show emotion was almost too much for him to bear and the last thing he wanted to do was to break down in front of his mates and the other men. In an all-male environment when there was barely enough food to go round, it didn't do to be seen as weak.

Most of the men were unusually quiet after the service and conversation was muted until they were told they could have a bath. As always, clean water on their skin, even if the water was only lukewarm, lifted their spirits again and when Ted went to sleep that night he felt as if both his body and his mind had, in some way, been cleansed. The good mood remained with them throughout the next day as they again went to work on the lido. More accustomed to the work now, they even had some energy left in the evenings and it wasn't long before someone had the bright idea of having a singsong. It was ages since Ted had felt like singing and he joined in with gusto. To start with, the memories flooded back and he recalled them all sitting on the ship on the way to France, singing songs to stop themselves being frightened of the all-too-present threat of torpedoes and the aerial bombardment that was crashing all around them. Determinedly he pushed the memories away and concentrated on singing his heart out.

```
              OUT - SIDE   FOR   ROLL - CALL ,  TOMMY .
   _ _ _ _ _ _ _ _ _ _ _ _ _ _ _ _ _ _ _ _ _ _ _ _ _ _

A   whistle   shrills   and   ' Jerry '   bangs   the   door .

' Aufstehen ! " the   ' Kriegie's '   working   day   begins   once   more .

He   gulps   his   ' ersatz '   coffee ,   some - times   hot ,

And   if   he's   lucky ,   eats   the   crust   he's   got .

" Out - side   for   roll - call "   - - - stamping   in   the   snow ,

As   usual   the   guards   are   counting   slow .

" Two   men   missing ! "   screams   along   the   line .

" Stand   to   attention   - - - stupid   Englischer   schweine . "

Our   ' sotto - voce '   comments   give   no   aid .

" Square - headed   bastards ! " ,   another   count   is   made .

' ARBEIT   MACHT   FREI '   topped   the   wired   gate ,

But   for   some   - - - that   freedom   came   too   late .
                   _ _ _ _ _ _ _ _ _ _
                   R O L L   ON
                   _ _ _ _ _ _ _ _ _ _
   " Roll   on   my   boat ",   we   used   to   say ,
   The   one   that   takes   us   all   away .
   We   saw   around   us   the   lame - -  the   lazy ,
   Those   ' Goons '   in   their   boxes - -  the   ' wire   crazy ' .
   " Look   at   that   man ,   he's   a   fair   disgrace .
   It's   been   a   week   since   he   washed   his   face !  "
   Then   I'd   hear   some   taps ,   and   along   came   Tim ,
   Nothing   seemed   to   worry   him .
   He   was   always   cheerful ,   always   kind .
   As   a   prisoner - of - war ,   it   was   rough - - -  being   blind ! .


            ( Harry   Trotter . Ex R.A.M.C. - - Fort 13   Thorn . )
```

Roll call poem written by one of the POWs.

On 24 June they lined up as usual for the early morning roll call. The British were lined up along one side of the square, the Poles at right angles and the French opposite, about fifty yards away. After the usual numerous counts, punctuated by the normal heckling and jeers, the men were surprised to see the Commandant appear. Becoming curious, they let their catcalls die slowly away until there was silence. The Commandant looked round and then smiling announced that France had surrendered. Those in the British ranks were initially stunned into silence. But this reaction soon turned to anger and disbelief as the French, their allies, cheered and hollered with delight. Fury coursed through the British lines and within seconds they had broken ranks and rushed across the gap between the two sides. Once there, they threw punches, even though many were really too weak to have any strength in them. The Poles looked on in amazement and the Commandant shouted something loudly in German that no one could understand and which no one took any notice of. Eventually, unable to regain any sense of control, he ordered the guards to fire. As they fired first one and then two rounds into the air, the fighting ceased and other than some continuing verbal abuse, the men returned reluctantly to their ranks.

Not taking any chances, the Germans hustled them quickly into their work parties and out of the camp. This meant most of them did not even get their early morning imitation coffee which added to the bad feeling between the two nationalities. Like the others Ted was completely demoralized by the news which meant that Britain was now completely alone. He also couldn't understand why the French had cheered until one of the other men explained this was probably because they thought if their country was no longer fighting they would soon be going home. Unfortunately, their joy was short-lived as most French prisoners did not return home until the war was over in 1945.

The weather was too hot and the work too hard for the men to continue grumbling for long, and those who had rushed across the square to attack the French soon forgot their anger as the real reason behind the French reaction circulated. Although they were angry that the French had let them down by surrendering, they couldn't, in all honesty, really blame individuals for wanting to go home. After all, they had all fought hard, that was why they were here. It wasn't their fault that the politicians had deserted them.

As the sun rose steadily into a cloudless, blue sky and the men were driven relentlessly by their guards, their anger was gradually replaced by their need for food, water and shade from the heat. By the time they returned to the fort they were too tired, hungry and thirsty, to continue with the dispute and after their meagre meal they collapsed exhausted on the straw which served as their beds.

It was another hot and airless day on 25 June and the work was hard. Whenever they got the chance, the men gazed skyward, longing to see the approach of some clouds, preferably rain clouds, so that they could cool off and have a break. Quite a few of them were now suffering from sunburn as they had removed their shirts in an attempt to get cool. Ted had kept his on, but his face still felt like it was burning. He was even more grateful that he had traded his watch for the carpentry job. It was much less back-breaking than the work some of his friends were doing and he could at least take his time using the excuse that his work had to be accurate. The day wore on slowly and it was late afternoon when the pains gripped him. He felt as if his stomach was on fire and he only just made it to the latrine. The pains got worse during the rest of the day, but as he had very little food in his stomach his trips to the latrine soon became less frequent. He didn't want to go sick unless he absolutely had to as it meant less rations, although the way he felt now he really didn't want to eat. Somehow, Ted survived the rest of the day and once back on his bunk he tried to keep his mind off the pain by writing a card to his mother. The pains were no longer intense, sharp and shooting. Instead, they had coalesced into a continual dull ache that was bad enough to keep him awake most of the night.

Although he tried to go to work the next morning, he doubled up with pain when he stood up and collapsed on the floor in agony. Overcoming his fear, he realized that he had no choice but to report sick. Much to his surprise the doctor was not unfriendly and sent him to the sickroom for the day where he was even more surprised to find that even the guards were quite friendly. Towards the end of the day the pains had lessoned considerably and, feeling hungry, Ted was delighted to find that rather than a reduction in rations he was given extra soup plus a meat sandwich.

Felling much better he reported for work the next day, but they had only been working for a couple of hours when it decided to rain. It was a welcome relief from the hot sticky air and they stood for several minutes savouring it much to the consternation of the guards who obviously thought they had all gone mad. The guards threatened them and, laughing, they took shelter in a small hut.

The rain continued all day and eventually the guards gave up and returned the men to the camp. It rained all night and as it was still raining the following day they stayed in bed, enjoying the luxury of not having to get up. To make the day even better they were given a loaf between four of them instead of the normal six and, even more amazing, they were given honey to spread on it.

As Ted finished the last crumb and licked his lips to savour every last taste, he suddenly realized that there was a certain amount of tension in the cellar. He looked up to see Rob licking his finger and then wiping it round the inside of the tin.

'Any left?' asked Sandy, watching Rob's efforts with studied disinterest. If there was one thing that could cause dissention amongst them it was the sharing out of the rations. Fortunately, the five of them were all good friends having endured so much together, but there were still the occasional arguments over rations although they never amounted to much. The same couldn't be said about some of the groups in which fights over the meagre food rations were quite common.

'Nah, thought I might be able to squeeze another teaspoon out but no such luck.' Rob threw down the tin in disgust and looked round carefully for any crumbs he might have dropped. Not finding any, he turned over in his bunk and tried unsuccessfully to convince his stomach that he was full.

The others did the same. The one thing they missed more than anything was the feeling of being full after a meal. All their rations seemed to do was make them hungrier and remind their stomachs that they were being underfed. The only advantage Ted could see to their meagre rations was that it cut down the number of trips they needed to make to the latrines.

The latrines consisted of two planks of wood across a large, open cesspit in full view of the main building. The stench was horrendous and trips to use them were kept to a minimum because of the dangers of falling in, especially when

Cyril, one of Ted's younger brothers, in RAF Regiment Uniform.

Cyril's wife, May, in RAF Uniform.

the planks were wet during and after rain. Furthermore, even the most slovenly soldier worked out that using them was to put himself at risk of catching cholera and typhoid.

The rain continued to fall and the morning of 29 June was dark as well as wet. Again there was no work, and the men sat about playing cards and reading. As the morning wore on, the light gradually improved and the previous torrential rain suddenly eased up allowing a glimpse of blue sky to appear. The guards came for them about midday and they worked until 7 pm. Much to their surprise they were given macaroni stew and bread and cheese for dinner and they made the most of the unexpected treat.

The next day, 30 June, was a Sunday and once again church parade was held. This time Ted successfully chased away the memories and enjoyed the service. At lunchtime their rather boring stew had some rice in which made it thicker and more filling and Ted felt more optimistic. If he had to spend the rest of the war here it wouldn't be too bad. At least he had his friends and the guards weren't too bad.

Lying on his bunk after lunch he gazed up at the ceiling and decided that maybe life wasn't too bad after all. But it seemed he had relaxed too soon. That night when he checked the lists to see where he was working the next day, he saw that his number was now on the list of those to be moved. Frantically he checked the rest of the numbers but only Harry was there, the others were to remain. After everything he already had been through he was now to be separated from Rob who had become his only remaining link with England.

Dejected, Ted walked slowly back to the cellar and told the others. The mood amongst his friends was sombre as they realized that it was probably only a matter of time before they were all separated. This was deliberate policy by the Germans because by separating the men from those they trusted, it was much harder for them to escape or plan sabotage. Tired as he was, Ted was unable to sleep as he worried about what the next day would bring. It was at this point he realized that now he was on his own and that he could only really rely on himself. Yes, Harry was going with him, but for how long? How long before he too was sent somewhere else? To survive and for his own self-protection, Ted could no longer allow himself to get close to people. He would have to keep everyone at arm's length and never trust anyone completely. With that depressing thought circulating in his head he at last managed to fall into a restless sleep.

The morning came only too quickly and, reluctantly, Ted picked up his meagre possessions and said his goodbyes. As he left the camp with Harry and the others he turned round for one more look and wondered if he would ever see his friends again. His last glimpse as he turned out of the gates was of them waving. Then they were out of sight and he was being marched back down to the railway station where, after a short wait, they were crowded onto another cattle truck, their destination unknown.

Chapter 15

Goose for Lunch

Fortunately, this train journey was nothing like as long as before and within a very short time they arrived at their destination, Simonsdorf, about 150km from Stalag XXA and the site of one of the satellite working camps – Camp 5, number 2.

After the insanitary and crowded conditions at Stalag XXA Ted describes Simonsdorf as 'good camp nice bed and billet' and after a night's sleep he received some 'nice stew'. He reports 2 July as a 'fine day' and that the men spent the day 'clearing parade ground'. The following day their work party began in earnest and they started work in the sand pits at the railway station. The next few days were spent moving rails and tipping sand. The prisoners even worked from 7 am to 12.30 pm on the Sunday morning despite Articles 27-32

Ted while a POW (second from the left in the front row).

of the Third Geneva Convention stating they should receive one day off a week. After a 'scrub out' they held a church service. Afterwards, as always, a mood of optimism prevailed for a while and they would often have a singsong which had the added advantage of irritating the guards. But once the singing stopped and they settled down to try and sleep, conversation became more muted as the men tried to find ways of coping with their plight.

It was the not knowing that was the worst. They had no idea how long this captivity would last or whether they would ever go home. But they had to have hope or they would not be able to get up each morning and get through each day. Although they never doubted for one moment that England would emerge victorious, they had no idea how long it would take. In the meantime they had to endure the constant abuse from the guards who seemed to have lost the ability to speak in reasonable tones. Everything said to them was shouted and Ted often queried the sanity of his guards who seemed to take delight in torturing them, physically or verbally, for no particular reason.

It was back to work the next morning and the next few days continued in this vein, the only excitement occurring on 13 July when five trucks derailed allowing them to finish early. On 21 July they went to Sturm via Marienburg (now Malbork) to fetch some railway sleepers. This was at least a change of scenery, although initially it caused them considerable anxiety as they had no idea where they were going or why. They also had to leave without their meagre possessions and feared they would never see them again. So it was with a sense of relief that they were taken to a yard and made to load heavy sleepers into the truck. The next day was even better for Ted as a new sergeant arrived in the camp with news of his father. Knowing his Dad was part of the BEF, Ted had wondered if he too, had been captured, so he was relieved to find out that he was one of the lucky ones evacuated from Dunkirk.

As July turned to August the weather deteriorated and they were plagued with torrential rain. For the most part, they worked through the rain with little cover, the rain soaking their thin clothes and leaving many sick from fevers and colds. They were now engaged in a variety of tasks, one day unloading thirteen trucks of fish and mash to the cookhouse and, on another, digging numerous holes in the soggy ground and putting poles up. Then, on 11 September, rumours circulated that yet again they were on the move - this time back to Thorn and the horrors of Stalag XXA. But before this could happen two of the trains derailed and crushed the foot of one of the men. Ted never found out what happened to the man as on 14 September they were put back in the cattle trucks at 7.30 am and sent back to Thorn. He arrived at 3 pm to find that Stalag XXA was just as bad as he remembered. In fact it was now even worse.

It was more overcrowded and there was a serious diphtheria epidemic in one part of the camp. However, during the day the work parties continued unabated, and Ted found himself unloading numerous coils of barbed wire. Without gloves or protective clothing, this was very painful and Ted was relieved when he was moved onto another work party. Bartering was common practice and the men used their precious items from the Red Cross parcels to buy food or bartered their cigarettes for food. Those lucky enough to still have watches were able to secure extra food or cigarettes from the odd guard who was happy to exchange a POW's possessions for something they should have had anyway. Other ways of filling the time included reading, playing cards and competitions for all sorts of things, including some of a rather dubious nature. [13]

Ted's father, Henry George Taylor.

Fortune-telling was also very popular with the POWs, even though the fortune-tellers were strangely reluctant to give an exact date when they would all be going home. They were, however, frowned on by the guards who were understandably worried they might predict that Germany would lose the war. But by far the most popular method of entertaining themselves was through concert parties. Despite the constant exhaustion, Ted became very involved with these, as he needed to do something to keep himself sane. On one occasion he even went to Fort 13 to entertain the other prisoners.

But the continual lack of food and the harsh conditions eventually took its toll on his health and on 29 September he was again gripped by severe pains in his abdomen. Although he tried to ignore the pain, it became so bad that it overrode the constant fear of reporting sick and he was put in isolation. Fortunately, he did not have diphtheria and the epidemic now seemed to be over. To his surprise he was again given reasonable medical treatment and even a cheese sandwich to eat instead of the normal pigs swill masquerading as soup. Ted remained in the isolation ward for over a week which gave him some time to recover and was then sent back to the main camp.

October continued in much the same vein as September except the weather became much colder. To their relief, the men were eventually given British Army greatcoats which had been delivered by the Red Cross. Concert practices continued in their spare time and food was still the main preoccupation and topic of conversation. On 17 October they were sent to Fort 17 for yet another delouse. Although the process was humiliating it did at least offer some brief respite from the constant itching. It was at Fort 17 that Ted stopped writing such meticulous daily entries. The rest of his story has been pieced together from several sources: the tape he made which gave a potted history of the rest of his time in captivity; the little he said to family and friends over the years, and from research into the lives of POWs in Poland.

But what is clear is that for Ted the next four years were to continue in this same pattern. As soon as he settled and made friends, he was moved again. Although some working camps were better than others, underlying them all was the same senseless, cavalier cruelty, unremitting boredom, lack of food and continual fight for survival. The ongoing brutality Ted witnessed and suffered was made worse by its seeming casualness. Men could be executed for the most trivial of reasons and, even worse, were the random executions to provide entertainment or to help relieve the boredom or grudges of the guards. Beatings and assaults were a common occurrence and also happened for little or no reason. Dogs were used to intimidate, inflict punishment or to kill, and fear permeated every aspect of camp life.

Wherever Ted was, the day would start and finish with the iniquitous Appel, or roll call. Occasionally extra roll calls were made throughout the day. In the summer the men stood and sweltered, and in winter they froze as the Germans counted them several times and then counted them again. During these interminable counts the men either stood quietly and ignored it or, more often, jeered and heckled the guards. No one ever understood why the Germans could never agree their figures and came to the conclusion that it was just another way of humiliating and torturing them.

Although 'goon baiting' did happen it was carried out carefully and those who did it were often taking their lives in their hands. Some of the simplest were the most effective. To liven up roll call someone would suddenly start looking skyward for several minutes as if watching something. The man next to him would join in and they were then joined by another and then another, all staring upwards in fascination. Eventually the guards looked up to see what they were looking at, and then unable to see anything, would turn their attention back to the men, who by this time were looking straight ahead as if whatever it was they had been watching was gone. This could also be done at any time as the men could stop what they were doing and look up. Once others had joined in, the guards would also look up and the men would then walk off chatting as if what they had been looking at had gone. Others involved pretending to be deaf, pretending not to understand or being asleep. But with all these caution had to be undertaken and the guard carefully selected. If they picked the wrong guard or over did it they were likely to suffer severe punishment. Punishments included beatings as well as solitary confinement, reduction in their already paltry rations or death at the end of a rifle butt or bullet. But the POWs need to do something to keep up their spirits so the practical jokes continued despite the risks they ran in perpetrating them.

Occasionally other things happened to brighten up the men's existence and break the monotonous drudgery and boredom that was every day camp life. One such incident was when a goose flew into the camp in the middle of a freezing cold winter. Unable to believe their luck, the starving men immediately grabbed it and attempted to wring its neck by twisting it round and round. Unfortunately, as soon as they let go the goose's neck it unwound and escaped and they had to start again. As gruesome as this sounds to those of us who have full stomachs and can get food whenever we want it, for the starving men this was a gift they could not afford to reject. Their task was made more difficult as they had to somehow find a way of keeping the goose quiet when they carried out its execution because if the guards had seen it they would have confiscated it. Eventually, after several attempts, the men succeeded in killing it and then came the difficult task of trying to cook it without the smell reaching their guards! But incidents like this were few and far between and most days were indistinguishable from the next, just another day they had to find the will to try and survive.

Another real hazard they faced was becoming ill. Hygiene and medical treatment were virtually non-existent in some of the camps, and in Stalag XXA, eventually led to the serious diphtheria epidemic mentioned earlier in which more than 200 men died. Lack of water and soap, overcrowding and lack of clean clothing, meant the smell in the huts and sleeping places was often overpowering and something they never really got used to. Even worse was the likelihood of injuries while working. These were common as there was little health and safety practised, and many men died as a result of their injuries and the lack of adequate medical treatment. For the Germans the Allied prisoners were just slave-labour to be used and abused as necessary. They had more than an adequate supply of labour and those injured or dying could always be replaced.

Although Ted considered escaping several times, he eventually decided that it was not worth it. There was nowhere to go. On one side there was the Baltic and to escape you either had to head down through Germany or up through Russia, neither of which was particularly realistic. The chances of success were so thin and the severity of the punishments meted out to those who failed convinced him of the futility of trying.

His world became the camps and his fellow POWs became his family. Each year the outside world receded until it became little more than a distant memory.

Each day was almost identical to the one before; a constant struggle for survival that meant ensuring you had enough food and trying to avoid irritating the guards beyond the normal banter that was almost becoming acceptable. However, although they were POWs, they were still soldiers and as such they still wanted to be part of the fight. So, although they had to be very careful, the men still managed to carry out small acts of sabotage, anything that would allow

HUT NO. 5

RECREATION FOR PRISONERS OF WAR

YOU have seen for yourself, now, the surroundings in which a prisoner of war lives. You have seen the treasured arts and crafts over which he bends in concentration to forget his captivity; the Chapel where in spirit he is linked with those who offer up the same prayers at home. You have seen the food and medical supplies with which the Red Cross and St. John keep him fit for the future. Now turn your attention to his recreation.

It is a part of the Geneva Convention that prisoners must be given space and time for exercise. Not all men are employed in work-parties and so, of course, exercise is very necessary. But there is little sport in which they can indulge without equipment.

The Red Cross provides all camps with equipment for cricket, football, tennis, boxing, swimming, and other outdoor sports. This

A Christmas party at Stalag XXA. Red Cross parcels, musical instruments, are well to the fore. No doubt the decorations were made from scraps of wrapping and packing in which they were delivered.

Stalag XXA. Ted in POW magazine.

them to do their bit to help the Allies win the war. The trick was to try and make it look like an accident or incompetence, as obvious sabotage would have been punished severely, most probably by torture and death.

One of the easiest 'accidents' was to ensure the skips full of earth that were being used in the construction of the roads they were building, tipped over while they were being pushed along railway lines. This successfully delayed construction for several hours while the mess was cleared up. Although the guards often suspected that these accidents were deliberate, the innocent denials of the POWs were usually sufficient to ensure they were not punished.

After his return from Simonsdorf in September 1940, Ted remained under the Stalag XXA administration area until 1941. He worked in a number of camps including 3a and did a variety of jobs ranging from hard manual labour on building sites, digging up and laying roads, repairing and laying railway lines, and labouring on farms. In the winter he cut blocks of ice from the frozen rivers and shovelled coal from trains into sheds. His active membership of the concert parties in whichever camp he was based helped in a small way to alleviate the pain of such a long separation from those he loved, and filled the time when he wasn't working. But it was in the main fort of Stalag XXA that he experienced his first Polish winter. It was nothing like he had even experienced before.

From October to April/May time the snow was at least two feet deep. The biting wind and freezing temperatures, often down to minus twenty-five degrees below and sometimes minus forty, were almost unbearable. Despite the cold, the camp was still overrun with lice which not only drove the men mad with continual itching, but also spread typhus. Almost more irritating were the rats which constantly foraged in the open for food, something there was very little

POW group. Ted is fifth from back on the left row. Standing next to Ted on his right is David Black, a Sapper with the Royal Engineers. His army number was 1909493 and he was captured in Boulogne, France, almost as soon as he had landed and spent the next five years in the POW camp XXB. He was born on 29 July in Airdrie, Scotland and died on 4 June, 2011, in Liverpool, Australia. He was 91. His son, Douglas Black, remembers him telling a story of a mass escape, and how one of the guards told him to run away, but his father knew if he did he would have received a bullet in his back. He also remembers him speaking about being sent to labour camps and possibly even a concentration camp.

of. They overran the huts and in several cases men were bitten in their sleep. In most places the latrines were open cesspits which often overflowed. In the summer the stench was dreadful, as were the flies that swarmed round incessantly. Their constant twin companions of lice and rats continued to plague them throughout the heat of the summer, together with the additional danger of typhus and diphtheria.

As winter came the stench from the latrines no longer bothered them as the cesspit was frozen solid. The danger now came from the ever-present rats that tried to attack their private parts as they crouched precariously on the slippery planks. The only way to use the latrine was to take a stout stick with them to hit the rats as they put in an appearance. The huts were little warmer inside than outside and the one wood-burning stove meant to heat the whole hut devoured their meagre ration of firewood in a very short time. Most men resorted to going to bed as soon as the fuel ran out, although the one thin blanket they were allowed did little to keep them warm.

Eventually though, the weather gradually warmed up and spring arrived bringing torrential rainfall which very quickly soaked through to their skin and played havoc with what was left of their uniforms, often shrinking them and rendering them little more than rags. Clothing was an ongoing problem as new uniforms were virtually non-existent, especially in the early days. The biggest shortage was of greatcoats and underwear. Ted had been very lucky to be given a greatcoat as many were not as fortunate. Many only had the uniforms they were standing up in and had no winter clothing at all or any other underwear. Many lost their 'housewife kits' when captured, or had already used all the contents, so had no way of repairing the rips and tears in their clothes, and their underpants and socks soon wore out and perished.

The Geneva Convention stated that the detaining power was meant to provide clothing and footwear for its prisoners and this caused problems for both sides. Although the Stalags often had large quantities of captured uniforms they would not distribute them. The Germans were short of adequate clothing and were not prepared to divert resources so that they could clothe POWs. They cut replacements in an attempt to force the Allies to provide clothing and footwear via the Red Cross, just as they had done with food. As the supply of Red Cross parcels took some time to become a more regular service for the first year, the only replacement uniforms came from combinations of the remnants of other nationality's uniforms, leaving POWs looking like tramps and indistinguishable from each other for some time. Some managed to make their own unit badges out of bits of material. This made them feel they were still defying the enemy and were resisting attempts to remove their sense of identity and pride in who they were.

Footwear was even harder to come by and many men spent the war with only the wooden clogs provided by the Germans. Others saved their boots for best and wore their clogs during the day. In some camps their underwear was removed whether it had fallen to bits or not, and in their place they were given vests and pants made of Baumwolle (wood wool). The remnants of their socks after the forced marches were also taken away to be replaced with Fusslappens (foot cloths). These were squares of wood-wool cloth that they had to wrap round each foot and tuck into their boots.

As the war went on the situation resolved itself to a certain extent as new sets of battledress arrived via the Red Cross. These uniforms were often sent by the families of pre-war regulars who, having gone off to war, had left their service dress behind. But the problem of underwear persisted. Even when the Red Cross did ship 4,000 sets of underwear for British POWs in Germany, the Germans sent them to a camp housing Croatians instead. Furthermore, sometimes the Germans refused to give out new items until the old ones were handed over. For those captured in hot climates in lightweight clothing, this was disastrous and many were sent on work duties in winter in sandals and shorts. This was all the more ridiculous as some POWs were not allowed to wear shorts in the summer, instead being made to wear the thick, winter, woollen battledress. Others were made to work in the same clothes they wore at night.

Having survived the arctic conditions throughout the winter, the POWs hoped the summer would be better. But summers in this part of Poland were very hot and dry so for many the torture continued as they sweltered and burned in the heat and tried to make a choice between wearing their coarse, scratchy shirts, or removing them and suffering sunburn and heat exhaustion. In Stalag XXA, water was in short supply as the one standby pipe in the courtyard dripped water rather than dispensing it with any enthusiasm.

Throughout the working camps and Stalags conditions varied. In most camps baths were extremely rare and access to hot water intermittent. Often hundreds of men would have to share one shower head and as many as sixty men had to share one cold tap. Some of the work camps provided no water at all and POWs had to draw it from lakes, wells or streams. If they were lucky enough to have piped water, they often found that the pipes were rusty, and the water was stained red or brown, even after they had boiled it. This lack of water often meant they had to make a choice about whether to wash or drink, but even if they did wash, they frequently only had one small towel on which to dry themselves. These towels were not replaced and so soon became filthy and worn thin by constant use, leaving the POWs with no option but to use rags to dry themselves.

Stuck in the camps so far from home, news of the war was also intermittent and often out of date. Mixing with the Polish civilians allowed them to keep up with the news from outside and as the war continued and the POW camps became more established, radios were often smuggled in. These were often

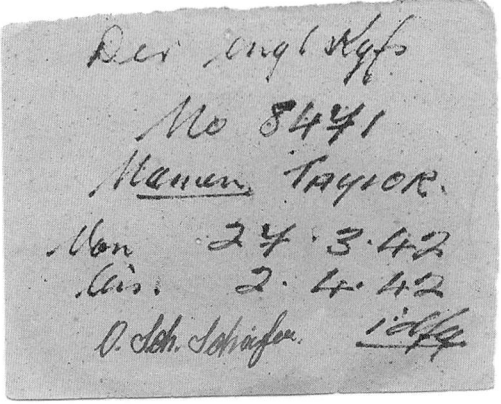

A receipt of some kind issued by the guards to Ted in 1942.

A boxing competition programme, 1942.

bartered for or even provided free of charge by the Polish civilians they met when on the working parties. War news was also imparted by the guards who couldn't wait to boast about how it was as easy to overrun Russia as it had been the rest of Europe. They also took great delight in reporting how much damage the Blitz was doing to British cities. The post from home gave little information about the war as the letters were heavily censored, but many POWs devised codes so they could get information through.

The post from home was sporadic throughout the whole of the war and Ted did not receive any at all until 1941. Writing home was just as difficult and many letters and cards never reached their destination. Correspondence was restricted to one month sending a postcard and the following month an airmail letter.[14] Because they were only allowed one of these at a time they had to spread it out. This was quite difficult when just the simple act of writing home made them feel closer to those they had left behind, even if it was only for a little while.

Ted remained at Stalag XXA until the autumn of 1941 when, with the prospect of yet another winter of unbelievably cold temperatures and little food facing him, he was heartily relieved to find out that he was about to be moved.

Chapter 16

Stolzenburg

Stalag XXB was similar to Stalag XXA in that it was a large base camp with lots of satellite camps, farms and factories, and located on the plateau at the top of a hill with the town of Marienburg below. Alongside it ran the river Nogat which was overlooked by one side of the camp. The Commandant, Unteroffizier Poznasky, was well-known amongst the POWs for his bike and for the numerous Appels that seemed to last forever, day and night. These were made worse by the POWs who would move around confusing the count even more. Occasionally, the POWs would go too far and the Germans would bring up a machine gun and threaten to shoot them if they moved again.

Ted's first view of Stalag XXB was its bleak exterior building surrounded by the usual double barbed wire fencing, lookout towers and floodlights. The guards were housed outside the main gate in a compound, and the other side of the river was no man's land. There was a single strand of wire about two or

A postcard addressed to Ted at one of the satellite camps of Stalag XXB at Stolzenberg.

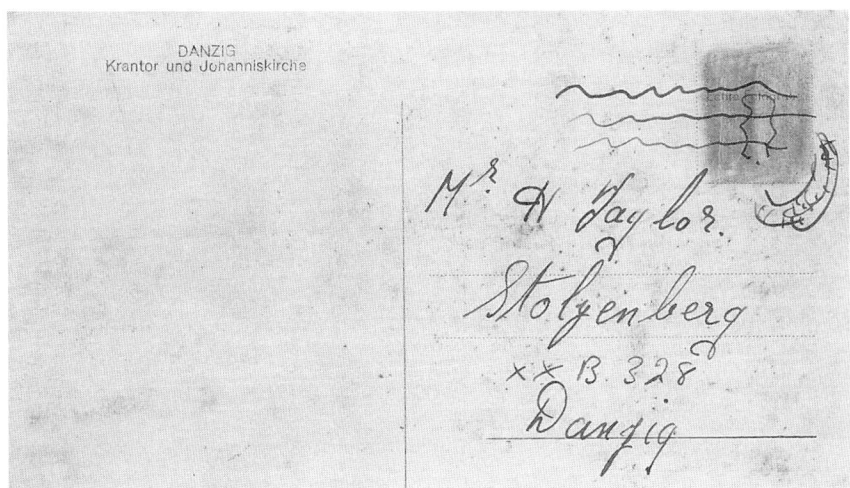

three feet off the ground with lots of black-painted skulls to deter anyone from escaping. The ground was in full view of the lookout towers and there were rumours that the land was mined. About six feet from the barbed wire were two eight-foot fences, four feet apart with rolls of barbed wire in between. Anyone straying beyond the wire was likely to get shot.

One of the buildings by the gate was the cookhouse. All the cooking was done by the POWs, closely watched by the Germans. Behind that was a brick building that was the cell block or bunker. There was room for about twelve POWs in there in solitary confinement and it was fenced off from the rest of the camp. Above the cell block was the Straflager, the place where prisoners were kept on remand if they were waiting for trial or for sentencing.

Another building by the main gate was the prisoners' library in which the men played cribbage and whist, and there was a small shop with ersatz goods which prisoners paid for with ersatz money. The sickbay was in the same block and next to this were the Belgian and French quarters.

" The Friedrichshain Players "

present

a stage version of Walt Disney's screen success

" SNOW WHITE and the 7 DWARFS ".

Cast:

A.Willcock	as	"Snow White"
J.Clifford	"	"Prince Charming"
A.Divers	"	"Queen Acida"
T.Kerr	"	"The Witch"
R.Jones	"	"Captain of the Guard"
R.Russell	"	"Huntsman"

J.Limer	as	"Doc"
J.Cremer	"	"Dopey"
H.Herbert	"	"Grumpy"
L.O.Rourke	"	"Sleepy"
J.Gilchrist	"	"Sneezy"
J.Bremner	"	"Happy"
J.Budgen	"	"Bashful"

J.Meadway	as	
J.Bartlett	"	"Queen's Guard"
E.Jackson	"	"Flunkey"
G.Halley	"	"A Mother"
J.Monaghan	"	"A Child"
D.Dewson	"	"Animal of the Forest"

W.Bowden	as	"Pagliacci"
H.Taylor	"	
E.Brand	"	"The Two Teddy's"

Music: P.Hickman and his Band.

A concert programme from Christmas 1941.

The latrines were on the same side of the river near the French and Belgian quarters and were just a large pit that drained down to the river. They were the same as the one at Stalag XXA and had crossed poles at either end and a pole on the middle on which the men were expected to perch. The washing facilities were a simple pipe with holes banged through it. Ted saw the water trickling through slowly and his heart sank.

In the middle of the courtyard there was a hole the size of a large swimming pool, filled with water. The POWs soon learnt that this was in case of fire and that the Germans did not appreciate them jumping in to it when it was hot. The camp had its own doctor and also two padres, one Roman Catholic and the other Church of England.

The men were told they could send home four postcards and two, three-sided letter-cards each month. There were also regular searches by the military police.

After a few months Ted was moved again. This time he was sent to camp 328 at Stolzenburg (about 422km from Marienburg) to help build a new camp.

Camp 328 came under the administration area of Stalag XXB and, as usual, the prisoners were piled into cattle trucks without food or water to be transported slowly towards their new destination. The only redeeming feature of this journey was that it was not baking hot. Also, conditions in Stalags XXA and XXB were so bad that Ted felt optimistic that wherever they went it would have to be better.

They eventually arrived at Danzig railway station and marched along a wide road until they came to a large building with a 'Café Fredrichstrasse' sign outside. Ted recalled this was a 'big old café at the bottom of a steep hill. The café had once been 'a big old dance hall' and after Thorn and Marienburg, Ted considered it to be 'surprisingly comfortable.'[15] Over the door was a large dilapidated sign proclaiming it to be a Beer Garden.

Some signatures of the cast of the Christmas concert.

However, Ted's elation that they were to be housed in a Beer Garden was soon replaced by amusement as they realized that it was nothing of the sort. What had previously been the bar was now behind a strong wire fence which was suspended from strong wooden struts that stretched from floor to ceiling. There was no beer in sight! Located about five feet away from the bar there was another similar wire fence with a gate in it. The men were herded through it into a large room which had obviously once been the main dance hall with a stage at the end. It was now filled with bunks from floor to ceiling. The gangways in between each row of bunks were approximately one foot wide and the main gangway was only about two feet wide. There were five bunks in each column and there was an immediate scramble for any empty top bunks as at least here you wouldn't get trodden on or covered in dirt and dust from the ones above. As they settled wearily into their bunks they began the normal ritual of checking for lice, under the watchful eye of those already there. After their long journey the thought of being able to wash was appealing and to their delight they were shown another door at the front of the hall which led to a long room with toilets and wash basins. Life in the camps had long removed any vestiges of dignity as far as privacy was concerned, so Ted hardly noticed the lack of partitions between the toilets or wash basins.

The back garden could be reached through another doorway that was kept barred and securely locked at all times. There was also no access to the rest of the building that consisted of the accommodation for the German guards and Commandant, a store room and a kitchen, which were all surrounded by a strong wire fence.

The only time the POWs were allowed in the garden, which had a large lawn and various shrubs surrounding the asphalt, was for roll call and occasional exercise. Ted was relieved to find that Sundays were still work-free days so he assumed that was the day they could exercise in the garden. He soon discovered, however, that it was surrounded by a very high wall with rows of coiled barbed wire strung out along its entire length, and that there were always armed guards patrolling whenever the men used the garden for exercise. Any thoughts of escape over the wall, therefore, even if they could have climbed over the barbed wire, were soon forgotten.

As Ted stood and listened to the instructions about what they could and couldn't do, he tried to ignore the continual grumbling of his stomach. They had not eaten anything that day having been moved straight after the ersatz coffee that pretended to be breakfast. They had consumed what was left of their Red Cross parcels a few days earlier so until the next ones arrived they were reliant on the Germans for their food. At Thorn and Marienburg the prisoners had been able to share a loaf of bread with their own combine, but here the guards divided the loaf into five pieces and handed it out. This meant you could be lucky and get a large piece or unlucky and receive hardly anything, but at least the bowl of soup actually contained some small pieces of potato, much to Ted's amazement.

The chronic shortage of food was to continue throughout the war. Eventually the Red Cross parcels did come through on a more regular basis, in many cases not a moment too soon as the men were very nearly starving by the time they did arrive. The food parcels came in shoe-sized boxes and were meant to supplement the rations given to them by their captors. Unfortunately, they were often used as the main source of food as German rations were usually deliberately poor and invariably only consisted of watery soup, ersatz coffee and small amounts of bread. This was a calculated policy of the Germans to try and force the Allies to feed their own prisoners through the Red Cross system, and was done despite the Geneva Convention stating that POWs should receive the same amount of food with the same calorific value as their own depot troops.

These Red Cross parcels were made up from charitable donations which were used to purchase foodstuffs throughout Europe. Although the contents varied, they normally comprised things like tinned butter, cheese, fish, apple puddings, jam, margarine, curried mutton, peas, corned beef and condensed milk. They also usually included sugar, tea and cocoa as well. The contents would vary depending on which nationality was sending them. The Canadian parcels were highly prized for their food and the American ones for their cigarettes. Although the British ones occasionally had some rather strange contents like Coleman's mustard, most POWs would not have survived without these food parcels. When the first ones arrived they were divided up so that each prisoner only had one item, but as the supply improved the men sometimes received one parcel a week each. But this often depended on where the POW was. For those outside the main camp on work parties the supply was often interrupted and they would sometimes go for weeks without receiving one. When they did arrive, distribution was reliant on the Germans and although some handed out the parcels intact, others would open them and hand out only some of the contents. In some places the men were given parcels weekly, in others, only half a parcel each. Tins were often opened so they could not be hoarded and used to aid in escaping, and the contents poured directly into mess tins. No account was taken of the contents so sometimes the men were given jam and sardines for one meal and meat and condensed milk for another. At other times all the tins were given out at once, but only after the Germans had made holes in them. Again this was to prevent hoarding. This led to men gorging themselves when the parcels first arrived or the food would go off. They would then have to wait ages for the next parcel and be starving when it did eventually arrive.

Despite the difficulties of storing food, some did manage to hoard it and were careful about not eating it all at once. This was known as 'mossing' but it carried its own problems as it meant men often ate while others went hungry

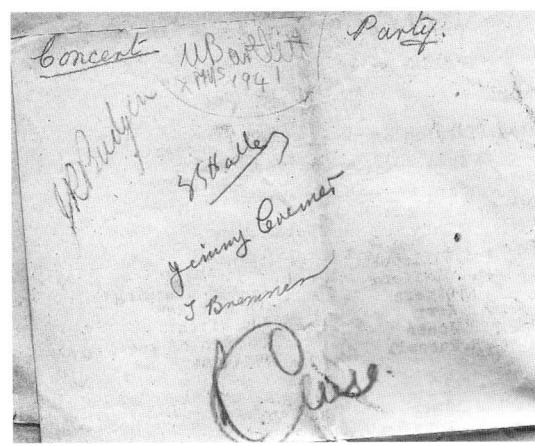

Signatures of the POW band Christmas 1941.

More signatures from the POW band.

because they had eaten their rations in one go. Cooking the food also had its own share of problems as there was only one stove in each hut. One way of resolving this was by allocating set times to each combine to cook their rations.

For most POWs the Red Cross parcels were all that stood between them and starvation and many would not have survived without them. But once the tide of the war turned against the Germans, Ted recalled 'the bombing broke down a lot of the bridges and railways and there wasn't much transport so you started only getting bits and pieces.'

Cigarettes were also in short supply which caused even more problems. Although the POWs were paid wages for their work, it was in Lagergeld or Lagermarks which had little value in the camp and no value at all outside. Up until 1942 these wages could be exchanged for various items from the German-run canteens although the items available were virtually as useless as the money itself. Things like ersatz soap, soup powders and cigarettes were not worth buying and after 1942 even these were unavailable. Cigarettes became the currency of the camp and the supplies sent in by the Red Cross and families were highly prized even by those who did not smoke. Those who did often suffered more as the need to fulfil their craving meant they would swap food for cigarettes even though they were starving. Conversely, cigarettes helped stave off the craving for food and when they weren't available then substitutes, which ranged from leaves, grass and even manure, were smoked instead.

Not knowing if camp 328 was going to be better or worse, Ted climbed onto his bunk. He'd finished his meagre rations and as he listened to some news about the war from the other POWs which had come from the Polish civilians, he wasn't sure how long it would take to settle in. Eventually he fell into a restless sleep punctuated by bouts of uncontrollable scratching as the lice moved in to colonise the new arrivals.

The men were roused at 5.45 am by the guards who took delight in pulling them off their bunks if they didn't respond quickly enough, and then taken outside for roll call as the Germans went through the numerous counts needed to ensure the paperwork matched the number of prisoners. They were subsequently marched out through the bar area, round the side of the building and onto a footpath which took them through a large field and up to the top of the hill.

Stolzenburg literally meant 'Proud Hill' and although the camp was mainly built by the Germans, Ted and his fellow POWs did all the 'donkey work, making the roads and levelling off and all that'. Building had started the previous year, but as the POWs who were originally assigned there had spent almost as much time finding ways to avoid working as they did actually working, it had not progressed very far by the time Ted arrived. The freezing winter weather also delayed progress as the POWs were sent to do other work.

This included unloading timber from the barges moored alongside the jetties on the river. This was particularly dangerous as the timber was slippery because it was covered in snow and ice. The banks too, were so slippery that there were numerous accidents and several broken bones. But by the time Ted arrived the weather had improved and the building was once again underway. He was assigned to digging trenches and laying foundations and drainpipes, and like the others, soon found ways to slow up the work. From what Ted could see the area was very old as they kept digging up cannon balls from previous wars. Although the work was hard he was grateful that at least they didn't have far to march back to the cafe. They continued to live in the cafe until the huts they were to live in on the hill were finished which took about another six months.

Once these huts in Stolzenburg were completed, Ted and the other POWs were able to move in. On the way there they were first taken to the delousing centre. For Ted this recalled memories of when he had first arrived in Poland but at least he could now stop itching for a while.

The new camp consisted of five single-storey, 200ft-long wooden huts. The first three huts each had two large rooms with twelve sets of double bunks up against the walls and a large round iron stove in the centre. The room was about twenty feet square and each hut had another room of a similar size which contained tables and benches to be shared between them all. The entrance to the rooms was through the communal dining/leisure room. The fourth hut was the same length and contained showers, toilets, accommodation for an officer and warrant officer and a sick bay. The fifth hut housed the kitchen, storerooms and a large concert or recreation hall.

There were air raid shelters between each hut. These had been constructed by digging a six-foot trench and placing old railway sleepers across the top and then covering the top with the earth that had been dug out. The whole camp was surrounded by two high wire fences about three feet apart and covered by double rows of barbed wire along the top. There were watchtowers at each corner, permanently manned by guards with machine guns, and outside the main gate there was a manned sentry box and accommodation for the German guards. Compared to the depravations of Stalags XXA, Stalag XXB and the other camps he had experienced, not to mention the overcrowding of the cafe, the new camp was so different that Ted had to pinch himself to make sure he hadn't died and gone to heaven.

But once the huts were finished Ted was sent outside the camp to be part of the working party constructing flats and houses for the workers in the submarine bases in Danzig. For Ted this was one of the best times while he was a POW. The camp was so much more comfortable than any of the others and the work was not too hard. There were also several opportunities for sabotage. The men fixed the front door bell so that when it was pressed the lights in the kitchen

Danzig during the war.

A German staff car in Danzig during the war.

Another scene of Danzig during the war.

came on affording them several laughs as the guards tried to work out why the lights kept coming on when there was no one there. They also put the opaque glass in the bathroom in the wrong way round 'so you could see in and you couldn't see out! The floorboards were just pushed together with wedges and not nailed down so when the Germans walked on them they sprung up!' recalled Ted. 'When the Germans complained they just looked blank and said, "well we don't understand, we're not them sort of workers" and they brushed it aside.' Others cemented the chimney stacks so the smoke from the fires couldn't get out. These lighter moments, few and far between, were what helped them through the harshness of their incarceration.

As the building progressed, supplies of tiles, wiring, plugs and ovens arrived, much of which found its way into the hands of the POWs. Brick ovens and ceramic tiles were added to the large iron stoves in the centres of the huts and heated by running the chimney from the original stove round the metal oven inside the brick and tiles and up through the roof. The men also burnt floorboards in the fireplaces at night to help keep warm.

Warning against escape notice given to all POWs. It was a source of amusement and also proved useful in the latrines.

While in Danzig, Ted again considered escaping, especially in the short, warm balmy months of the Baltic summer. But although there were boats going from Danzig to Sweden these were heavily guarded by the Germans who would go out on any boats heading to Sweden and then come back in again on them making escape virtually impossible. The problem for most POWs was that escaping would invariably mean involving civilians, and if the Germans caught them it would not just be the civilians who would be imprisoned, tortured and shot, it would also be their families who would suffer the same punishment. This effectively prevented many POWs from escaping as they did not want to be responsible for the unnecessary deaths of women and children.

Life continued in much the same vein with little happening on a day-to-day basis, the only excitement to their routine provided when, after yet another failed escape attempt, the Germans handed out leaflets at roll call one morning warning of the dangers of escaping. The leaflets pointed out that the men were much safer in the camps than outside where they would be shot as enemy agents. This was greeted with waves of laughter and grateful thanks for some toilet paper at last.

Chapter 17

Liberation

The Allied Commando raid in Dieppe in 1942 caused problems for POWs all over Germany and Poland as reports filtered through that the commandos had been instructed to handcuff German prisoners. In retaliation, orders were sent to all camps that POWs should also have their hands tied behind their backs from morning until night. However this was not practical for working camps, so instead, the guards removed all the men's trousers, boots or clogs in the evenings. This only lasted a couple of days though as the POWs took so long to find their own trousers and footwear the next morning the Germans soon gave up and life returned to what passed for normal in the camps.

As the years passed, the camps had become better organised, and nearly all now had hidden wirelesses. This meant that the news about the war was much more up to date and not so reliant on new POWs, whose own news was often old by the time they arrived. In Stolzenburg, the Germans produced their own POW magazine called *Camp*. It was full of propaganda but the prisoners soon learnt to read between the lines, and as time went on it was obvious there were not quite so many things for the Germans to boast about. As the war gradually

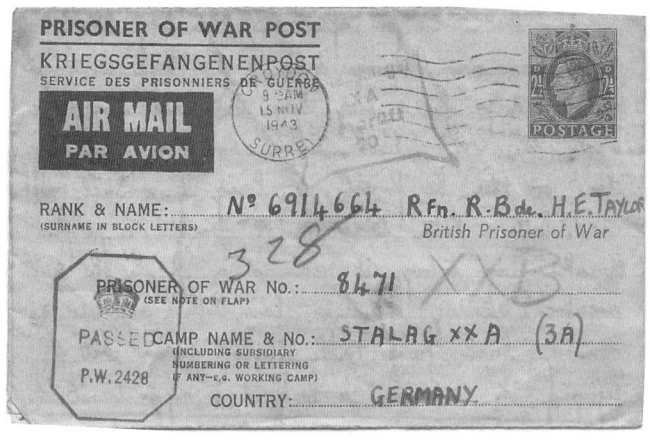

A letter to Ted at Stalag XXA dated 15/11/1943.

POW postcard from Ted to Brenda, 1944.

Kriegsgefangenenpost

Postkarte

PASSED
P.W.3287

Gebührenfrei!

Absender:
Vor- und Zuname:

Gefangenennummer:

Lager-Bezeichnung:
    M.-Stammlager XX B

Deutschland (Allemagne)

Empfängsort:

Straße:

Land:
Landesteil (Provinz usw.)

begun to turn in the Allie's favour, treatment of the POWs became slightly less harsh and the flow of Red Cross parcels improved. They were also amused to be given leaflets inviting them to join the British Frei Corps at one of the morning roll calls. This caused hoots of derision and catcalls as the men vented their disgust on the Germans. However, although they treated the German's offer with mocking amusement, they were not so forgiving of the accompanying British man who tried to persuade them to join the German's fight against the Soviet Union. The guards had to withdraw him rapidly as the POWs explained their point of view rather forcibly to someone they considered to be a traitor.

So the monotonous routine of the camps continued and for Ted, his family and Brenda remained the rock he clung to and his reason for surviving. But over the next two years they faded even further and took on a dreamlike quality that he knew, in his lucid moments, bore little resemblance to reality. This feeling of dislocation was exacerbated by the fact that contact from home was still very intermittent, and moving camps always meant even more delays for any post.

Like many others Ted looked forward to the post arriving, but this anticipation was always accompanied by an underlying fear that the letter would contain bad news such as the death of a loved one, or would be a 'Dear John' letter signalling the end of a relationship. For some, losing the anchor that was providing something to cling to, signalled a decline into depression and eventually some gave up completely, preferring death to a continued existence without hope. The letters also renewed the link with home which only reinforced the feeling of hopelessness of their current situation and highlighted how much of their life was passing them by while they languished in the camps.

The propaganda photographs the Germans sometimes took and circulated, were often sent home but gave entirely the wrong impressions of the men's

157

captivity. They did not want to worry their loved ones and always tried to look happy. Coupled with the nice clean uniforms that were always miraculously available when the camera appeared, these pictures almost implied they were on holiday. This would prevent some ever speaking about the horrors they'd experienced and witnessed. Others received some rather unpleasant letters suggesting the POWs were having a very cushy time compared to those on active service or on the Home Front. These letters were a devastating blow and caused many to give up the struggle. Life was hard enough especially when they were moved again and again and separated from the friends who could have supported them.

Cover of the Christmas menu, 1942. Ted and his friends called themselves 'The Amalgamated Moaners Ltd.'

Ted lost count of the friends he had made in the various camps and on the working parties and then lost touch with as he was moved somewhere else, and he often thought about whether he would ever see them again. He tried hard not to think about them and would do everything

Inside the 1942 Christmas menu. This was the POWs' Christmas Day food which was normally saved from their Red Cross parcels. Without these they would have starved – unfortunately they were intermittent and those on satellite camps often went months without them.

"GUNFIRE" (8AM IN BED)

BUTTERED BISCUITS
    & JAM.

BACON WITH MEAT ROLL
    & TOMATOES
BUTTERED BREAD. JAM.
    & MARMALADE.
TEA.
    — x —

DINNER
SOUP (AS SUPPLIED BY OUR HOSTS)
XMAS PUDDING & CUSTARD.
STEWED FRUIT
BISCUITS & CHEESE.
MINERALS (HOT OR COLD)
    — x —

TEA (5 PM)
FRUIT + CUSTARD.
CHOCOLATE & FRUIT CAKE
BUTTERED BREAD. JAM.
TEA
    — x —
SUPPER
SANDWICHES (MISCELLANEOUS)
MINERALS (SERVED HOT)

he could to distract himself when he felt the darkness of depression descending on him. He gradually became as self-reliant as it was possible to be in the camps with their culture of interdependence and eventually, through bitter experience, Ted learnt not to really trust or rely on anyone. Despite his gentle upbringing even he was defeated by the brutality of his treatment and of those around him and he began to change, imperceptibly at first. Then gradually the gentle boy disappeared to be replaced by a man who had somehow found an iron will within him to survive. He was never actively cruel, nor would he ever seek to actively harm those around him, but he learnt to rely on himself and not get involved. The changes in his personality happened so slowly that he was almost unaware of them, and because all those who had known him before were elsewhere, he was totally oblivious as to how much he was changing.

Ted had made a conscious decision to suppress any memories of his friends who had died in battle and under the brutal camp regimes. To remember and mourn them now while his own situation was so perilous would serve no purpose and could sap his own will to survive. But even more deeply buried than these memories of his lost friends was the fear that he would never actually go home at all.

One of the bunks in Majdanek.

Accommodation in Majdanek. Each block held many more men than there were bunks and hundreds ended up sleeping on the floor, squashed up against each other.

Bath House. The blue staining is from the Zyklon B gas.

A view of the camp perimeter.

View of the camp perimeter showing its proximity to the main road.

The crematorium at Majdanek.

The Germans made little attempt to hide their atrocities from the local community. The public road ran alongside the camp and its inmates included local resistance fighters as well as farmers who did not hand over their full quota of crops.

The sign stating 'Showers'. They were actually the gas chamber.

161

For the first couple of years there had been the very real fear that the Germans would win the war and that Britain would be invaded. Once that fear subsided and the tide turned, this was replaced with a new fear for the men - that they would die before it ended, either through the ill treatment, cruelty and casual brutality that was an everyday occurrence, or through sickness, injury and lack of medical treatment – or simply because the Germans would want to try and hide their atrocities by just killing them all out of hand. Now the Germans were demonstrably losing the war, the fear that they would just shoot their prisoners before closing the camp and escaping back to Germany had grown considerably and rumours were rife to the effect that this was already happening. The numbers of SS in the area were increasing and although they had not yet taken over running the camps, there was an ever-present fear that it was only a matter of time.

The other fear that haunted Ted came from rumours about camps where several of the men had gone to work and never returned. These rumours suggested there were extermination camps dedicated to killing as many Jews as possible. When he had first heard the stories, Ted, like many others, had scoffed. There was no way on earth he could conceive of something so completely diabolical. Surely it could not be true. But the rumours persisted and came from too many different sources for him to continue to deny them. The day he was eventually forced to confront the ugly truth was the day his faith finally left him. Since his capture and brutal experiences at the hands of the Germans, his faith had wavered many times, but somehow he had always managed to hold on to it.

But then he heard first-hand accounts of working parties who had passed these camps and seen SS guards encouraging their dogs to chase Jews round the compound of the camp and, even worse, encouraging the dogs to savage them. Others told him of young boys hanging from gallows on ropes while SS guards swung on their legs. Ted had already seen emaciated Jewish women and girls in thin, striped dresses and with shaved heads, being made to climb on top of wagons in the burning sun to unload coal with their bare hands while the guards stoned them or clubbed them with pick axe handles and anything else to hand. Recalling how the Jewish girl on the train a lifetime ago had said she was going to Poland to start a new life, was for him, the final straw. No God he could ever place his trust and faith in could let something so monstrous happen.

We knew that Ted spent some time on a working party in one of the concentration camps, but until recently we weren't sure which one. He certainly knew other POWs who went into these camps as he talked about them, but his reaction to hearing Jewish songs later in his life indicated he had witnessed atrocities as well as hearing about them second-hand. He also talked about POWs not returning from these working parties. It is well-known that several hundred British POWs were kept in the part of Auschwitz known as Monowitz, and that British POWs were amongst those who were used to build some of the camps. Other prisoners were made to work in some of the war industries that were located within them like IG Farben – the company that made the Zyklon-B gas used in the Nazi death camps - Krupps, Siemens and Schukert.

What is not so well-known is that a number of British POWs, including Ted, spent time in Majdanek. This was a concentration and forced labour camp located in a suburb three miles from Lublin. It later became a death camp. Majdanek opened in September 1941 and was initially for Soviet POWs, but fifty-four different nationalities from twenty-eight countries passed through its gates. These were mainly Jewish, Soviet or Polish, but there were also ordinary POWs from Britain who were probably there to help build or extend the camp – which covered an area of 667 acres and was surrounded by an electrified barbed wire fence.

Majdanek had seven gas chambers, two wooden gallows, a small crematorium and, from 1943, a larger crematorium. It was located by the side of a main road and the Germans did little to disguise the purpose of the camp from the ordinary Polish civilians. There was room for up to 45,000 prisoners although the Germans once had plans to extend it to house up to 250,000. There are no accurate figures as to how many people died in Majdanek. The Germans

One of the gas chambers.

163

Inside accommodation blocks at Majdanek.

A store of Zyklon B. The Russians arrived so quickly in 1944 that the Germans were unable to destroy the camp or the evidence of their atrocities.

Gas ovens in Majdanek.

A watch tower.

Some of the thousands of victims of Majdanek.

Zyklon B canister.

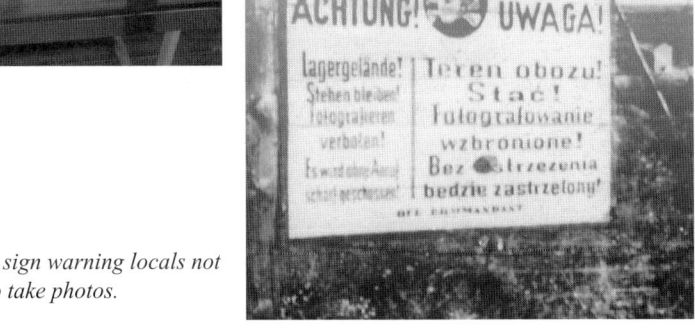

A sign warning locals not to take photos.

destroyed the records on the eve of the Soviet liberation in 1944 and they also used a rotational system of numbering people which ran from one to 20,000 and then started again. The best estimate puts the total number deported there at no less than 250,000. After the surrender of Italy in autumn 1943, many Italian officers who had refused to continue fighting, or who began fighting against the Germans, were also sent to Majdanek to be executed.

Ted's first sight of Majdanek would have been a large wooden gate, on either side of which were sentry boxes painted with black and white chevrons and manned by armed guards. Once they had passed through the gate, the men were in the inner compound which was divided into sections, each surrounded by a double row of barbed wire fencing. Encircling the compounds was a line of nineteen watchtowers manned by SS guards with loaded machine guns, rifles and grenades. In the distance Ted would have seen a tall, brick chimney belching continuous white smoke into the air from the top of a slope and there would have been a strange smell in the air. Near one of the main streets he would have seen a large field on which stood a solitary, white stucco house which was the Commandant's home. Further inside the camp was a gravel-covered square in front of a large building which had a small, black guard-tower to its right. This square was called 'Rosenfeld' (Rose Field). This was the German's idea of humour as Rosenfeld was a Jewish name and the square was where families were separated, men to one side, women and children on the other. The Germans would then repeat the separation process, this time deciding who looked fit enough to be useful as a worker and consigning the rest to the gas chambers.

Ted's other nightmare was being sent to work in a salt mine. This particular threat had been made not long after their surrender and played on his mind in the intervening years. Again, this was something Ted said virtually nothing about to his family, but which he did mention to his friend. Among the many POW pictures Ted kept was a picture of prisoners in a mine of some sort. Other POWs reported working in salt mines in Silesia and in Germany. At these, the men would go underground to mine the salt while others worked on it above ground where it was crushed, mixed with water and left in saltpans to crystalize. The water was then pumped off leaving wet crystals. Some POWs went into the saltpans and loaded the wet crystals onto carriers which ran round on a rail above them. After several hours their feet were in a terrible state as the wet salt made their flesh raw. The wet salt was finally taken into heating sheds where it was dried, and then there to a silo where it was put into paper bags and loaded onto trains to be exported around Europe as fertilizer called kali.

Other British POWs were sent to work in coal mines in Poland. Conditions in these mines were terrible and, as well as the ever-present danger from explosions, many workers died from infections of relatively minor wounds because medical treatment was non-existent.

POWs in a mine.

A part of Ted expected his loss of faith to leave a gaping hole in his life but somewhat to his surprise it didn't. The horrors of his experiences had gradually begun the process of enabling him to shut down emotionally, a self-protection mechanism that often results from considerable trauma. He found that whereas earlier he would have reacted to the continual atrocities around him, they now left him almost unaffected. Many of his companions were experiencing the same so his reactions were considered normal. The idea was to survive and you couldn't do that if you raised your head above the parapet. The old army adage about never volunteering for anything stood him in good stead and he concentrated on taking one day at a time.

Then suddenly, after nearly five years in captivity, there was a light at the end of the tunnel. The news had continued to improve for several months after D Day as the Allies swept eastwards and the Russians swept westwards towards them. The POWs had witnessed American Fortress bombers dropping bombs on Danzig and as the year progressed, they could hear the shelling and see the red glow in the sky that told them the Russian artillery was getting closer. The camps were alive with rumours and speculation and it was all the NCOs could do to prevent riots and attempted breakouts. Although the Germans were losing the war they were stubbornly holding on and the NCOs feared a massacre if the prisoners rioted. However, together with the rising excitement there was also rising tension as it was feared the Russians would arrive first. The Germans were petrified of the advancing Russians and the POWs were wary of the treatment they might receive.

The prisoners were also anxious about the increasing involvement of the Gestapo in the day to day running of the camps, particularly where escapes were concerned. Just as worrying was the increased action of the SS in some of the areas around the camps. Although the Germans had been threatened with severe punishments if anything happened to the thousands of POWs under their care - not to mention the fact that the Allies now held thousands of German POWs - it was already known that various fanatical SS units had shot surrendering troops as late as 1944. This dangerous mix of chaos, anarchy and fanaticism that swept through eastern Europe as the Russian onslaught quickly overran or skirted German defences in their race westward, meant that nothing was certain, least of all that the POWs would be liberated.

And then on 18 January 1945, their lives changed irrevocably. The Russians were now so close the men could hear the gunfire and see the shells dropping on the city. Panicked, the Germans evacuated the camp and drove the POWs westward away from the advancing Russians and towards Germany. For Ted and his fellow prisoners this looked like the beginning of the end of their imprisonment, but there was still one more cruel twist of fate awaiting them.

Chapter 18

Death on the Road
January – May 1945

It was not only the reaction of the Germans to the POWs that the Allies were worried about. They too had heard the rumours about the way the Russians behaved towards the POWs, often not bothering to distinguish between them and their captors. As the Russians rapidly moved westwards, concern amongst the Western Allies grew about what would happen to the POWs if they overran the camps. There was also the very real fear that POWs could get killed and injured purely because they were situated in the middle of the fighting. In an attempt to ensure their safety, the International Red Cross insisted that POWs should be moved to a place of safety to prevent them becoming caught up in any fighting. The Geneva Convention also stated that POWs should be removed from the frontline. As soon as it became obvious that Germany was losing, and as early as 1944, plans were prepared to begin evacuating the camps. Although the reasoning behind this was sound and well-intentioned, no one could possibly have imagined it would add a new dimension to the suffering of the already starving POWs.

And so, in 1945, came a new chapter in the horror of the POWs lives as the infamous death marches started. Together with the inmates of the concentration camps, thousands of Allied prisoners were force-marched across the frozen wastes of Europe ahead of the Russian advance. Ted had experienced the forced march eastward five years earlier and thought nothing could possibly be worse, He was about to find out just how wrong he could be. The only advantage this time was that at least he was heading towards his family and home and not away from them. But in the summer of 1940 he had been relatively fit and healthy. Now he was a mere shadow of his former self; starving and malnourished he was about to undertake the same journey on foot, in the depths of winter with little clothing, and virtually no food.

Evacuation day had started the same for Ted as any other, and although rumours had been rife for some time that the Russians were coming, he had long since given up on listening to rumours; especially ones that related to the end of the war or going home. He had heard too many over the years to listen any more and like many others, he knew that any march across Europe would be a million times worse in the winter than it had been in the heat of the summer. But despite his scepticism he, like the others, tried to prepare as best they could. While many men got rid of any unnecessary possessions like books and musical instruments, some made gloves and hats out of scrap material. Others already had balaclavas or gloves sent by their families so spent their time resting or trying to barter their possessions for food. They all knew that food was the key to survival and that there would be little opportunity to scavenge in the depths of the Polish winter.

Ted rested on his bunk. He knew he would need every ounce of strength he possessed to survive a forced march given his already weakened state, and he hoped that the rumours were wrong. Perhaps the Americans or the British would get there first; perhaps the Russians were not as bad as rumour suggested. But deep down he knew that it was unlikely the Germans would hang around long enough to let them find out. The big question that haunted him and many others was whether the Germans would really evacuate them or whether they would kill them before they fled. There were already stories that detachments of SS had thrown hand grenades into huts of other camps killing all the occupants on their way eastwards; others that POWs had been buried underground in mines. These rumours, coupled with the very real fear that the Russians would just kill everyone they came across or take them prisoner and transport them further eastward, added to the men's fears.

Each day that passed brought more tension. The POWs were told several times they were leaving and then the orders were countermanded and changed. This happened so many times that Ted seriously doubted whether anything would ever really happen. Every day more men returned from outside working parties to join the increasingly overcrowded and overflowing huts. Lack of space meant they were now forced to sleep on the floors of the huts and in the washrooms, and food was becoming even scarcer than before. The stench of the unwashed bodies, even in the freezing temperatures, was appalling as men became frightened to remove their boots or clothing in case they were stolen for the possible march home.

But even Ted realized that something was happening when they were woken early and made to line up at the gates with what few possessions they had. Like the others, he grabbed as much as he could before they were hurried out of the hut. Experience of instant moves had made him a past master at packing his meagre possessions up in the shortest possible time. In any case, this time there had been plenty of warning that something might happen. Like the others, Ted had begun sleeping in his boots and wearing all his clothes just in case they had no time to grab them. Amongst the possessions he had with him were his letters from Brenda and his diaries which were mostly written at the beginning when he still dreamed of going home quite soon. He also found room for the photographs of his friends taken at the rehearsals and performances of the concert parties that he had been so heavily involved in. Although they were frequently exhausted and almost always starving, the men had still found some time to amuse themselves as well and it was this that had kept most of them going, especially in the early days when the news of the war was almost always bad.

Once Red Cross parcels began to arrive the POWs were able to occasionally get hold of gramophone records and a gramophone on which to play them, as well as musical instruments. Red Cross boxes were broken up and made into stages, vacant buildings were turned into concert halls and old, discarded uniforms turned into costumes. Some plays and variety shows were very professional and often had some of the men acting and dressing up as women. Ted and his party had even gone to a couple of the other working camps to entertain them in the early days. For Ted, this involvement in concert parties was one of the things that kept him sane as it represented another world from the one of misery, boredom and senseless cruelty he inhabited every day. He could not leave his photographs behind as they represented the only good things in his life over the past five years. Fortunately, they didn't weigh much and he was able to pack them in some waxed paper from one of the parcels which he hoped would ensure they didn't perish if he got wet. Although it might be a long time before he was able to look at them without anger, rage or sadness, he felt he owed it to all those who hadn't made it to take them with him.

As he lined up with the others the temperature almost took his breath away. It was twenty-five degrees below zero outside the hut and the snow was at least a foot deep in some places, even deeper in others, especially where it had blown into drifts. There were nearly 3,000 men in the camp and most were lined up in the normal columns as the Germans began to count them. The count seemed much shorter than usual to Ted and then they were walked out through the gates for the last time. The few remaining men were left there to continue to produce bread for the Germans. Ted did not know if they would ever be seen again. But there was no time for speculation and, as he turned his attention to his own plight, he shivered in the freezing wind that was howling off the Baltic.

Although prisoners in some of the camps were either given Red Cross parcels before they left or raided the stores and took them, for Ted and his companions the parcels had stopped several months ago so the only food they were given was a small loaf of bread, 'about the size of a small Hovis between five men'. They were told that food was to be provided on the way by a wagon following them. Most of them never saw this wagon, so other than the odd Red Cross truck that appeared, all they had was whatever they could scrounge on the route westwards. But that was all in the future and probably, if they had known just how horrendous it would be, many of them would have given up as soon as they left the camp. Now, although they had their fears, they also had the eternal human hope that things would be all right in the end. The one thought that kept going through their minds was that this was just the beginning and that soon they would be free. So, despite the cold and freezing conditions when they set off, things didn't seem too bad. To Ted, the guards 'were a bit like home guard and for the first two days we were walking along, weren't marching, more of a shuffle than anything else. We hadn't got the energy to walk through that snow.'

Ted's last view of the camp was the fleeing Germans and he couldn't help feeling a small glow of satisfaction that at last his captors were feeling the same fear he and his friends had endured for nearly five long years. His elation was short-lived however, as he realized that wherever the Germans were taking them it was probably Germany and that Germany was a long way away. There were no trains or trucks now; the Allied bombing had destroyed most of the transport links so the Germans obviously did intend to walk them there. The enormity of this task gradually dawned on him again. It was freezing cold and snowing again. Having endured four Polish winters he was not under any illusion as to just how cold it could get and yet the Germans were obviously intending to march thousands of undernourished POWs westwards towards Germany through the thick snow and ice.

Ted shivered, as much from fear and dread as cold. Although during captivity his body had slowly acclimatized to the icy cold and biting wind of a Polish winter, he was not sure he could survive a march of thousands of miles with little food, worn boots, just his uniform, coat, and a blanket to protect him from the cold. Fortunately he also had gloves and a hat he had made from the inside lining of his coat, but even they would not protect him from the freezing conditions as the weeks went on.

The wind howled round them and within minutes they were engulfed in a blizzard. As Ted glanced back, unable to resist a last look at the camp, it disappeared into a white swirling mist and was gone from sight. He turned his head and looked forward, his face enduring the snow and icy pellets of hail that were increasing in intensity. The cold was so intense and the fury of the hail so violent that he was almost unable to breathe, a sharp pain piercing his lungs every time he inhaled the icy air. When he breathed out, the air was so cold that it froze the lapel of his greatcoat. Putting his head down and gritting his teeth, Ted inwardly made himself a promise that he would survive this. He had come too far and endured too much horror and suffering to be defeated now. He glanced at the men either side of him and felt that they too nodded imperceptibly as if they had read his thoughts.

Although Ted did not know it, this forced march was not an isolated event. It was, in fact, one of several 'death marches' taking place across the bitter wilderness of Poland as the Germans fled the rapidly advancing Russians. January and February 1945 were among the coldest winter months of the twentieth century, with blizzards and temperatures as low as –25 °C (–13 °F), and even until the middle of March, temperatures were well below 0 °C (32 °F).

In most camps, the POWs were broken up into groups of 250 to 300 men. The inadequate roads and the flow of the battles raging around them meant they did not all take the same route and their treatment varied. On average they would march between ten and twenty miles per day depending on the conditions. Several times on the march the columns of men were separated into different groups and they soon lost contact with many of those they had been imprisoned with. As they continued westward others joined them including civilians, those from other camps and even those from concentration camps who then just as quickly disappeared. These were the easiest to identify as their skeletal frames were even less able to cope with the privations of the march and their corpses soon littered the roads, a reminder as if they needed it, of the way the Germans treated their prisoners. Men lost track of friends and companions and often never found out what had happened to them. And still they marched on, each day a living hell, each day's survival a miracle.

If they were lucky they found factories, churches and barns to take shelter in overnight. When they were unlucky they spent nights in the open. Some Germans provided farm wagons pulled by other POWs for those unable to walk; others simply shot them where they had fallen. Some guards and prisoners became interdependent on each other while other Germans became increasingly hostile to those they were guarding and their behaviour became even more callous, often taking delight in their suffering. In some villages the men passed through people came out and fed them, in others they threw bricks and stones at them and jeered in a way reminiscent of their treatment so many years earlier.

Some of the columns reached Western Germany and liberation; others were marched towards the Baltic Sea where they were held hostage by the Nazis and used as hostages and human shields.

But Ted knew none of this; his only thought was to keep going, that each step was taking him nearer home. He was glad that Harry was with him as he knew he could trust him. Harry was one of his oldest friends from the camps and although they had been separated several times for some reason, they had at last been reunited just before Christmas. If Ted had still believed in a God he would have thought it was His doing, but he no longer thought like that. It was just pure luck that had brought them together, a fortune he was grateful for.

He closed his ears to the moans and groans of those who were already struggling and concentrated on putting one foot in front of another, allowing his thoughts to focus on Brenda and his Mum for the first time in ages. Maybe this time he was finally going home.

Hour after hour they trudged wearily on. Despite the hard physical work most of them had been subjected to, they were not used to walking long distances. Finding themselves on a forced march in good weather would have been hard enough, but in the current weather and given their poor physical condition, it was almost impossible. The snow was thick and slowed their progress considerably, and before long daylight faded and the guards looked around for somewhere to shelter. But there was no shelter to be seen in the vast, empty snow-covered fields and Ted despaired of ever stopping. The snow was so deep that they had hardly travelled any distance; at the most about ten miles and they were already exhausted. But that was just the beginning.

As the days wore on the conditions deteriorated. Dysentery and sickness were rife and men often dropped out of the column, too weak to carry on. They lay down in the snow and went to sleep. Within a very short time their bodies were frozen solid. Even now the persecution from the guards did not stop. Although some just ignored anyone who dropped out of the lines, others took a sadistic delight in humiliating the POWs and would shoot those who stopped for a rest or tried to get food from some of the isolated farmhouses they passed. On a couple of occasions, when a civilian gave some of the men warm drinks, the guards knocked them out of their hands. When they protested, the Germans shot them in the stomach leaving them to die slowly and in agony, laughing while their blood seeped slowly into the pristine white snow, staining it a dark red. Inured as the men were to the casual brutality they had witnessed over the last five years, this unnecessary torture almost excelled anything they had previously experienced and only added to the misery.

About every thirty miles there were huge barns, obviously erected for the purpose of providing shelter to the fleeing Germans and their prisoners. But because conditions were so dreadful, they did not always travel far enough which meant on some nights they could not find shelter. On the nights no shelter was available they paced up and down, frightened to go to sleep because they knew that if they laid down they would freeze in temperatures that would often drop to minus forty degrees. The roads were icy and extremely slippery, and many men broke ankles or legs as they slid over, especially those unlucky enough to be wearing wooden clogs, but they had no option but to keep walking or they would die. In some places the snow had been blown into ridges and then frozen leaving a kind of corrugated iron effect. Unable to walk over the ridges because they were so slippery, the men were forced to crawl over them.

Each day saw fresh nightmares as more and more men died or just disappeared. Each night was worse because they fought over the limited space in whatever shelter they had been lucky enough to find as to be left outside meant certain death. Sometimes they knew that other POWs must have come through before them as they found remains of Red Cross parcels and discarded cigarette butts on the floors. In some places there was straw to wrap themselves in, in others there was nothing and they lay shivering in the vast empty space knowing that at least it was marginally warmer than outside.

On the odd occasion the men found a two-storey barn, they fought for places upstairs. Once they had secured a spot they didn't dare move and would urinate where they lay. But even huddled together on the floor below with urine trickling down was preferable to sleeping outside. For those unable to find shelter, anything was better than lying in open fields. Some slept in dung heaps, so desperate were they for warmth. Others slept in pig pens and fought the pigs for food, the swill being preferable to starving. This added to their dysentery and stomach complaints and made their lives more unbearable, but the need for food, any food, to try and stop their organs from shutting down, was preferable to nothing at all.

In the mornings the men would stamp up and down and slap their frozen hands against their bodies in an attempt to get the circulation moving again. Those lucky enough to have any food in tins found that it had frozen solid overnight so was completely inedible. Those who risked taking their boots off found the perspiration and sweat from the previous day's march made them too frozen to put back on, so had to walk without them in the hope they would thaw out before they got frostbite. Men who left their boots on overnight found they were frozen to their feet in the morning. This meant they were agony to walk in until they had thawed out. Some men managed to stuff paper into their boots which was a great help in retaining heat until they began to sweat and then it was useless.

Although they had been told a wagon would be following them carrying bread, invariably it was nowhere to be seen, so with little food they were reduced to scavenging to survive, even eating cats, dogs, rats, and grass. On one occasion one of the horses pulling a refugee wagon collapsed and died, and instantly the starving men hacked pieces out of it, unable to believe their good fortune. They quickly built a fire and used sticks, bits of wire and anything they could find, to roast the meat. But this was an exception and for the most part there was no food other than the bread ration, if they were lucky. Already underweight, many reached the end of their march weighing less than half the weight they started the war at.

There were no medicines and no help for those who were unlucky enough to get sick, and they soon became filthy because they dare not risk taking off their clothes to wash for fear of frostbite. Not that they had the energy or the facilities to wash or shave even if they had been able to. Their clothes were soon alive with lice and although for many this was just another minor irritation to add to their discomfort, others caught typhus from them. Malnourished and underweight, many succumbed quite quickly to pneumonia, diphtheria, pellagra and exhaustion. The men were told that a wagon following behind would pick up the sick and those who collapsed, but, like the food wagon, no one ever saw it. Frostbite became everyone's fear as their extremities froze in the extreme temperatures and amputations were common. Even those wearing gloves and boots were not immune.

Friendships that had survived years of incarceration began to fracture as the instinct for survival took over. On the odd occasion when the Germans did appear with food or the Red Cross managed to get through, there were no orderly queues just a mad scramble to get as much as possible. Being polite would not keep you alive and staying alive was the driving imperative behind behaviour most of them would never normally have considered.

As January passed into February and then into March, the surviving men noticed that the weather was beginning to get a little warmer, although it was often still below freezing at night. At first they realized it was no longer as bitingly cold and then, that the snow was beginning to melt. Initially this did not bring any relief as they now found they were shuffling through inches of wet slush. Although they thought it was impossible to be even more uncomfortable they were wrong. The slush soaked through whatever coverings they had on their feet, even those lucky enough to be wearing boots, leaving them struggling with feet that were both cold and wet - ideal conditions for trench foot. They were continually plagued by driving rain and blustery winds, but as the thaw progressed, green shoots appeared on the trees and they wondered if they would actually survive after all. But their ordeal was still not yet over.

At first, as they shuffled down the Baltic coast, they were subject to intermittent bombing raids by the Russians who possibly thought they were retreating Germans. The men had to take cover each time the bombers came over, but fortunately many of them were not particularly accurate. Eventually the POWs were out of range and the bombing stopped for a while. But then they came within range of the American and British bombers who also mistook them for retreating Germans and who bombed them with considerable more accuracy. Bombing raids by the Americans and British increased steadily as the men gradually made their way west and although the sight of the bomb damage inflicted did wonders for their morale, they had to keep taking cover and several of them were killed. In a village called Gresse, sixty Allied POWs were killed by RAF Typhoons.

Although the Germans were obviously losing the war, they continued to fight on and the POWs were still a good source of slave labour. Exhausted as they were, they occasionally found themselves clearing bomb damage and repairing roads so the war could continue. Some were made to help dig out the bodies after bombing raids and others were housed in cattle trucks in stations and made to repair the damage to the railways while the Allied planes roared overhead and saturated the surrounding area with bombs. There was no food other than the watery soup, black bread and ersatz coffee the Germans provided which was hardly appetising or even particularly nourishing, but at least it was regular.

Somehow, throughout all this chaos, Ted and Harry had managed to stay together and to look out for each other. By working as a team they had survived in slightly better shape than many of the others and having each other to rely and depend on, reinforced the iron sense of determination that had got them this far.

As March passed slowly into April, they were still heading westwards. By now, in Ted's group, the guards had handed over their weapons and surrendered to the POWs and yet still they walked on and on, taking weary step after weary step. Each day merged into the next and many no longer had any idea what day it was or how long they had been walking. The only thing they knew was that each painful step was taking them a little closer to home. The constant struggle to find enough food to keep them going for another day occupied all their waking thoughts and the thought of getting home occupied their dreams at night.

Although each step took them nearer home, the danger of being killed by Allied bombing or straying into small local skirmishes increased. The shelling and artillery of the Russian advance provided constant background noise as they continued westwards. The ground shook continually with the vibrations caused by 'Stalin's Organ', the multiple rocket launcher that had so terrorized and demoralized the Germans on the Eastern Front. But that, at least, was behind them and not a real threat. The threat now came from advance scouting parties of Russians or fanatical SS divisions dug in and ready to fight to the death. Both posed a constant danger to the POWs and the Germans who now walked at their side, uneasy comrades as they tried to avoid the dangers all around them.

They tried to keep off the main routes and often resorted to only travelling at night. In the distance, in all directions, they saw the red glows of the fires started by bombing on the various towns and cities and they used these to navigate by. The noise of shelling, mortars and artillery filled the air and the ground shook as the shells found their target. At times the men found themselves making their way through smoke, and the smell of cordite and the noise of the distant battles reignited Ted's memories of 1940, causing him to pull up sharply. But there was no time for memories, no time for mourning his friends, no time for anything but to keep walking. The present was much too dangerous to spend time thinking about the past. That would come later. Now, he needed all his strength to keep putting one foot in front of the other. For the most part they had given up thinking about when they would reach their destination, they just knew that they had to keep walking.

Unsure of their reception, most of the time they hid if they saw or heard any Russians, but there were exceptions to this rule. Several times the POWs, Ted included, went to the assistance of local women and killed or wounded the Russian soldiers who were attempting to rape them. On other occasions they prevented isolated farms from being looted. But most of the time, common sense and the determination to survive that had kept them alive this long, overrode their compassion and they had to ignore the cries for help.

By the beginning of May, some had walked over 500 miles and others as far as a thousand miles. In these horrendous, chaotic conditions they had not been walking in a straight line, so although the distance between Marienburg and Barth is about 572km by road, most of the POWs had walked considerably further. They had taken diversions to avoid fighting and to avail themselves of what little shelter was available. Before the guards had surrendered to them, the men had been marched into towns to help clear bomb damage and to bury the victims of bombing. They had been marched to railway lines and stations to help clear the lines and then back to the roads to help repair them.

Once the guards had surrendered, the POWs faced even more danger as they added the retreating Germans to the list of those to avoid. Now they were forced to take back-roads through forests and hills and to cross fields and rivers, often only travelling at night as it was too dangerous to move about during the day.

But for Ted, almost at the limit of his endurance, the walking was mercifully coming to an end. On the evening of VE day they found themselves on the outskirts of Stalag Luft 1. At first, Ted thought that the lights in the distance were some kind of hallucination but as he shuffled closer he realized what it was. The men were so tired and exhausted that they no longer really cared whether it had been liberated or not. It represented shelter and possibly food and an end to the endless walking.

On 30 April 1945, things in Stalag Luft 1 had reached a head. The Commandant had received orders to move the POWs to Germany to prevent them falling into the hands of the Russians. But the Senior American Officer (SAO) informed the Commandant that the POWs would not evacuate the camp unless force was used and after some time, to avoid bloodshed, the Commandant agreed not to carry out an evacuation.

At about 10 pm the guards turned out the perimeter and internal street lights and were then seen leaving the camp. The SAO then took control of the camp and ordered the MPs to make sure the POWs remained orderly and did not try to leave and guards were posted all round the camp to protect it from any stray parties of retreating Germans or fanatical SS units entering the camp. On the 1st May scouting parties were sent out to try and make contact with the Russians and after two or three days contact was made with local Russian commanders and arrangements were made to bring in some food for the POWs. Despite their being under the control of the Russians nothing was done to remove them from the camp and on 6 May Colonel Byerly left the camp with two officers from a British Airborne division and flew to England where he reported to the 8th Air Force HQ. It was here that arrangements were made to evacuate the liberated POWs by air.

However, things were not as simple as first appeared. The British and Americans were still in negotiations with the Russians over the release of the POWs because, quite simply, the Russians would not let them go without the release and repatriation of several thousand Soviet POWs who were in camps in England. Many of these Soviet POWs had been forcibly enlisted into the German army at the point of a gun; others had enlisted willingly seeing the Germans as liberators against the Soviets. Once enlisted the Germans, sensibly enough, put them to fight on the Western Front where considerable numbers of them immediately surrendered to the Western Allies as soon as it was expedient to do so. They were then shipped to England and placed in POW camps. Later these numbers were swelled by several thousand Soviet POWs liberated from German POW camps by the Western Allies.

Having spent the war promulgating the lie that there were no Soviet POWs, that no Soviets had defected to fight with the Germans and that all patriotic Soviets had died defending the Soviet Union, Stalin was forced to rewrite history yet again. He now wanted all these Soviets back. The demands for their return had begun much earlier in 1944 but both the British and US governments had been wary of the possibility of the Soviets holding British and American POWs as hostages if they liberated the Eastern camps before the Western Allies. They had therefore delayed responding, wanting to ensure they retained some bargaining power should this situation occur.

They had finally run out of time and although they had a reasonable idea of what would happen to those returning to the Soviet Union they considered they had little choice if they wanted to ensure the safe return of their own POWs. In the case of Stalag Luft 1 there is speculation that the liberation of the POWs there was wholly reliant on agreeing to Stalin's demand for the repatriation of a particular White Russian émigré. Until his demand was met Stalin would not agree to the release of the men incarcerated there.

Therefore, although the camp was in the area liberated by the Russians they had left the running of the camp to the Americans and taken no further steps either to help in their repatriation or to move them anywhere else as negotiations continued. In other areas British and American POWs were taken by the Russians to Odessa and then sent home from there by ship. However, some 30,000 British POWs appear to have been unaccounted for at the end of the war.

Of the 199,592 captured British and Commonwealth POWs known to be in German camps in Eastern Europe at the beginning of 1945 only 168,746 returned. While many undoubtedly died on the death marches through malnutrition, illness, casual shootings and beatings by their captors or simply froze to death, others were killed by bombing and strafing from Allied aircraft or from being caught in the cross fire between the advancing Allies and retreating Germans. Some are believed to have simply moved in with girlfriends and families they met when working on farms and in Polish factories and some may have just wanted to disappear. However, there have been persistent rumours that some British POWs were taken east and ended their lives in Soviet Gulags never to be seen again. There is still no conclusive proof that this happened but neither is there any to the contrary.

So when Ted and his weary companions entered the camp on the eve of VE day they were delighted to discover that although the camp had been liberated by the Russians, it was under the control of the Americans. However, Ted had no idea of the delicate negotiations that were going on or that his freedom and the freedom of the other POWs still hung precariously in the balance. Like the others, all he felt in his weakened exhausted state was an overwhelming sense of relief that maybe this was the end at last. Perhaps now he could go home.

Chapter 19

Home
May 1945

As the plane landed Ted found he was suddenly unable to move, the shock of finally being home was just too much for him. Then his legs started to work again and easing himself off his stomach, he gratefully alighted the plane and set foot on English soil for the first time in five years. Everything seemed really strange, the activity around him seemed alien, and he felt an odd sense of dislocation. It was strange; he had waited so long for this moment and now he was terrified. A part of him wanted to get back on the plane and return to the familiar, to the place that, ludicrously as it seemed, had become more real to him than his own home.

Events had moved very quickly after the men had walked in through the gates of Stalag Luft 1 only five days ago. Ted shook himself as he realized that it *was* only five days ago and yet his life had now changed irrevocably. At first they had been interrogated by the 6th British Airborne who wanted to make sure

On arrival at Stalag Luft 1 Ted was interrogated to make sure he was not a German fleeing from the Russians.

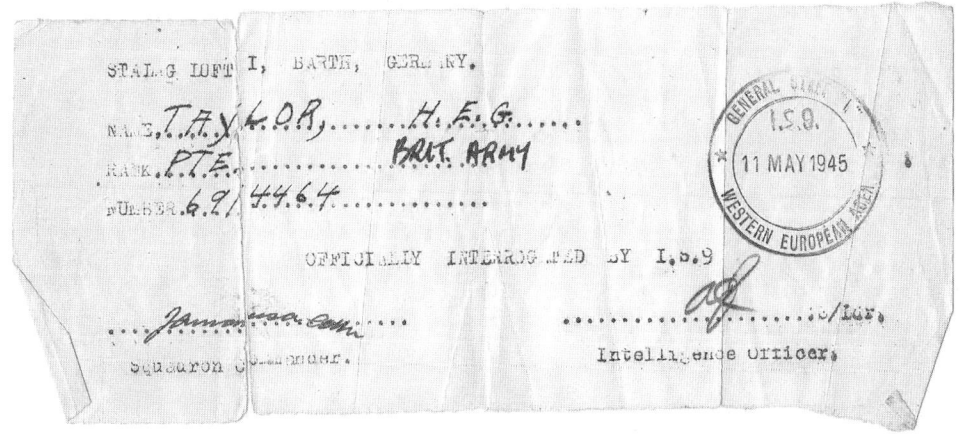

they were not Germans trying to escape the Russians. He was asked numerous questions about where his depot had been, where the nearest pub to it was, and various other details about life in Britain. Given his experiences and the length of time he had been a POW, he was surprised that he actually remembered enough to answer their questions, let alone enough to satisfy them that he really was a British POW. After this they were given more food than they had seen in months and allowed to rest. Ted had only been able to eat a tiny portion despite his hunger. Even that proved almost too rich for him even though it was only rations from some Red Cross parcels, 'liberated' by the camp's inhabitants as the Germans fled. Years on starvation rations and the last few months with so little food had shrunk his stomach considerably, but he had done his best. He then had the best night's sleep he could remember, although he woke early in the morning with stomach ache and for a few minutes was unable to remember where he was. When he remembered he hardly dared believe it and it was only when he had walked around the camp a couple of times without guards questioning or threatening him, that he accepted he was almost free. A couple of times he stopped and watched warily as large formations of bombers flew over the camp but nothing was dropped on them. He soon forgot about them as he deliberated on how much longer it would be before he went home.

But the men's ordeal was not quite over and Ted soon learnt that although technically they were free, the Russians would not let them leave. On 4 May 1945 the RAF, through Bomber Command, launched Operation Exodus and the first of 72, 500 POWs were repatriated over twenty-three days in over 2,900 sorties, but there were still delays and problems further east.

For the prisoners in Stalag Luft 1 the wait went on as the Americans were still busy negotiating permission to airlift the POWs home. The Russians wanted to take them by land to Odessa and then send them home by ship which would have added considerable time onto their journey home. But that wasn't the only reason the POWs objected. Rumours were already circulating that if the Russians took them they might never go home so they were understandably concerned. To keep them occupied and to minimise tension, those POWs who were fit enough were instructed to begin clearing the nearby airfield of mines and bomb damage so that the American planes could land.

Other than the POWs who had 'wandered in' the majority of prisoners in Stalag Luft 1 were American and British aircrew and, on the whole, had been much better treated than Ted and his fellow POWs. Up until October 1944 the average calories per day were between 1,200 and 1,800 per day. The normal menu would consist of six potatoes, one-fifth of a loaf of bread, some margarine, a small piece of meat (normally horse meat), two vegetables (cabbage, parsnips, beets or turnips), tea, coffee and some sugar, plus a thin barley soup. By January 1945 that had rapidly reduced to 800 calories and by March 1945, German rations and the lack of Red Cross parcels meant many men were even too weak to get out of bed. The American MPs were even ordered to guard the rubbish bins to prevent POWs raiding them and making themselves sick. However, on 1 April a shipment of Red Cross parcels arrived from Lübeck via Sweden and after that the situation improved and the men again had sufficient food.

By 11 May the Allies secured permission to use the airport next to the camp, but only for the a few hours on 12 and 13 May. The evacuation plan was to first take those who were wounded or sick, and then the British POWs, many of whom, like Ted, had been in captivity since 1940. These prisoners were either marched to or taken by tractor and trailers to the airfield in batches of twenty-five to avoid clogging up the road and loading area.

The first plane that arrived on 12 May was a B-17 with the Commander of the 1st Air Division of the Eighth Force. This was followed by a C-46 with officers of General Eisenhower's Staff. Then came two more B-17s with personnel and communication equipment and next, the first of the evacuation B-17s which were equipped with wooden decking material to provide a floor. All weapons and armoury had been removed to ensure maximum room for the POWs. The crew of each B-17 were told they could take no more than thirty-two men otherwise they would not be able to take off safely. The sick and wounded were evacuated in six C-46s which also joined in the evacuation of the other POWs. By the morning of the third day, 14 May, the last of the men were flown out, one of these being Colonel Zemke.

Ted's army book stamped with his date of discharge, 29/09/1945

Although Ted had no idea of the considerable activity going on behind the scenes while they were waiting for the evacuation to begin, he had heard the rumours circulating the camp. After everything he had already endured, it seemed that yet again some capricious God had stepped in to place one more obstacle in his way and he was almost paralysed by fear that he might still be prevented from returning home. But once they were told it was going ahead he surrendered to the first stirrings of hope that maybe this time he was going home after all. Knowing there were thousands of men all waiting to be evacuated and having no idea of the planned timetable just added to his anguish and sleeping was even worse as he was petrified he would miss the call and be left behind. But eventually exhaustion overtook him and he fell into a deep sleep, only to be awakened at 4 am and told to be ready to go almost immediately.

Ted had plenty of experience at that and almost in a dream he picked up his meagre possessions and followed the others. They were marched down to the parade ground where they were counted out into batches. Then several farmers with tractors and trailers came along and the men got on and were taken down to the airfield a couple of miles away. When they arrived at the airfield they were lined up again and one by one the Americans drafted in the Flying Fortresses. As each landed, the men climbed aboard and it took off. In all, the Americans evacuated 8,487 POWs over the three days.

Destinations were varied; all over the UK for the British POWs and France for the American POWs, but the men didn't really care where they were going to land. The only important thing was that they were going home. Ted had waited patiently for his turn and then he was in the gun turret, lying flat on his stomach and looking out of the Perspex window onto the field below. The plane took off, next stop Ford Aerodrome, near Arundel, in Sussex. As the plane headed towards England, Ted watched the countryside shrinking away beneath him and suddenly realized that his eyes were watering. He blinked the tears away angrily and then smiled. It was all over, the horror, the brutality, the fighting, the starvation, everything he had endured for five years, and somehow, against all the odds, he had survived to tell the tale.

He was suddenly aware of Harry nudging his arm, and bringing himself out of his reverie he once again took stock of his surroundings, unable to quite believe that he was really here. Breathing deeply he nodded and they headed towards the numerous tents set up to process the returning POWs.

The next couple of hours passed in a kind of trance as kindly WRVS ladies pointed them in the direction of the delousing area. Ted sighed as he headed towards the tent for yet more humiliation, but to his surprise it proved to be a form of emotional, as well as physical, cleansing. As the lice fell off his body it was as if he was also shedding his POW identity ready to start anew. After all the hair was removed from their bodies and their lousy rags of uniforms were destroyed. They were then given new uniforms which, to their now louse-free bodies, felt strange and wonderful, if rather scratchy. But scratchy from newness, not lice, was almost a pleasure and yet another sign that his ordeal was almost over. The next stop was the doctor who gave them a rather cursory medical while asking numerous questions and then they were given some food and emergency ration books which entitled them to double rations for a month. Afterwards they were asked to fill in some Liberation Questionnaires which asked for information about POWs who had collaborated with the Germans. Although some did name names and give details, others just used them to complain about the treatment they had received. Others saw it as an opportunity to praise the NCOs who had tried to make their lives bearable and those who had saved lives. Once they had finished they returned to the WVRS ladies who kindly sewed on their new Regimental Titles, Division Signs (in Ted's case the Black Cat), and any badges of rank, medal ribbons etc.

Then it was all over and they were given ten shillings and travel warrants and sent home on six weeks' leave with orders to report back to the depot afterwards for a further medical which would determine whether they should be retained or discharged. Although the war in Europe was over, there was still the war against Japan to be won.

Having experienced how fanatical the Japanese were, the Allies knew they would have to fight for every inch of captured territory and every foot of land in Japan before they would even consider surrendering. In May 1945 it was expected that this war would last at least another year, possibly longer, and that it could cost the lives of over a million men even if the Western Allies could persuade Stalin to join in the fight against Japan which was still not certain. This meant automatic discharge was not a certainty as it was assumed that although the returning POWs would not be eligible for overseas service for at least six months, after that they could be sent out to fight in the Far East.

But Ted was still blissfully unaware of this threat to his future as they were driven to the station and he prepared himself to say goodbye. As far as he was concerned he was home for good and thoughts of being sent abroad to carry on fighting never even entered his head. The journey to the station was quicker than expected and as the truck drove off they stood looking at each other awkwardly. After everything they had been through they were unable to think of anything to say so they simply shook hands and walked into the station, Ted to go to London and Harry to Hampshire. Ted still couldn't get rid of the feeling that he was in some kind of dream and that he would soon wake up and find himself back in the camp. This was a feeling that would stay with him for a long time and be the cause of numerous nightmares in the future. He closed his eyes and pinched himself and then opened his eyes again. But nothing happened, he didn't suddenly wake up and the station was still there so, reassured, he took a deep breath and entered the building.

Despite the fact that he had been sent to Danzig by train, a journey that had been nothing like the awful earlier train journeys organised by his Nazi captors, the station immediately conjured up memories of that horrendous journey east across Germany and Poland in 1940. Ted hesitated and it took him several moments before he could persuade himself to board the train. In an effort to distract himself he decided to buy some chocolate from the station vending machine, but it was empty and had been for a long time. Like many other things he recalled from life before 1940, it was a victim of rationing and it would take him several weeks to come to terms with the fact that England was not the land of plenty he remembered.

Sighing heavily, but now feeling calmer, he boarded the train and found himself enjoying the simple pleasure of deciding where to sit. Having not had a choice for so long, he was surprised at just how hard this was and changed seats several times before deciding that he was comfortable. Once seated, Ted felt slightly better as sitting on proper train seats held no memory of Germany. Their journeys as POWs had always been on the floor of cattle trucks, and he began to slowly relax. Within seconds though, other memories flooded in, memories of the journey he had made back to Winchester after Christmas in 1940 – five years and another lifetime ago. He fought back the rising sense of panic and inwardly chastised himself for being so weak. He had survived 'hell on earth' so a simple train journey home was not going to defeat him.

Ted knew he needed to concentrate on something else so he looked out of the window and watched as the countryside flashed past. Despite his determination not to let the memories flood back in, he found he was now powerless to stop them. It was as if the floodgates had opened and he was no longer able to control his thoughts. As the train headed towards London the memories continued to flow: the journey in the trucks to Southampton, the crossing to Calais, the fighting, the noise, the smell and taste of the smoke and the cordite, and the screams and moans of the wounded and the dying. He mentally shook himself and immediately blocked out any thoughts of his friends and how they had died. He couldn't remember that now or he would start crying and if he started he might never stop and that would never do. He dug his fingernails hard into the palms of his hand and tapped his foot on the floor of the train, ignoring the concerned glances of the young woman sitting opposite him.

Eventually Ted successfully managed to calm himself down and started to relax. Knowing it was best to keep his mind occupied on something else he concentrated his attention on the view out of the train window. It looked so different from the Polish countryside, so tiny and compact after the vast

Ted's first certificate of service 1939-1946.

expanses of the European countryside that he had become so used to seeing, but it wasn't just that. This was not the same countryside that he remembered, with its patchwork of fields and hedges and picture postcard villages. The villages he passed showed considerable signs of bombing and the roads had armed checkpoints at every crossroads. Most of the traffic he saw on the roads seemed to be American jeeps and military transport, although there was the occasional private car and, in the villages, an odd bread delivery van.

It was no good. It no longer seemed familiar at all so he closed his eyes and allowed his thoughts to wander to Brenda. How much had she had changed? Would she recognize him? He hadn't seen a mirror yet but he knew he must look completely different. But he hadn't just changed on the outside. Somewhere within he knew that he was irrevocably different and he didn't know if their relationship would survive the changes. Ted's experiences had altered the way he thought about things. He could no longer remember how he had thought back in 1940 and was sure the same must be true of Brenda. After all it had been five years. Five years of intermittent contact but a lifetime of experiences and he was not sure if either of them would ever really recover from the things they had witnessed.

A surge of gratitude suddenly swept through him as he thanked providence, (he could no longer thank a God who allowed such atrocities as those he had witnessed to take place) that Brenda had waited for him. Like all those with

187

girlfriends, fiancées or wives, Ted had lived in fear of receiving the so-called 'Dear John' letter telling him she had found someone else. Almost worse was the letter from the 'well-meaning friend or neighbour' who thought a POW should know that his loved one was 'keeping company' with someone else. Sometimes these were genuine and were meant with the best of intentions, but others were malicious with no basis. Ted had often wondered whether those who sent them had any idea of the damage they were doing. Some POWs who received them just gave up and slowly lost the will to survive even though everyone tried to help them through it. Others had deliberately thrown themselves at the wire or attacked a guard so that their pain was over. But Brenda had waited for him and whatever happened he knew he should always be

A picture of Brenda after the war.

eternally grateful to her for that. He swiftly pushed away the thought that he had no idea what she had been doing while he was locked up and successfully managed to suppress it. She had waited; that was all that was important for now. Feeling much better now and beginning to really look forward to seeing his family and Brenda, Ted turned his attention back to his fellow travellers and the activity around him.

He found himself listening to the conversations of the people around him and was bemused. He couldn't understand many of the things they were talking about and he realized with a sharp pang that he would never know what they had experienced in those missing years. The fear that he would always be an outsider in some way, a stranger in his own country, struck him. Then a new feeling started to grow within him, one that at first he had difficulty identifying but that he later recognized as guilt. He felt guilty that he had spent the war safe in a camp on the other side of Europe while they had all suffered. He turned to speak to Harry but of course he wasn't there. There was no one he could talk to who would understand how he felt, and his euphoria at the thought of being home soon was gradually replaced with a feeling of dislocation and detachment.

On the seat opposite was a young woman with a child. Seeing him watching her and looking less stressed than he had earlier, she smiled and asked casually if he was on leave. For a moment he was unable to answer. It was five years since he had spent any time with women and he found himself unexpectedly tongue-tied and shy. He also remembered at the very moment he was about to open his mouth that he mustn't swear. In the camps swearing every other word had been normal as it made it harder for the Germans and the civilian guards to understand them. Before he'd been conscripted Ted had never sworn and it had taken him several months to get into the habit. Now he would have to unlearn the habit and the words froze on his lips. It didn't help that the only women he had seen in the last five years had been East and Central European women and most had not worn any make-up. To him the young woman opposite seemed to have a mask on her face and he asked himself if all British women now wore thick make-up.

When he did eventually find his voice and explained that he had been a prisoner of war for five years, she nodded and then changed the subject asking what he was going to do now he was home. Ted had no way of knowing that she wasn't being disparaging because he had been a prisoner. Her response was the normal reaction of the majority of people in Britain as the war was nearly over, they didn't want to talk about it. They wanted to look forward to the future and to get on with their lives. Everyone had a war story to tell, they had all been there in one way or another, but that was the past and no one wanted to listen any more.

For Ted and many of those returning from the camps, this was particularly damaging as no one could understand what they had experienced and the numerous films made about POWs after the war mainly concentrated on the officer camps. These were very different from the camps the ordinary ranks

On arrival home, Ted was sent to a Polish Repatriation Camp in Gloucestershire to try and help him adjust.

were sent to, but even the portrayal of the officer camps was sanitized to a certain extent and the true horror rarely emerged. This left the public with the false perception that those who had been imprisoned in the camps had somehow had an easy war. Even the Red Cross newspapers for the families of POWs for the most part presented a picture of contented prisoners planting tomatoes and taking exams. Although there was mention of insanitary conditions and lack of food and clothing, it was quite low-key so the impression of a 'holiday camp' atmosphere prevailed. Even the SHAEF (Supreme Headquarters Allied Expeditionary Force) Report which highlighted their plight was never made public.

The POWs themselves did not want their loved ones worrying about them so they smiled in photos and in their letters said very little. In any case, much of what they wrote was heavily censored anyway. After a very short time Ted was no longer able to find the words to express the horrors he had seen. He buried them deep within himself so that the nightmares would stop and he could forget.

But that was all in the future and he knew from bitter experience that there was no point dwelling on things he could do nothing about, so he did his best to ignore the growing conflict within himself and buried it with all the other things he wanted to forget and concentrated on just getting home.

Eventually the train pulled into Waterloo Station and Ted stepped out into the familiar streets that he had not seen for so long. His first reaction was one of shock and disbelief as he searched for a familiar landmark. After several moments acclimatizing himself, he worked out where he was and headed purposefully towards 62a Stondon Road. Everywhere he looked there was bomb damage and large craters. He worried that the house might no longer be there and he fought hard to quell the rising panic that it might have suffered the same fate as so many others.

He had been completely out of touch since the last of the post had arrived way back in 1944. Although some men telephoned ahead or sent telegrams to let their families know they were coming home, he hadn't bothered. Now he wondered if perhaps that had been a mistake. What if they were all out and he couldn't get in?

This last thought made him smile as he thought that after all the things he had been through sitting on the doorstep for a while would not really be that much of a hardship. He looked round at the remains of the celebration bunting that was fluttering gently in the wind and wondered what it had been like here on VE night, the night the war ended, the day he had reached Stalag Luft 1 and found freedom. The only celebration in Stalag Luft 1 was the ceremonial burning of the watchtowers which he had watched with quiet satisfaction. But Ted needn't have felt left out because celebrations across the country were for

Ted with his mother Lou and Brenda, 1946. Ted still looks very thin.

the most part quite muted as people greeted the end of the war with more relief that anything else.

The announcement that the war was over had gone out on the radio at 7.40 pm on 7 May 1945. It said the treaty was expected to be signed at 2.40 am on 8 May. The church bells which had been silent since the beginning of the war – and were to be rung only to warn of invasion - signalled that the war in Europe was finally over. The war in Japan would of course continue for several more months. But peace was at last in sight and people waited in anticipation for the ringing of the bells. However, for some reason this didn't happen and many people were caught out and turned up to work only to be sent home again, so other than in the major cities celebrations took a little while to get going.

At 3 pm Winston Churchill addressed the nation from Downing Street, his broadcast being transmitted on radios throughout the country and on numerous loud speakers. This was followed by the 'Last Post' and 'God Save the King'. People also listened to the radio - 'Bells and Victory Celebrations' went down particularly well although some objected to the constant commentary all the way through. For the most part people decorated their homes and celebrated quietly with family or went to the numerous thanksgiving services that took place in the churches throughout the country.

Ted suddenly realized he had been standing on the pavement for several minutes without moving and was beginning to draw attention to himself. He took a few steps forward and noticed a corner shop. He thought about the money in his pocket and decided it might be nice to buy some cigarettes. The novelty of actually being free to go into a shop and buy something struck him and for a moment he felt paralysed. Then he found his legs and went in. The shelves were pretty much empty, and not as he expected and certainly not how he remembered. Although he knew there was rationing, he had somehow expected the shop to be exactly as it was before he went away. He went up to the counter and nervously asked for some cigarettes only to be told, sorry, they kept what little supply they did have for their regular customers.

Ted wandered back out into the street confused; this wasn't what he had thought it was going to be like. He felt like a complete stranger in the place he had lived and worked for several years and the feeling of disorientation he had felt earlier swept over him again. He took a deep breath and pulled himself together. Never mind, he was almost home now, then it would be different. He was so deep in his thoughts that he almost walked past the house. Something made him look up and there it was, right in front of him and, to his intense relief, almost exactly as he remembered it. Well, the front door could probably do with a lick of paint and the plants he remembered growing in the front garden had been replaced by what appeared to be vegetables, but otherwise it was the same, almost as if he hadn't been gone. As he had done so many times in his dreams over the past few years, he walked slowly up the path and knocked at the door. A few seconds passed which to Ted seemed like hours and then the door opened and his mother was standing there. For a split second she just stared at him and Ted feared that she didn't recognize him. Maybe this was just another dream after all and he would wake up and find himself back in the camp. But then, as he was engulfed in her arms, he knew that this time he was not dreaming, that this was the real thing, and he was truly home at last.

When his mother eventually pulled back and let him go, she was laughing and crying at the same time. She fired questions about when he had got back and how, and then she hugged him again and told him there was plenty of time for that. Ted felt completely overwhelmed and knew he was on the verge of crying, something he couldn't let himself do so somehow he managed to interrupt and ask about Brenda. Smiling through the tears that were still streaming down her face, his mother stepped back and pointed down the hall to the kitchen.

In the same dreamlike state he walked passed her into the hall, the calming rhythmic ticking of the hall clock taking him by surprise for a few seconds. He glanced into the dining room and found his eye drawn to the clean tablecloth, the knives and forks all laid out neatly. Ted couldn't remember the last time he'd sat down at a proper table and used knives and forks. In the camps they'd used their fingers and licked the plates clean, so scarce was food. The food given

Ted and Brenda's wedding in September 1945.

to him by the WRVS had been a spam sandwich and some biscuits, so even then there was no need for cutlery.

As he turned back he caught a quick glimpse of himself in the hall mirror and froze, totally shocked. No wonder his Mum hadn't recognized him, he hardly recognized himself. His skin was grey and lined and he looked several years older than he actually was. His body was painfully thin and hairless, and the hair on his head had been shaved off when he landed at Ford. Ted wondered if when it regrew it would be grey like the hair that they had shaved off or would regain its previous colour. Some of his teeth had become loose as his gums had receded through lack of food and vitamins. His cheeks were hollow and sunk into his face.

He gazed in horror for a few moments and almost ran away. What would

Brenda think when she saw him? How could she possibly still love him when he looked like this? How long he would have stood there if his Mum hadn't nudged him forward he didn't know. But he found himself automatically taking the final steps and opening the door into the kitchen and there she was.

Brenda had her back towards him, her hands in the sink busy washing up. The radio was playing music so she hadn't heard him knocking at the front door. Hearing the kitchen door open she turned round to speak expecting to see his mother and almost dropped the cup in her hand as she stared at him in disbelief and total amazement. Within seconds this had turned to joy and, as if the past five years had never happened, she ran towards him and allowed him to enfold her in his arms. Ted closed his eyes and held tight. She had recognized him, she was still here, and she had waited for him. He felt as if a great weight had been lifted off his shoulders. He could let go of his fears and worries now. He was safe at home with those he loved. Somehow he had survived against the odds and his reward was to live to see this day.

Ted's service details and medals. POWs could always recognize each other as although they would have had the 1939-1945 Star, they had fewer campaign medals.

Abroad—Theatres

Medals, clasps, decorations, mentions in despatches ; any special act of gallantry or distinguished conduct brought to notice in Brigade or Superior Orders.	*Long Service and Good Conduct Medal.*

Date *9 Jan 1962*   Signature of C.O. _____ *E.O* _____ Unit

for Officer i/c Records, Exeter.

Previous Service in H.M. Forces

Royal Navy, Royal Marines, Army (showing corps) or R.A.F.	Period		Rank on Discharge	Medals, etc.
	From	To		
THE RIFLE BRIGADE	15-9-39	8-6-46		1939/45 STAR
CLASS "Z" RESERVE	9-6-46	13-2-47		WAR MEDAL 1939/4
THE RIFLE BRIGADE	11-2-47	28-1-58	Cpl	

The government was very concerned about the mental health of those returning from POW camps and asked some prisoners who had returned earlier to produce some leaflets that could be distributed to the families. These contained useful advice suggesting that families and friends let the returning POW to do exactly what he wanted for the first few days to allow him to get used to the idea of having choices again. If he wanted to stay in on his own then let him. If he wanted to spend all his time outside then he should be able to do this. Being able to make choices again was something that would take time, even with simple things like which radio station to listen to or about whether to go out or not. The leaflets also advised that the returning POWs might experience periods when they were really chatty and cheerful and others when they were very depressed and craved solitude. If a POW wanted to talk they should encourage it and listen, if he didn't they should not push it but wait until he was ready, if ever. Having spent years crammed together in unsanitary huts with hundreds of other men, many just wanted to be left alone and enjoy not having to share everything. Some simply found everything so frightening that they hid in their bedrooms and refused to come out. Many didn't want to be the centre of attention and found continual visits by family members all asking for information, totally draining however well-meaning they knew it to be. The men just wanted to quietly settle back into normal life. Others wanted to try and cram all the things they had missed into the first few days. This was rarely possible as most were not physically capable of much exertion.

Many married men who had dreamt of taking their wives to bed the minute they returned home found they simply didn't have the energy, or were too shy, after such a long enforced absence. Many were too ashamed of their emaciated, hairless bodies to risk making advances that might be rejected. As the years passed many never wanted to go on holiday and others wouldn't take their children to zoos or let them have birds or animals in cages. Some like Ted would never have dogs or go anywhere near holiday camps. The leaflets also contained lots more useful advice such as not over-feeding the returning POWs or allowing them to have too much strong alcohol as their weakened bodies would never be able to tolerate it. However, these leaflets were never published by the new Labour Government leaving the returning men and their families to muddle through as best they could.

Another bone of contention was the wages that were owed to them. As serving members of the Armed Forces, the men's wages had continued to accrue during the time they were prisoners. However, these credits as they were called, had deductions taken out for the wages the Germans had supposedly paid them when they were working in the camps. It would seem that the British Government paid the Germans money which was supposed to be given to the POWs as their wages. Of course many had never received any wages and those that had found considerable discrepancies between what the British Government said the Germans had paid them and what they had actually been paid.

This was a sore subject for many years and was exacerbated when the Germans put together a financial compensation package to help those who had been used as slave labour by the Third Reich which excluded British POWs. This matter has never been resolved despite various promises from Parliamentary-seat-chasing MPs, and as yet no British European POWs have received any money or compensation. Even when the Japanese POWs rightfully received all their money, the European POWs were still studiously ignored and have never received the money owed to them.

But for Ted all these things were for the future and at that moment he was content to stand quietly in the kitchen holding tight to his fiancée. As far as he was concerned it was now time for life to begin again. It was time to make up for all those lost moments, those lost years they could have spent together if war and life hadn't got in the way.

Postscript

On 6 August the USA dropped the first of two atom bombs on Japan. On 2 September, Japan formally surrendered. The war was finally over leaving an estimated fifty to seventy-plus million dead and several more millions displaced and homeless. Instead of being retained, most of the returning POWs were discharged along with thousands of other servicemen. Ted was sent to an ex-Polish patriation camp in Gloucestershire where he remained until he was discharged on 8 June 1946.

Ted and Brenda married on 15 September 1945 and had three children; David who was born in October 1947 when Ted was in Germany, Jennifer in 1950 when the family was based in Winchester, and Christopher in 1952, while the family were based in Tidworth. Christopher sadly died when only a few days old. The family line continued with four grandchildren and four great-grandchildren. Against all the odds, the note Ted had hastily written on the discarded signal pad at the end of May 1940 and handed to a Frenchman, had found its way home to his Mum, Lou, in June 1940. She was not officially notified that he was alive and a prisoner until late September 1940.

After being demobbed Ted found it really hard to settle to any of the jobs he tried. After his experiences during the war being a milkman or working on the buses held no appeal and so eventually he decided to rejoin the army. In February 1947 he rejoined the 2nd Battalion the Rifle Brigade and was part of the Army of

Ted and Brenda at a friend's christening, circa 1945.

Occupation in Germany. Coincidentally my own father, Anthony McEntee, also joined the 2nd Battalion, The Rifle Brigade in 1945 after lying about his age in an unsuccessful attempt to see action before the end of the war. He too was a member of the army of occupation and was based in the same place, at the same

Taylor family picture, circa 1950. Ted and Brenda and their two children, David (aged about three) and baby Jenny.

Ted's papers stamped to say he already had civilian clothing – ie, his 'demob suit'.

time as Ted. It is entirely possible that their paths would have crossed although, of course, there was no reason at that time for either of them to have been aware of the other.

In 1948 the 2nd Battalion the Rifle Brigade was disbanded and Ted transferred across to the Kings Royal Rifle Corp (now 2 Rifles). Throughout his sixteen years' service, as well as being part of the Army of Occupation, Ted

Ted's discharge certificate dated 1946.

took part in the state funeral of King George VI and the Coronation of Queen Elisabeth II. The Rifles 'family' continued to look after him and during that time he spent several years as the Batman/Driver for a young officer, now Field Marshal Lord Bramall, which led to a lasting friendship between the two men. Bramall, then a Lieutenant Colonel, was also Commanding Officer of Ted's son David when he was in Malaya in the 1960s.

In the early 1950s Ted was transferred on attachment to the TA, running the Messes in Buckingham Gate. While there he had a rather unfortunate accident, although he never elaborated too much on the details. It would appear he was driving round the Palace grounds in the Austin Champ he had been allocated (the Rolls Royce of Jeeps) when he hit the Queen's car. He hastened to reassure us that she was not hurt but never told us what happened to him as a result, although it possibly didn't help any prospects of promotion! Ted remained in the army until 1963 when he retired having reached the rank of Corporal. After his retirement from the army he found a job at Lorilleaux and Bolton of Templefieds, Harlow, where he worked for twenty-one years as an ink and varnish-maker and driver until he retired in 1983.

Ted was an active member of the Royal British Legion for several years and

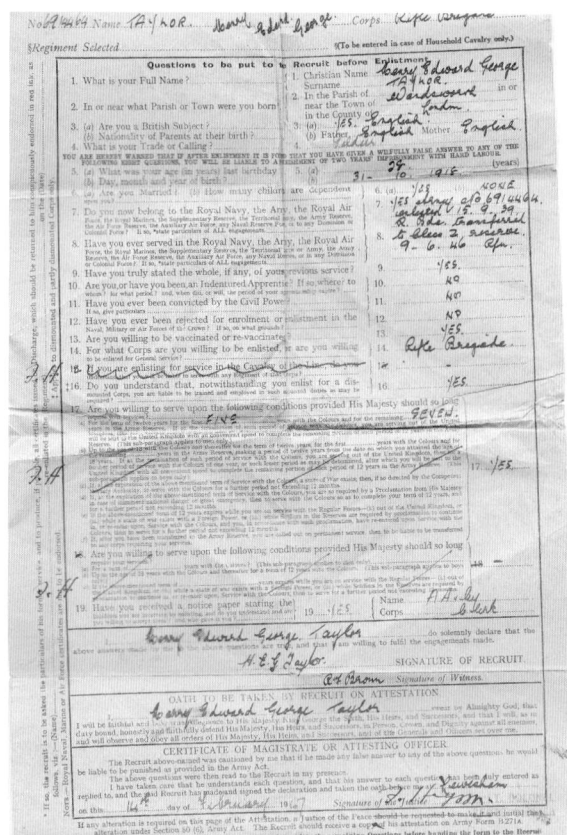

Unable to settle, Ted rejoined the army. This is his enlistment document.

Ted after he re-enlisted, (third from the left with his mess tin).

Ted in Germany post re-enlistment.

as well as helping to raise money for them he was also the standard bearer for the Harlow and Roydon Branch. He had never spoken to his family about his experiences and when young, David couldn't understand why his father wouldn't take them to a holiday camp and why he had such a dislike of dogs, particularly Alsatians. Like many surviving POWs Ted also hated to see food left on the plate, always slept with his bedroom door open and suffered for many years with nightmares.

On 20 October 1994 Brenda sadly died and Ted was, once more, alone. Although the war had left both of them different people and their marriage had not always been easy, he missed her very much. He left all her everyday things in the same places they had been before her death, as if she had just 'popped out' for a few moments. In 1995 Ted attended a Second World War World Victory Memorial Service in the Harlow Synagogue as the standard bearer for the Royal British Legion and they sang some of the songs he had heard in the camps. Ted broke down and began to speak about some of the atrocities he had witnessed. This was the first time he had really said anything, but even then his account was muted and sanitized as everything had been blocked out for so many years that he was now unable to find the words to really describe the horrors he had experienced.

Ted went back to Poland in 1984 and visited the cemetery where many of his friends were buried. The cemetery was immaculate having been looked after by the children of the nearby orphanage. Ted and those who went with him took sweets, oranges, toiletries and stationery to give to the children in grateful thanks for their care over the years. In 2004, when the 65th anniversary of the beginning

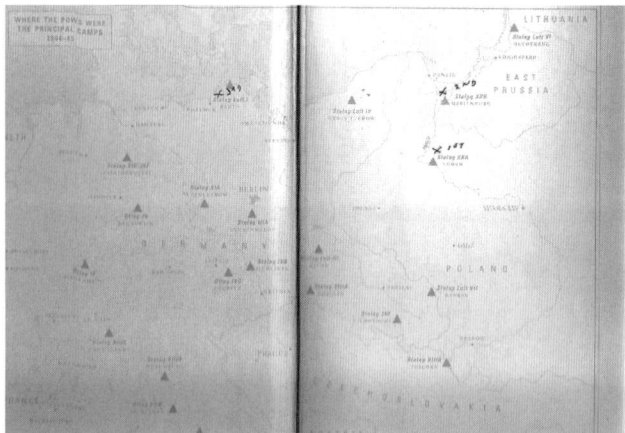

Ted marked the camps he spent time in.

Ted by the Calais Memorial.

Ted as RBL Standard bearer on a trip to Calais cemetery to remember his friends who died.

The Calais memorial.

Ted went back to Poland in 1984 to visit the cemetery there.

Ted paying his respects in Poland to the many who did not return.

of the war was commemorated, the National Lottery offered funding for war veterans to revisit the graves of their fallen comrades. Although the few surviving members of the POW group Ted belonged to applied for funding so they too could make this pilgrimage one last time, for some reason, known only to those on the Lottery funding board, they were refused. For the few remaining survivors this removed their last opportunity to return to the cemetery to pay their respects.

Like the majority of the general public, I knew very little about those few days in Calais in 1940 or the subsequent treatment of the ordinary POW at the hands of their captors. I had grown up on a diet of sanitised POW camp films (there was even a comedy, *Stalag 17*) but none bore any reality to the truth. As far as the Defence of Calais was concerned attention is nearly always focused on the evacuation from Dunkirk and even modern documentaries on the Second World War hardly mention Calais at all. So in 2005, when BBC Radio Essex took part in a wartime memory project, I asked Ted if I could write about his war. I managed to get him to speak on tape about his experiences which I then transcribed into a short story which Ted was delighted with and showed to many of his friends. For the time being that was it.

Majdanek has been preserved as a museum. This is its memorial.

The gas chambers were also used to dispose of prisoners from other nationalities, including British. This plaque commemorates them.

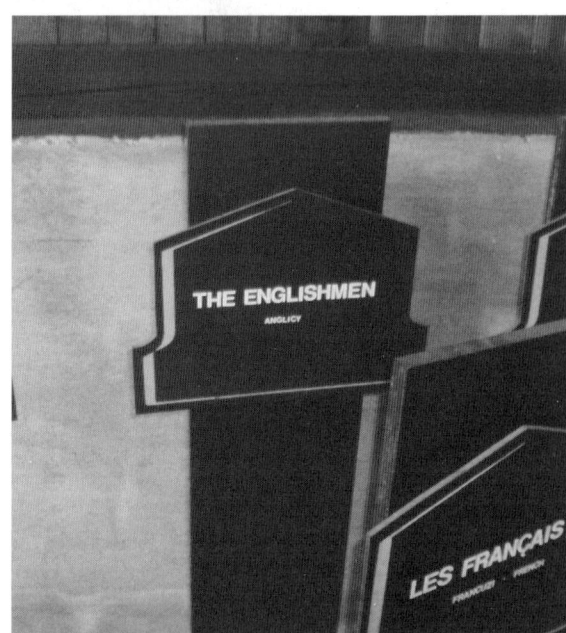

Memorial to the Rifle Brigade in Calais.

Ted met up again with Field Marshal Bramall at one of the Queen's garden parties. He was always immensely proud of this photo.

Ted at Buckingham Palace. Fortunately, he was not driving this time!

In the summer of 2005 we went down with Ted to Winchester to celebrate the 250th Anniversary of the forming of the Royal Americans and the final muster of the Kings Royal Rifle Corps. We had a lovely day and Ted was able to meet up again with Field Marshal Lord Bramall who stopped and spent some time chatting to him.

On 26 April 2007, Ted was invited to Winchester by RSM John Allen of the 4th Battalion the Rifles. He was the guest of honour at the Sergeants' Mess Optelic 10 Pre-Deployment Regimental supper before their tour of Iraq. He went with his son David and they both had a wonderful evening, although Ted was rather bemused to find himself treated as such a hero, something he had never considered himself to be.

Ted continued to live independently until he suffered a massive stroke in August 2008 and after several months in hospital he had to go into a nursing home. As a way of trying to cheer him up I suggested writing his story as a book.

Although Ted counted himself as one of the lucky ones in that he came back alive, he and the other POWs who were treated as slave labour by the Germans were considerably damaged by their experiences. Many adjusted on the surface but many others, like Ted, were unable to reconcile the experiences they'd had with the cheery, holiday-camp-style films that were the public's only window into the POW experience. Initially no one wanted to talk about the war and then, when they did, people only wanted to hear about those they considered to be 'the action heroes'. Many POWs didn't talk about their experiences because they wanted to forget, others because they feared they would not be believed, and most because to do so would reawaken the nightmares.

After Ted died on 4 April 2009 at the age of ninety, we found the diaries he had written in 1940, together with numerous photos of the POW camps and letters from Brenda to him in the POW camps. It is these treasures from Ted's past, together with extensive research to fill in the gaps, which form the basis of this tribute to Ted and all those other heroes of the Second World War 'who gave their tomorrows so that we could have our todays'.

Carole McEntee-Taylor 2010

Ted's medals.

'The task of the Garrison was hopeless from the start. From the moment of arrival, Calais was in horrid confusion owing to the swarms of civilian refugees and the arrival of hospital trains carrying hundreds of wounded.

The two supply ships were the natural means of evacuation, and they were used to take away sixteen hundred non-combatants and four hundred wounded, but no one was allowed to depart before she was completely unloaded: as a result part of the garrison was short of ammunition throughout the battle. Moreover, on the second day a sortie showed it impossible to carry out the original mission of opening the road to Dunkirk, and instead of becoming a new base of supplies, Calais became the altar of sacrifice...... The Commander of the garrison and his men deserve outstandingly well of their comrades and of their country.'

The Times Leader, 2 October 1940,
quoted in *The Rifle Brigade Chronicle* 1941, p84.

Notes

1. Quoted in *Rifle Brigade Chronicle* 1940.
2. An impressive aircraft in every respect, the B-17G had a wing span of 103ft 9in (31.6 m), was 74ft 4in (22.6m) long and had a height of 19ft 1in (5.8m). The four supercharged Wright R-1820-97 Cyclones engines gave it a top speed of 287mph (462 km/h) and it could cruise comfortably at 182 mph (293 km/h). The highest it could fly was 35,800ft (10,850m), and it had a maximum range of 3,400 miles (5,471km).
3. Second in Command.
4. The King's Royal Rifle Corps were the 60th (Rifles) and the Rifle Brigade were the 95th (Rifles).
5. If you would like to know more about Brenda's story then you might like to read *The Cat & The Nightingale Saga*. This is the docu-drama version of Ted and Brenda's war and covers Brenda's life as a nurse through the Blitz.
6. In 1974 a war game between the German generals who had planned Operation Sealion (the name of Hitler's planned invasion of Britain) and those who had designed the defences, came to the following conclusion. Although the Germans could have landed, they would only have managed to progress about fifteen miles inland before being beaten back.
7. In five trips between 28 May and 2 June the Mersey ferry *Royal Daffodil* evacuated 7,461 service personnel from Dunkirk. This was the highest number evacuated by any passenger vessel involved in the Dunkirk operations. On 2 June *Royal Daffodil* was attacked by six German aircraft. One of the bombs penetrated two of her decks and blew a hole below the water line, but she managed to limp back to port. *Royal Daffodil* was the second Mersey ferry of that name. The original *Daffodil* was given the honour of being renamed *Royal Daffodil* following her involvement in the First World War operation to block the harbour at Zeebrugge, on the night of 22/23 April, 1918.
8. Ted's words.
9. Unfortunately I was unable to read these words as the diary was written in pencil and had deteriorated too much.
10. The Depot Letter, p61 The Rifle Brigade Chronicle 1940.
11. Quoted in T*he Rifle Brigade Chronicle* 1940 p48.
12. Ersatz is a German word meaning substitution. It became a common word during WW2 as other ingredients were substituted for those that were no longer available.

13. One person reports competitions to see who had the largest penis!

14. I have read elsewhere that they were given four postcards and two letters per month but this is not what Ted said. It may that it varied from place to place.

15. Other descriptions I have read are not quite so complimentary. The different accounts may be because the camp was much better than the appalling conditions Ted had come from, or because he wanted to play down the horror of his experiences in front of me and his son.

Index